With love from
Marjorie.

WHERE MAN BELONGS

By the same Author—

THE WISDOM OF THE FIELDS
THIS PLOT OF EARTH
DOWNLAND MAN
SHEPHERD'S COUNTRY
REMEMBRANCE
THE ENGLISH COUNTRYMAN
THE TREE OF LIFE
MEN OF EARTH
  ETC. ETC.

ÆSVÆ 24 · 1·5·8·8·

THE "GRAFTON" PORTRAIT OF SHAKESPEARE

Reproduced by permission from the original in the John Rylands Library, Manchester.

WHERE MAN BELONGS

by

H. J. MASSINGHAM

Collins

14 ST. JAMES'S PLACE LONDON

1946

Dedicated to the shades and presences
of those who head these chapters.

CONTENTS

PREFACE

My obligations in this book are to those who head its chapters.
I also owe a new debt of gratitude to Mr. Arthur Bryant, who
has read the manuscript, as he did that of my last book. He
has been a tower of strength to me in suggestion and in criticism, but most of all in the warmth of his generosity. His
appraisal has renewed me; his criticism nerved me to practise
it continually on myself. No author can do more for another.
To the bounty of Miss V. Sackville-West I owe her splendid
"A Sussex Song" as the heading to Chapter XII. Practically
all the book is new. A very little of the material, but worded
rather differently, appeared in *The Geographical Magazine*,
Time and Tide and *The Field*.

The portrait of Shakespeare is reproduced from the original
in the John Rylands Library, Manchester, by permission of
the Governors of that institution.

CHAPTER I

WILLIAM SHAKESPEARE OF WARWICKSHIRE

"He was the man who of all modern, and perhaps ancient poets, had the largest and most comprehensive soul . . . He was naturally learn'd; he needed not the spectacles of books to read Nature; he looked inwards and found her there."

JOHN DRYDEN.

I

I SO RARELY go to a London play that I have one advantage, if only one, over the professional critic. I can view the performance with an eye not dulled by familiarity. When the play is one of Shakespeare's country comedies, I have the further advantage of realising, like other countrymen, his dyed-in-the-wool ruralism. The *Midsummer Night's Dream* was acted by a celebrated repertory company well disciplined to the revival of old plays and composed of seasoned actors. I found myself not merely disappointed but convinced that the company had wholly misinterpreted the meaning, concept and purpose of the *Dream*. It was originally acted as a courtly Masque to celebrate the marriage of Essex with the widow of Sir Philip Sidney, and the obvious references to Queen Elizabeth make it almost certain that she was present at the first performance. It was therefore stylised according to the customary rubric of the Masque. This depended upon formal patterned spectacle, derived from the traditional pageants acted on festival days by the trade guilds in the country and market towns, and in post-Reformation days given the classical settings of the Renaissance.

Everything about the *Dream* suggests that this was exactly how it was played. It *is* a dream—an idyll, a pastoral, a flight of exquisite fancy, where love is under the dominion of magic and human reason the sport of the fairies. It is a world of moonshine, mummery, marvels and metamorphosis, a world as fragile as a drop of dew, as inconsequent as the airy gambols

9

of a butterfly, as irrational as the jests of Edward Lear, as purely lyrical as the folk-music of Handel, and as fantastic as fairyland should be. So at the end of his life Shakespeare used music and Masque once more, but this time to foreshadow the ultimate mysteries of life.

Shakespeare loved to mix up many elements of life in the same play, comedy with tragedy,[1] pomp with farce, the alehouse with the reception-room, and the sweetest and most spontaneous poetry ever written with ceremonious prose and buskined verse. Therefore, "The most lamentable comedy and most cruel death of Pyramus and Thisby," acted by Bottom the Weaver and his fellow village craftsmen, is rehearsed among the secret and haunted glades of Arden. We should feel the spiced contrast but not incongruity. For this village drama parodying the London thriller sprang from the same stem as the Pageant and the Masque. Both were hawked round by the travelling players that Shakespeare must often have seen not only in the guild hall at Stratford or Coventry but in many a farmhouse kitchen in the Avon country. I have myself seen exactly the same kind of thing as the Pageant of the Nine Worthies in *Love's Labour's Lost* performed by the locals in a pub at Chipping Campden.

So far from conceiving the *Dream* in this spirit, the London players acted it semi-realistically, as though the shuffling and reshuffling of the four lovers in the forest were after the fashion of a modern problem play. Helena, the despised of Demetrius, was a highly sophisticated lady of fashion. Full of airs and tricks and mannered archness, she might have been in the boudoir of the Restoration theatre, the mysterious depths of the elvish woodland Ranelagh Gardens or Hyde Park. Oberon spoke his wild woodnotes like an after-luncheon speech at the Mansion House. But worst of all were the antics of the hempen homespuns. The way to do their stuff is with the most profound and solemn gravity, a wooden pomposity, a deadly earnestness. So is thrown into relief the double satire upon themselves and upon the play they act, which is a travesty of the blood-and-thunder melodrama of Kyd's *Spanish Tragedy* and its type on the early Elizabethan stage. But *Pyramus and*

---

[1] In Dame Quickley's description of the death of Falstaff in *Henry V*, comedy and tragedy become completely fused.

Thisbe was acted as second-class music-hall slapstick, highly self-conscious and as urban as it well could be. Villagers were degraded into comedians of the practical joke order.

The question is whether the London stage is capable of performing rural drama. If so, can it perform that of Shakespeare, the supreme genius who embodied the whole culture of England, sprung direct from her native soil? For all true culture is organic and rooted in the traditional forms evolved out of a rural matrix. Culture cannot exist in a vacuum. Our urbanism has become completely severed from its roots. Or, to change the figure, it is like a soil that bears only by the stimulants of chemicals. It is without living nourishment. It thus simulates life rather than lives. It has sucked the rural life dry. But that life-blood in its veins cannot remain so without being continually recharged through and from the heart. Unless its organic source is active it turns to chlorinated water.

II

It is the religious and rural bent of Shakespeare's art that makes him no longer understood by ourselves. Two different concepts to us, but they were once related in the mediæval "natural law," derived from its origin in the country tale of the Gospels. In his own way Shakespeare also related them. But he did so more from the rural bias of his nature than because he was a religious man. It was from tradition and his experience of life, both rural and the reverse, that he developed his religious philosophy. His intense ruralism in its turn proceeded both as cause and effect from his birth, upbringing, and education as a Warwickshire countryman. It was fed all through his life by constant visitings to Stratford during his dramatic career in London. He purchased property there in house and land when at the height of his metropolitan fame, and retired to them in the September of his life. It is a mistake to think that Shakespeare ever lost touch with Stratford. He was there for a prolonged period in 1596, bought New Place in 1597 and rehabilitated his family. In the corn shortage of 1598, when he was thirty-four and fourteen

years before his retirement, the yields from his acreage were
the third largest in Stratford. The universal artist and the
star of the London crowd and the London Court remained a
provincial all his life.

Shakespeare's biographers are usually scandalised by the
contrast between the author of the plays and the owner of land
and house property in Warwickshire. And not even the
worshippers can feel quite happy about his going to law against
certain debtors of his in Stratford. For the rest, the contemporary urban prejudice against land ownership has beyond
all reason distorted his property holding as reflecting upon his
glory. Every countryman, no matter what his station in the
rural economy, desires, or did desire, to possess property in
land. No society except our own plutocratic one, composed of a
few holding irresponsible property and most of the rest of the
nation holding none, or of the all-propertied State masquerading
as "The People," has ever dreamed of regarding individual
property holding as in itself anti-social. Shakespeare was not
acquisitive by nature and prosaic off the stage simply because
he was a land-owner, as some of his biographers maintain.
His active share in the agitation of 1614 against the plot to
enclose the common land of Old Stratford and Welcombe
acquits him of coveting his neighbour's landmark. Through
his cousin, Thomas Greene, he pleaded the cause of the
Commoners in London, and, as was ratified soon after his
death, successfully.[1] Shakespeare's relations with Stratford
prove him to have been the traditional countryman and a good
provincial.

As such, he worked and thought from the opposite direction
to Whitman. Whitman was one of the least regional of poets.
He did not confine himself to a single continent. He was the
"world-citizen." His eyes were fixed on the horizon rather
than on the ground at his feet. He embodies the spirit of
modernism, which in a hundred different ways is expansive.
The sense of mass, of speed, of size, of distance, of "the conquest
of nature," of cosmopolitan vastness, Whitman expresses all
these distinctive elements of the modern spirit.

Shakespeare was at the other pole. He was regional and
universal. His approach to life and to human nature was

---

[1] C. M. Ingleby: *Shakespeare and the Welcombe Enclosures* (1883).

realist, based on his own observation and his own experience. He never idealised crowds as Whitman did. His Greeks, Romans, Italians were Englishmen all. His imagination was contractive, individual, selective and organic, not expansive and generalised. When the very globe seemed to be wrenched off its axis by the power of evil in *Macbeth*, the firmament to be convulsed in *King Lear*, these paroxysms of nature rose like the Djinn out of the bottle from *this* castle and *that* heath. In *Romeo and Juliet*, Phaethon, as remote in the skies as in human interest, is the "wagoner." Shakespeare brings him down to earth quicker than his own rashness. In *Lucrece* and *Venus and Adonis*, which Hazlitt described as "a couple of ice-boxes," the only pieces that come alive in these academic studies of "lust in action" are the natural history ones: the dive-dapper (dabchick), the milch doe, the snail, the hunting of "poor Watt," the hare, the horses, particularly the stallion, and the country callings of the dyer and the careful housewife. All are described with an air of easy but sensitive familiarity. In the 'prentice thriller of *Henry VI*, Henry's ache for the ordered shepherd's life and the less familiar farewell of Suffolk and Margaret:—

> "Even as a splitted bark, so sunder we
> This way fall I to death.
> This way for me"—

are like bunches of flowers in a clearing-station.

In Shakespeare, the best is always personal. It is to be noted that the first figures to take flesh and blood among the dummies of the earliest plays are countrymen—for instance, Launce and Speed and the Host in *The Two Gentlemen of Verona*, Costard and Sir Nathaniel, the country curate, in *Love's Labour's Lost*. The last pair strike sparks from each other when Costard says of Sir Nathaniel playing Alexander in the Masque:—

> "a foolish mild man, an honest man, look you, and soon dashed! He is a marvellous good neighbour, faith, and a very good bowler; but for Alisander,—alas, you see how 'tis—a little o'erparted."

Nobody but a countryman could have written this about

a countryman. In so stiff a period piece, this burst of natural-
ness and the songs with it are like glimpses of a garden seen
through the windows of a museum. In Shakespeare, the rural
bias prevails even in the indoor plays. In *Twelfth Night*, lovers,
plotters, gulls and clown do most of their stuff in a garden;
the dancing duelling wits of Benedict and Beatrice in *Much Ado*
yield to their hearts in an orchard. The grandiose abstractions
of Whitman would have been as abhorrent to Shakespeare's
qualitative spirit as the cloudy rhetoric of Marlowe (which he
first imitated and then parodied) actually was.

III

The countryman has from time immemorial been concrete
and realistic in thought where the townsman has tended to
theorise and generalise. This habit of mind in its higher
ranges expresses itself in natural symbols as abstraction rarely
if ever does. The extent of Shakespeare's natural and rural
symbolism based on his organic and pictorial sense was not
realised by Shakespeare commentators until the appearance of
Dr. Caroline Spurgeon's masterly study of *Shakespeare's
Iterative Imagery*.[1] She has given a detailed analysis of the
types of images, metaphors and similes used by Shakespeare.
He systematically used associated clusters of these natural
images as symbols of each play. Those of light blaze and
flicker through *Romeo and Juliet*, and *Macbeth* is sticky with
those of blood. Those of sickness are the key to *Hamlet*, of
fawning dogs to *Timon*. Dancing, music, birds and outdoor
sport are the main imagery of *Much Ado*. Beatrice was born
under a dancing star. It was W. H. Hudson's eye which
saw
> "where Beatrice like a lapwing runs
> Close by the ground, to hear our conference."

You not only see Beatrice making a dash for cover but her very
stoop and gait. But you must have noted with Shakespeare
how the lapwing runs.

These country symbols cover a wide field:—birds, mammals

[1] 1936.

and insects; the weather and the seasons; clouds and the sky; the River Avon on whose banks he was born; country sports and games and the natural scene but not landscape; wild flowers; husbandry.[1] The smith, the butcher, the potter, the country tailor, the weaver, the glover, the solderer, the dyer, the lacemaker, the cooper, the tinker, the joiner, the thatcher, the needleworker of samplers and particularly the carpenter, stock the plays with abundance of imagery. The crafts of the housewife, particularly cooking and baking bread, are as busy in them. Princess Imogen is described as a good cook. The hunter blows his horn through the enchanted glades of his poetry, though his sympathies were always with the hunted. But of all these rural images those of gardening play by far the most varied and copious part. The plays and poems are stuffed with horticultural analogy and illustration. The gardens of New Place must have been constant in his thought when Hamlet's nightmare disgust at his mother's incest, the diseased court and the time "out of joint" are summed up in "Ah, fie, 'tis an unweeded garden." The contrast between the flower and

"the fat weed
That rots itself in ease on Lethe's wharf"—

is constantly used in the play as symbolic point and counter-point. The agony in Othello's mind sees Desdemona as weed and festered lily. Some of these images, of course, are borrowed from Pliny and the herbalists. But they are so often precise and true that they must have come out of his own personal observation and predilection. What else was he doing at New Place but farming and gardening?

The records of his fellow dramatists in this respect are extraordinarily meagre. Though poets like Drayton, Vaughan and Traherne were ruralists, the only ones over the whole range of seventeenth century poetry who made rich use of proverbial idiom and the folk tradition were Shakespeare—and George Herbert. Country imagery in Marlowe, for instance, is extremely rare. As the doctrinaire Machiavelian, the poetic imperialist, the daring free-thinker, he was a townsman true to type. But Shakespeare took a heavy crop of rural images

[1] Gleaning, threshing, winnowing, haymaking, etc.

from his native Warwickshire. He was as regional a poet as Thomas Hardy or John Clare. What the Suffolk Stour was to Constable, the Warwickshire Avon was to Shakespeare. The painter of "Dedham Mill" wrote: "Shakespeare could make anything poetical; he tells us of poor Tom's haunts among 'sheep cotes and mills.' As long as I do paint, I shall never cease to paint such places." In Constable's paintings there is the same husbandly intercourse between man and nature as in Shakespeare's plays and poems. The same sense of the inexha tible variety of nature is in them both. No days, no hou   two leaves, have been alike, wrote Constable, since the   of the world. Constable related the natural with the   ural as Shakespeare did in his later plays—"At every   ake, and on whatever object I turn my eyes, that sublime pression of the Scriptures, 'I am the resurrection and the life' seems as if uttered near me." The profound differences between the two do not obscure a fundamental likeness in their mental attitudes to English country.

I wish that Dr. Spurgeon had explored this particular ground of Shakespeare's regional loves. But she does give one striking instance. Under the eighteenth arch of Sir Hugh Clopton's 15th century bridge over the Avon just above the Memorial Theatre, the current forms a spiral eddy and turns back upon its course. This freakish habit is minutely described in ll. 1667-73 in *Lucrece*. How rich, then, the intimacy between the greatest of all poets and his native place that Henry James called "the core and centre of the English world, midmost England, unmitigated England"! Milton understood this well when he spoke of Shakespeare "warbling his native wood notes wild."

Shakespeare's poetic debt to what he actually saw in Warwickshire and the Cotswolds has never been closely examined. But the following is to the life one of those sweeping floods of the great plain I have watched from the Saxon Tower of Deerhurst Church, making the trees of the fertile fields islets of an inland lake:—

"The ox has therefore stretch'd his yoke in vain,
The ploughman lost his sweat; and the green corn
Hath rotted ere his youth attain'd a beard;

The fold stands empty in the drownèd field,
And crows are fatted with the murrion flock.
The nine men's morris is filled up with mud
And the quaint mazes of the wanton green
For lack of tread are undistinguishable."

So Titania, fresh from India.

This concrete rural warmth of colour is in a different world from Marlowe's cold, majestic, starry but not earthly imagery. The water-meadows of the Avon that

"makes sweet music with the embroidered stones,
   giving a gentle kiss to every sedge,"

have for centuries been a paradise for cattle. In describing the flight of Cleopatra's galley at the battle of Actium, Enobarbus says:—

"The breeze upon her, like a cow in June,
   Hoists sail and flies."

The word "breeze" has foundered many an editor of Shakespeare's text. It is Midlands vernacular for the gadfly that stampedes the summer cows, *holding their tails vertically like the sails of a ship*. So did our soldiers and sailors "babble o' green fields" among the sands of Libya or in the fabled Mediterranean. None but Shakespeare has thus made them one. Warwickshire is a land of hedges, which, when neglected,

"Like prisoners wildly overgrown with hair,
   Put forth disordered twigs."

But they were not all neglected because the Midlands were a regional capital of the craft of pleaching or laying a hedge, and FitzHerbert's *Boke of Husbandrie* (1528) has a section, "To plashe or pleche a Hedge." The Midlands technique was diffused to my own region, where laying a hedge is still called "plushing." The "thick-pleached alley,"

"Where honeysuckles ripened by the sun
   Forbid the sun to enter,"

is referred to many times in the plays.

On his way to the Cotswolds to see Captain Dover's Games on Dover's Hill, north of Chipping Campden, Shakespeare passed the Vale of Evesham, a fruit-growing region since the foundation of Evesham Abbey. For miles around, the old pear trees creep along the ground like great horned snails. Everybody knows the wonderful lines about grafting in *The Winter's Tale*. But if I, who have read them fifty times, now write them down, the reader can bear with them once more:—

> "You see, sweet maid, we marry
> A gentler scion to the wildest stock
> And make conceive a bark of lesser kind
> By bud of nobler race; this is an art
> Which does mend nature—change it rather, but
> The art itself is nature."

What a world away from the Miltonic set piece! On Dover's Hill, Justice Shallow had his greyhound "outrun on Cotsall" (*King Henry IV*). On the Wolds, Falstaff, with a nature broad as theirs and wit as nimble as their breezes, bilked the Justice whom some say was Sir Thomas Lucy of Charlecote, Shakespeare's boyhood enemy, on the stage. But he paid a tribute to his husbandry. From Stinchcombe Hill, Harry Percy saw Berkeley Castle "by yon tuft of trees." It is the only promontory along the Edge where the Castle can be seen.[1] In this neighbourhood Shakespeare had family connections, and at Nibley Justice Shallow once sowed his red wheat. In our own period, ignorant of the arts of life, its ideal properties for reed-thatching go by default. Every thatcher always speaks of his wheat-straw as "reeds." *Ariel*:—

> "His tears run down his beard, like winter's drops
> From eaves of reeds."

Not eaves of thatch, be it noted.

[1] There is no landscape painting in Shakespeare except Edgar's description of Dover Cliff—to his blinded father. Only when society became urban in the late eighteenth century did views became fashionable. The country scene was in Shakespeare's bones, not in a picture for his eyes only.

Fourteen years ago, in Cotswold field and cottage and over mugs of "scrumpy," I collected a glossary of Shakespearean words still in Cotswold currency. I can scarcely believe to-day that I once heard "good-speed" for our trite "good-bye," our repulsive "bye-bye" or cheap and lazy "so long." I heard "lush" as Shakespeare used it in *Henry IV,* "mazzard" for head as in *Hamlet* and *Othello,* "plash" for pool as in *The Taming of the Shrew,* "orts" for leavings as in *Troilus and Cressida,* "slobberly" for sloppy as in *Henry V,* "scathe" for harm as in *Richard III,* "twit" for blab as in *The Two Gentlemen of Verona,* and many others that Shakespeare spoke on these "high wild hills." Time out of mind, the Yabberton Yawnies (Ebrington simpletons, with wits "as thick as Tewkesbury mustard," as Falstaff said of Poins) were reputed to have mucked the church tower to make it grow as tall as Campden's. When the stone was seen to be discoloured a few days later, a wise yawny observed, "It a done he some good, cause he a growghed two inches." This was just the country clownishness that Shakespeare loved and in variants used over and over again.

The men who were speaking Shakespeare to me at the Eight Bells at Campden were nearly all illiterates. But they knew a thing or two the professors have forgotten. One of these Shakespearean countrymen, Reuben Smith, of Compton Abdale, aged seventy-five and still doing a score of jobs about the farm, talks Shakespearean to this day without, perhaps, ever having heard of him. That Shakespeare did lift the local idiom of his own country folk into his plays is shown by "on a line" for "in a rage," and Iago's "speake within doore" for "speak softly," both Warwickshire.

English lace-making, apparently founded by Catherine of Aragon, was widespread in the Midlands, its headquarters, and a body of folk-song, custom and ceremony gathered about it. The Duke in *Twelfth Night* asks Feste for one of these "antique" songs:—

"Mark it, Cesario, it is old and plain,
  The spinsters and the knitters in the sun
  And the free maids, that weave their threads with
                          bones (bobbins),
  Do use to sing it."

In my own village, years ago, I used to see the spinsters weaving their bones on their horsed pillows in the evening sun. Barton-on-the-Heath, in the Oxfordshire Cotswolds, was the home of Christopher Sly, the tinker, and Justice Silence's "By our Lady, I think 'a be but Goodman Puff of Barson" refers to the fat man of Barcheston. Here Richard Hyckes, under the enlightened patronage of Squire Sheldon, made the famous tapestry maps[1] and "arras, moccadoes, carolles, plonketts, grograynes, sayes and serges" on the local looms.

To Shakespeare's borrowings from the peasantry may be traced his love of lines of one-syllabled words:—

> " When we are born, we cry that we are come
> To this great stage of fools."—*Lear*,

is one of hundreds. Words to the peasant were like physical objects, " things that you may touch and see." It is possible that Shakespeare's transporting, terrifying or almost intolerably poignant use of repetition in words is derived from the same characteristic in countrymen. Justice Shallow of the Wolds repeats himself again and again. The Clown in *Antony and Cleopatra* iterates "I wish you joy o' the worm," and he is a typically Buckinghamshire yokel. So is Dogberry of Grendon Underwood in the same county, where, according to Aubrey, Shakespeare put up on his journeys between Stratford and London.

Repetition in words is one of Hamlet's modes of self-expression, and Hamlet was very near to Shakespeare's heart, if he was not his creation of a large part of himself. By repetition, a whole character is limned in a line. Octavia, standing between Antony and Cæsar:—

> "The Jove of power make me, most weak, most weak,
> Your reconciler."

The horror and anguish of Othello at his own deed smite us in the one-syllabled

> "My wife! my wife! what wife! I have no wife."

Repetition frequently occurs in *Macbeth*, and, of course, with

[1] *See* p. 129.

what might be called supernatural power in *King Lear*. "No, no, no life . . ." and the terrible quintet of "nevers" that toll out after them, by no poet before or since has the spectre of utter despair, and the irreparable loss of all been evoked by a simplicity so elemental. One last instance from *King Lear*. Cordelia confronts her father:—

Lear : But goes your heart with this?
Cordelia : Ay, my good lord.
Lear : So young, and so untender.
Cordelia : So young, my lord, and true.

Their reunion when Lear awakes from his madness:—

Lear : For as I am a man, I think this lady
            To be my child Cordelia. (he kneels)
Cordelia : And so I am, I am. (she kneels)

Thus, by the repeat of the very simplest of words, the wrestling of a dual pride and the reconciliation of a dual humility, are matchlessly evoked.

The songs scattered over the plays are either the peasants' just as they sang them or touched with the wand of their supreme fellow-countryman. Some of the folklore came from Scot, Roger Bacon, Ovid, Pliny and other scholars. But most of it his country neighbours knew by heart:—

"In winter's tedious nights sit by this fire
With good old folks, and let them tell their tales
Of woeful ages, long ago betid,
And send the hearers weeping to their beds."

They were not "tales told at the Mermaid," but tales of the far away and long ago, stored from who knows what sources into the timeless memory of the peasant. Troilus's "As true as steel, as plantage to the moon," is an old wives' tale that some moderns consider a biological truth. The fairy lore, with its charms and spells, is much of it a relic of the ancient nature-worship locally handed down, like the horse-brasses of the moon and other symbols. Shakespeare's "beldam trot" is the peasant's "old wife," the corn-spirit of the ancients, recollected in the "Old Wife Trods" of the archaic green ways and ox-droves.

So with games, dancing and ballads. The home-made has to be sifted from the imported. But foot-racing, football, wrestling, loggats, quoits, shovel-board, prisoners' base, barley-break or last-in-hell, push-pin, cherry-pit, hoodman blind and handy-dandy, the guests of the plays, were all peasant field-sports. Not used in sport but to make the human play richer or more terrible. Lear speaks of the last in his madness, and Hamlet says to his mother:—

> "What devil was't
> That thus hath cozened thee at hoodman blind?"

Hamlet again in the charnel house:—

> "Did these bones cost no more the breeding, but to play at loggats with 'em?"

Traditional ballads, as distinct from the contemporary and usually scurrilous ones, are scattered in spadefuls over the plays, like rich earth round flowers of speech and character, Ophelia's, Desdemona's, the Fool's in *King Lear*. In what the Puritans called "the heathen devilry of dancing," again, the references to formal dances like the pavane and the galliard are in a very different category from such dances as the Morris, danced with treble, mean, tenor and double bells behind the team of forty oxen drawing the maypole to the village green. Both Feste, the clown in *Twelfth Night*, and Ariel in *The Tempest* play the pipe and tabor, the accompaniment to a country step dance. Many a time Shakespeare saw "greasy Joan," "keel the pot" at Mary Arden's farm in Wilmcote. Once he saw and incomparably reported the two carriers in the grey dawn of the inn yard at Rochester (*Henry IV*). The first carrier swears "by the mass," as Justice Silence swears "By our Lady." Yeoman-bred Shakespeare, the Midlands gardener and freeholder who put his country-mindedness upon the London stage, lived on the time-borders of Gothic England. He had a much better right than Voltaire to say, *Il faut cultiver notre jardin.*

Lafeu's "I took this lark for a bunting" in *All's Well* and Warwick's :—

"His well-proportion'd beard made rough and ragged
Like to the summer's corn by tempest lodged."[1]

in *Henry IV* are two examples out of hundreds that show a poet rooted to his native countryside and enriching instinct with observation. He made use of natural symbols for atmospheric, emotional, and dramatic purposes, and grouped them together to form a power-station for each play. His theatre, depending for its effects not upon the scene but the spoken word, gave him full play in such imaginative symbolism. A similar effect can be seen in detached lines or couplets:—

"Light thickens
And the crow makes wing for the rooky wood"

is more than magic of description. The light clots or, as we say, "my heart stopped" or "I was frozen with fear." Again:—

"I have lived long enough, my way of life
Is fallen into the sere, the yellow leaf."

Macbeth becomes the dying year, just as the sick Fisher King in the Holy Grail Mystery romance was identified with the passing of summer into winter. Yet another instance of this subtle and masterly rural symbolism is the use of littleness to express greatness. John of Gaunt's speech about England is hackneyed enough. But it buds once more when it is considered in this antiphonal sense—"this little world," this "precious stone," this "blessed plot," leased out "like a tenement or pelting farm." Imogen's picture of England as a swan's nest in a great pool is even more striking. The Warwickshire man speaks out of his provincial experience. But the effect is of a mighty tree risen from an acorn, as the kingdom of heaven was likened to a mustard seed.

Parallel with this service of the small making greatness greater is that of natural or every-day sights and scenes making tragic and catastrophic events yet more tremendous. There are many examples of this audacious imagery in the last two Acts of *Antony and Cleopatra*. When Antony discovers he is betrayed:—

[1] "Lodged" is still a technical term among the more traditional farmers.

"O this false soul of Egypt . . .
Whose bosom was my crownet . . .
Like a right gipsy, hath, at fast and loose,
Beguiled me to the very heart of loss."

She had "packt cards with Cæsar." Cleopatra's great epitaph on Antony:—

"realms and islands were
As plates dropt from his pocket."

When the asp bites and Charmian cries, "O eastern star!"—

"Peace, peace,
Dost thou not see my baby at my breast,
That sucks the nurse asleep?"

Greatest of all when Charmian says:—

"Now boast thee, death, in thy possession lies
A lass unparalleled."

But there is yet a greater—when the dying Lear says:—

"Pray you, undo this button: thank you, sir"—

This is the concrete country mode of understatement enskied.

Yet a third element shows a further flowering. In the earlier plays, the natural forces and the rural scene are represented in an idyllic setting. Nature is pure poetry, the countryman pure comedy. But in the later plays, particularly in *King Lear*, *Macbeth* and the last three "Comedies," nature advances from the background into the foreground. The foolishness of Bottom and Dogberry becomes the wisdom of Lear's folk-singing Fool. The natural scene takes part in the play as an actor; its poetry assumes the grander function of a moral agent in the Tragedies and in the last "Comedies" a spiritual one. Nature becomes linked with supernature. The word is made flesh.

IV

Natural imagery in Shakespeare is thus woven into the very fabric of his art. It is only from such a foundation that we can understand what is meant by the statement that his creative powers are like nature's. Dr. Johnson said—"Shakespeare always makes nature predominate over accident," unlike Hardy, whose characters are so often the victims of accident. Dr. Johnson also paid a tribute to Shakespeare's "vigilance of observation," one not unlike Keats's. But the supreme creations which De Quincey truly said are like works of nature—go beyond observation. It has been well said that they become creatures independent of their creator, like Rembrandt's. They escape from their maker's control and are just as alive off stage as on it. They are so self-contained that they burst their dramatic framework, like a fermenting home-made wine bursting its bottle. Shakespeare's avowed purpose was to hold the mirror up to nature, and "truth to nature" was in his view the poet's criterion. The royal carelessness, the sublime simplicity, the secret complexity of nature are all there. Nature's craftsmanship is there. His superb stagecraft in his maturity, that is to say, is always organic. Character, speech and dramatic action all grow out of and illumine one another. The discipline of such freedom is not imposed from without, but comes naturally out of the interplay between them. The modesty of nature is there. Hamlet-Shakespeare rebukes the players because they have affronted it. A lightning example of this occurs in *The Tempest*. The original of the lines" Ye elves of hills, brooks, standing lakes and groves . . ." is in Ovid's *Metamorphoses*. Medea's power over the tides in Ovid is transformed:—

"And ye that on the sands with printless foot
Do chase the ebbing Neptune and do fly him
When he comes back."

And nature's profusion. Madmen, pimps, bawds, villains, comics, tender, sparkling, evil, or heroic women, men for good or bad of superhuman stature, pour out like some great natural flood or tropical heat. No genius has created people of genius like Shakespeare—Hamlet, Mercutio (almost), Beatrice, Falstaff, Lear, Perdita and Prospero. "The art itself is nature."

To the startled reader or spectator some of these creations appear like demigods. But flawed every one, except perhaps Prospero. So they are humanised and conform to the Christian doctrine of man's nature. "It is beyond the competence of the critic," Pearsall Smith[1] has said, "to explain such creative power; he approaches there the ultimate secret of existence, the mystery by means of which this many-peopled world has been brought into being." But this supernatural gift is based on, translated from the organic and the natural. How should the modern world, spellbound by the inorganic, or the amoral Freudian novelist, paddling about in the Styx of the unconscious, understand Shakespeare?

Modern life is overpoweringly social: there is little or no room in it for the eccentric, the solitary, the cat that walks by itself. But a good case could be made for Shakespeare, the lonely contemplative. Mixing with his fellow-actors and playwrights, enjoying brief friendships with the quality, fond of his glass, brimming with human feeling, over-sexed as he must have been, a practical man of business, favoured at Court, particularly under James, he seems the very last man to have courted solitude. Contemporary records testify to his good nature, wit and ease of manners. For years he was *the* popular playwright, the magnet of his age. But beneath the surface he appears as great a solitary as Wordsworth. At the Globe, he was a countryman in a company of urban professionals. He left Bankside for his little market-town in his prime (he was only forty-eight), nor does his will indicate that he left friendship behind. What intercourse of spirit did he find at Stratford? Dr. Hall, one or both of his daughters, John Combe? His intimates are much more likely to have been his own characters and his communion with his garden and the countryside.

The internal evidence is much stronger. Jacques—Hamlet—Prospero, it is more or less accepted that these were the characters of his character. Jacques, the earlier Hamlet, is an

[1] *On Reading Shakespeare.*

ironical Wordsworthian who walks through the play without being of the play. Hamlet's preoccupation with universals, his habit of seeing all things in relation to the stars and the moral order and his philosophic detachment from the life of the Court, make his immersion in the muddiness of its affairs half his tragedy. Horatio is his confidant but hardly the fellow of his soul. And what companionship could Prospero, the purged and matured Hamlet, have?

Jacques is a preliminary draft of Hamlet in another direction. Dilettante as he is, he declares his aim to be Hamlet's—namely, "to cleanse the foul body of th' infected world." When Prospero-Shakespeare drowned his book and returned with "every third thought" his grave, to Stratford-Milan, it was as one utterly disillusioned with city, stage and court. He was the man who in *King Lear* had seen the perdition of a world and redemption only in death, in *Macbeth* the futility of ambition and the nothingness of its triumph, in *Othello* the pity and tears of things, in *Hamlet* the warping of a supreme human spirit, in *Timon* the solitude of generosity, in *Antony and Cleopatra* the dissolution of an integrated State, in *The Tempest* the passing of human life into the consummation of dream. Had this Prometheus companions? He found his fellow in his native place, a green forecourt of eternity in which alone his spirit could rest. The last three plays are irradiated with the light of setting suns. Half the world was flooded by it, and that half was the rural heart of England. The other half lay beyond the horizon.

Shakespeare's solitariness and rural passion make logical and consistent his detestation of the mass-man. The collective smell of a crowd—"the mutable rank-scented many"—he loathed. There can be no doubt about this partly instinctive aversion, and it is the feeling of every countryman. But Shakespeare's anti-demagogy, summed up in Mark Antony's speech in the Forum which beguiles, plays upon and despises the pliable, ignorant town-mob, was also a political conviction. It was "the noblest Roman of them all" whose curt address disdained to "please the million", as Hamlet says. Collectivism and theoretic and ideological abstractions about equality—always the product of the urban mind—were antipathetic to the whole body of Shakespeare's beliefs. His view of the equality man is condensed into Jack Cade's "I will apparel them all in one livery, that they may agree like brothers, and worship me as their lord." Or, as we should put it, the ideal of the "common man" means levelling down to one common denominator, the natural prey of dictatorship. Shakespeare had no confidence in the "yes or no of general ignorance." Shakespeare's men and women are all uncommon people. The common man tears the poet Cinna to pieces in *Julius Cæsar*, forces Coriolanus to betray his country and would have made jeering bawdry of the shame of Cleopatra. So the wolfish mob howled "Crucify him!"

Another element was involved besides his country instinct and political faith. Ben Jonson's "understanding gentlemen of the ground," the apple-peelers, sausage-eaters and "stinkards" of the Globe Theatre pit had driven him to many a grisly sacrifice of his artistic conscience. The ranting and the blood-letting and such crudities as the cannibal dish of *Titus Andronicus* (if Shakespeare ever wrote more than a scene or two of it) were "commodity" for the multitude. But worse than these were such botchings as the Pecksniffian last Act of *Measure for Measure*, the squalid marriage of Hero and Claudio in *Much Ado*, the debasement of Joan of Arc and the speciousness of Prince Hal. Shakespeare cannot be acquitted of a dose of original sin in bad taste, bad feeling, the sophisticated innuendo of bawdry, so recondite that only scholars to-day can smoke out its meaning, lack of scruple, cheap-jackery, lily-painting and machine-work. It was not the Hydra in the Globe pit which in *The Two Gentlemen of Verona* drove Valentine to offer his faithful Silvia to her would-be ravisher. Perhaps his own responsibility for such lapses increased his hatred for a mob whose pressure compelled him to commit many others. And how well he was aware of it! "O, it offends me to the soul," says Hamlet-Shakespeare to the players, "to hear a robustious periwig-pated fellow tear a passion to tatters, to very rags, to split the ear of the groundlings, who, for the most part, are capable of nothing but inexplicable dumb-shows and noise." "Pox! Leave thy damnable faces and begin!" Hamlet cries furiously to the mouthing and gesticulating actor in the play-scene which is to confound Claudius and verify the Ghost's revelation.

Shakespeare's obvious love for country Tom, individual Dick and ribald Harry fanned his distaste for their multiplication in London. His clowns were all taken from their prototypes in country celebration and mummery. In his youth at Stratford he must often have seen the buffoon with his bladder and belled cap leading the procession of the Morris dancers. Yet he gives his fools and clowns some of his sweetest music, and transfigures them into oracles, satirists, philosophers and illiterate men of wit, wisdom and insight. Truth as revealed to the simple is in Shakespeare as well as in the New Testament. "Unto the Greeks foolishness;" unto the townsman likewise. For the mob to Shakespeare was not only the undifferentiated plebs. The fashionable, the usurer, the monopolist, the official "dressed in a little brief authority" (as distinguished from the country Dogberrys who were laughable, not an offence), these were to him parcels of the urban mass-man. It is to be noted that he never painted the citizens in the mode of Dekker and Middleton.[1]

The attitude of the "new humanism" is anti-Shakespearean at both ends. Shakespeare made his art intelligible to large mixed audiences. One type of modern humanist considers its work inartistic unless it is unintelligible to all but a few specialists. Another type at the other extreme[2] accepts the passing of "minority culture" and professes to appeal to a "mass-civilisation" whose culture is fed to it by a "mass production manufacturing goods of a sophisticated quality for a mass market." The humanist must no longer be the prophet or the critic of society; he has ceased to be the interpreter of universal truth and beauty to it. He flatters and woos, not guides and warns the mass-mind. Still less is his business with nature; he is to be the cultural medium of "the great urban centres." As Hamlet the humanist is obsolete. His rôle is that of Rosencrantz and Guildenstern. It is clear that Shakespeare has no points of contact with either type.

Shakespeare's anti-Puritanism was equally marked. Partly because he himself, as Lear's and Timon's crazy fulminations against sex reveal, recoiled with Puritan disgust and over-

[1] *The Merry Wives*, being written to royal order, is the exception that proves the rule.

[2] *Pilot Papers* (1945).

emphasis against his own sexuality. But his antipathy to the
Puritans was far more deep-seated and wiser than a distortion
of his own nature. The Puritans were the bourgeois party that
obstructed the freedom of the theatres and succeeded in closing
them after his death. The Puritans were the urban shopkeepers
and business men who persecuted the festal countryman and
withered the musical soul of rural England. Just over thirty
years after Shakespeare's death, the Puritans had all the
ballad-singers arrested, and there were holocausts of organs,
lutes, viols, flutes, theorbos and "harpsicons." Two years after
his death, James I had to restore the Maypoles and Whitsun
Ales in Lancashire, suppressed by the Puritan magistrates. The
virtuous Stratford of Shakespeare's return was a dull and
silent town compared with the Stratford of cakes and ale he
had left as a young man.

But for Shakespeare there was more in the Puritan suppres-
sion of country dance, song, pageant and mime than this.
Music to him was part of man's moral being:—

> "The man that hath no music in himself . . .
> Is fit for treasons, stratagems and spoils.
> The motions of his spirit are dull as night,
> And his affections dark as Erebus:
> Let no such man be trusted."

Music is the medicine for restoring Lear to his right mind.
He had a metaphysical love for music which in the heavenly
talk between Jessica and Lorenzo at Belmont takes on a purely
Gothic expression:—

> "There's not the smallest orb which thou behold'st
> But in his motion like an angel sings,
> Still quiring to the young-eyed cherubins—
> Such harmony is in immortal souls;
> But whilst this muddy vesture of decay
> Doth grossly close it in, we cannot hear it."

Exactly the same traditional thought appears in Cleopatra's
lament for Antony:—

> "his voice was propertied
> As all the tunèd spheres."

Nothing could be more mediæval. Somehow, he felt, the whole traditional fabric of human joy and sweetness and lyrical heart's ease was being threatened by the Puritans, and it is impossible to imagine the plays without the peasant's melodious voice in them. Angelo, the Puritan bureaucrat in *Measure for Measure*, is one of the vilest hypocrites in all fiction. His self-righteousness is worn like a suit of glittering armour which makes it even less tolerable than the oozing sort. He is corruption incarnate, and, as Shakespeare's Grand Inquisitor, prepares the way for the terrific judgments against authority in *King Lear*. It was on account of Angelo that the cosmic lines in the play were written:—

> "Man . . . like an angry ape
> Plays such fantastic tricks before high heaven
> As make the angels weep . . . "

Rural society has always been hierarchical in structure, so much so that it never could be anything else. That did not prevent the village community from being a thoroughly democratic institution. But it was a democracy within an aristocratic frame. It was a graded society of mutual obligations, duties and commitments because there is no other way of serving the land. Shakespeare's aristocratic and traditional principles, formulated in Ulysses'

> "The heavens themselves, the planets and the centre
> Observe degree, priority and place,"

were thus part of his organic ruralism. The individualism and sturdy independence of his yeoman stock were in no sense Victorian. They were perfectly compatible with hierarchy. His belief that, when this "degree" is overturned, chaos is come again, was as intuitive as it was reasoned. The whole cycle of the History Plays reveals a tension of conflict between the forces of disorder and those of a deeply moralised order. Their origins lay in the Morality rather than in the old Chronicle Play.[1] The nucleus of morality itself lay in the cohesion of the family:—

[1] See *Shakespeare's History Plays*, by Dr. E. M. W. Tillyard.

> "Filial ingratitude!
> Is it not as this mouth should tear this hand
> For lifting food to't?"

The enmity of the urban middle class to the aristocratic idea is vehemently expressed in *Coriolanus*, but blended with the lashing of the hero's own pride, the cardinal Christian sin with which Shakespeare was so preoccupied. The very play in which the Ulysses speech occurs is a savage parody of the romantic illusions to which conventional thought is prone. In fact, Shakespeare overdoes the satire on the picturesque heroes of the war for a drab. The sons of Atreus are dwarfed and vulgarised to the level of Thersites' spleen.

Why does Shakespeare make these ferocious attacks upon an hereditary leadership he believed to be the buttress of order and the arch of concord? Partly, no doubt, because of the distemper in his own mind when he wrote *Troilus and Cressida*. But his artillery is discharged at "the great image of authority" in many other plays. *Cymbeline*, *Timon*, *Hamlet* and especially *King Lear* reverberate with it. The answer is that the corruption of the aristocratic principle slashed through the network of obligations and responsibilities which justified it. Self-will is the besetting sin of Shakespeare's Titanic figures, and the duty of self-will is only to itself. But this aristocratic concept, upheld by the very attacks he made upon it, is wholly alien to the modern mind, whether in its moral or political aspect. By the irony of history, the totalitarian idea, whether Communist, Fascist or democratic, has shown itself even more prone to war, disorder and authoritarianism than the aristocratic idea, some sympathy with which (natural to the countryman and endemic to the mediæval mind) is necessary in order to understand Shakespeare. He accepted these traditional principles, just as he did the conventions of his theatre—the soliloquy, the dumb show, the pun, the rhymed couplet and the rest. But in accepting he transcended them.

These various aspects of Shakespeare's mind thus radiate from a common centre. The natural creator, the imagist of natural symbols, the exile from his native Warwickshire, the solitary, the natural philosopher, also showed himself as the anti-proletarian, the individualist who feared and recoiled from mankind in terms of collective numbers, the champion of an ordered hierarchy but the scourge of a corrupt aristocracy. All were branches thrown up from his deep-rootedness in the soil of his home. His reader would, then, expect to find in his art a coherent and unified reflection of this multiple thought. It is not only present, but, without stretching the plain letter of the text, can be crystallised into a kind of formula. It is, in fact, the contrast between the life of the town and the life of the country.

This contrast is not, of course, impressed like a post-office stamp upon every play he wrote. Such is not the way of art. But with variations both of form and idea it is a recurrent theme in play after play. Brandes strikes the keynote in his chapter on *As You Like It*:—

"First and foremost, the play typefies Shakespeare's longing, the longing of this great spirit, to get away from the unnatural city life, away from the false and ungrateful city folk, intent on business and on gain, away from flattery and falsehood and deceit, out into the country, where simple manners still endure, where it is easier to realise the dream of full freedom, and where the scent of the wood is so sweet."

This is obvious enough. But the motive of

"Away, away from men and towns
To the wild woods and the downs"

acquires much greater force and complexity when it is considered out of the context of the specifically rural plays and among scenes and characters not rural at all.

Hamlet, for instance, interlards his speech with as many old country saws, jigs, catches, ballads and proverbial lore as Edgar himself in *King Lear*. And Hamlet is driven half-mad and suicidal by the criminality of the court and its attendant sycophancy. The beastliness of the usurper King gathers to a head the diffused rottenness of the State of Denmark. When he contemplates self-slaughter, he thinks more in general than in personal terms:—

W.M.B.   C

"The oppressor's wrong, the proud man's contumely,
    The insolence of office and the spurns
    That patient merit of the unworthy takes."

"To be honest as this world goes, is to be one man picked out
of ten thousand." His picture of the piece of work that is
man, "the paragon of animals," the lord of the natural
kingdom, is in the bitterest contrast with the vicious world
of power-politics, time-serving, expediency, artifice, debau-
chery, idleness and busy intrigue. Lear: "change places; and
handy-dandy, which is the justice, which is the thief?" The
arrogance of the lords of Mycenæ and Sparta in *Troilus and
Cressida* is a counterpart of their meanness, brutality, treachery
and lust. Thersites is the stick of dynamite that explodes
Ulysses' "order" into chaos.

The snarling invective of Timon in his cave by the lonely
sea stresses the moral yet more plainly. The corruption of the
money-power is here as strong a poison as the ingratitude
taken up again in *King Lear*. Timon says to Phrynia and
Timandra, the concubines of Alicibiades, when they beg him
for gold:—

"Hold up, you sluts, your aprons mountant."

"There is more gold.
    Do you damn others and let this damn you,
    And ditches grave you all."

Lear :—
    "Plate sin with gold
    And the strong lance of justice hurtless breaks;
    Arm it in rags, a pigmy's straw doth pierce it."

The misanthropic indignation of Timon, scorching as Swift's,
is lightless. He has no refuge from the moral pestilence of
Athens but his "everlasting mansion" of death "upon the
beachèd verge of the salt flood." Lear has no refuge from the
torrent of evil in high places but death. But from the as
corrupt courts of Cymbeline, of Leontes in *The Winter's Tale*
and of Milan in *The Tempest*, as from the court of the banished

Duke in *As You Like It*, the escape is found. It was Shakespeare's own from London.

V

This rural "escapism," richly dramatised in these four plays, is set over against what is escaped from—the life of the town. The contrast appears in three different forms. The country plays of *As You Like It* and the *Dream* are very distinct in mood from the country trio of *Cymbeline*, *The Winter's Tale* and *The Tempest*. Another aspect is shown in *Macbeth* and *King Lear*, wherein the religious universals, especially in the latter, are much more detached from a moralised nature than in the last three "Comedies."

Shakespeare took *As You Like It* from Lodge's *Euphues His Legacie*. He left Lodge's lioness in Arden but imported Jacques, Touchstone and Audrey into it from his own mind. The spring-like temper of "when wheat is green, when hawthorn buds appear" contrasts with the autumnal sense of *The Winter's Tale* and its companions. But he was not content with borrowing the pastoral convention. Real country people walked into the tapestry. Rosalind and Orlando, woven into the pastoral design as they are, by their wit and health and freshness walk out of it. The sheep, though pastoral furniture, have "greasy fells." The air of delicate make-believe exactly corresponds with the Renaissance view of "sweetest Shakespeare, fancy's child." This fantasy is far removed from the realism of the shepherd's feast in *The Winter's Tale* and its meaning as the secret of the good life. But the touches of rural realism do not break the idyllic spell of Arden. On the contrary, they enhance it by making the dream closer to real life and the reality more dream-like.

But this blending of fact with fiction into a vision of wholeness is much more audacious in the *Midsummer Night's Dream*. The moon is the goddess of this passionless play. In the first hundred lines to Act I Scene I, which is Theseus' court, there are no fewer than five references to the moon. It is the moonshine of enchantment but also of ribaldry, of the clod-hopper and the sprite, of classical legend and peasant

folk-lore, of Indian groves and the meadows and woods of
the Avon. Magic and homeliness are at one. Ceremonious
masque-like lovers, courtiers and hunters are in and out of
fairyland whose gossamer elves sport in the village workshop
and the farm kitchen. The mysterious "little western flower"
grows among the flora and insect fauna of Warwickshire lanes
and woodland rides. No lyrical poet in the world has ever
done anything like this. Yet the moon of the *Dream*, shining
upon this motley company, is quite different from the moon
of Belmont that lights up the shores of old romance and
reveals to mortals the music of the spheres. Thus the traditional culture of the English countryside found in Shakespeare
its supreme embodiment. As nature and man had made it he
rendered it whole, the real with the fantastical, the poetry
with the practice. How should we, who have deserted it,
understand him? Only by the reawakening of a dormant
instinct. Only by passing through the fire that Shakespeare
himself endured. Only by emerging from the travail and
tribulation he foretold. Only by a return to the sanity and truth
he himself disclosed in the last plays. For the Tragedies are
symbols of our own tragedy. His escape to the country to find
a deeper reality in it than even he knew in the *Dream* may yet
be ours.

Pearsall Smith speaks of the Tragedies as darkened by
"an awful and enigmatic quality." No sensitive and unpre-
judiced reader can doubt that their gloom, their appalled
sense of the potency of evil, the superhuman passions of their
characters, the clash in them between the heights and the
abyss, the atmosphere of world-catastrophe that enfolds them,
were projected upon a gigantic stage from a spiritual crisis
in Shakespeare himself. They are preluded by "the unpleasant
comedies"—*All's Well* and *Troilus* (1602-3) and *Measure for
Measure* (1604)—in a bitter disillusionment with and contempt
for the false valuations of society. The world smiles upon the
acquisitive Helena, the hypocrite Angelo and the vain, cruel
and treacherous Achilles. But this crisis is not the most modern
view. The modern view has "seen through" the absolute
validity of moral judgments. Shakespeare could never have had
a spiritual crisis, because traditional values are meaningless.
His tragic cycle was in response to the veering of the popular

will from comedy to tragedy. Othello was taken in Iago's hook from no flaw in his own character, but in obedience to a stage convention by which the hero always believed the lies of the villain.

How could such blindness of perception have arisen? Partly, no doubt, as a reaction from the nineteenth century idolatry of Shakespeare. But the cause must lie deeper. It can only proceed from the hostility or, more likely, unfamiliarity of the urban mind to such Christian conceptions as sin, free will, the "creatureliness" of man, repentance and redemption. It is all at sea with so Gothic a scene in *Hamlet* as King Claudius' semi-contrite prayer which falls to earth like a wounded bird:—

> "My words fly up, my thoughts remain below:
> Words without thoughts never to heaven go."

It is not out of place, therefore, to refer very briefly to Reinhold Niebuhr's[1] definition of the "prophetic message" and the "prophetic judgment" in respect of "sin." "Sin is the unwillingness of man to acknowledge his creatureliness and dependence upon God." This is the sin against God. The "prophetic judgment" is relevant to "the self-sufficiency of modern man whose technical achievements obscure his dependence upon vast natural processes beyond his control and accentuate the perennial pride of man in his own power and security." This is the sin against nature. "For Biblical faith, God is revealed in the catastrophic events of history," caused by "the pride of man in vain rebellion against the structure, the law, the essential character of reality." This is the sin against reality. The Christian doctrine of sin is centred in self-will. Sin, that is to say, is a spiritual and not a natural flaw.

All the Tragedies without exception are dramatic commentaries upon the spiritual sin of pride and self-will or will-to-power. When self-will and self-interest wholly dominate a man, he turns into a devil like Iago, "more fell than anguish, hunger, or the sea." Where the sin of pride does not possess the tragic heroes to the exclusion of all else, they are engaged in an inward conflict with themselves, which convulses the

---

[1] *The Nature and Destiny of Man.*

kingdom, and in *King Lear*, the cosmos. The prides of Coriolanus, of Brutus, of Macbeth, of Timon, of Antony, of Lear, even of Cordelia, are all very different issues of pride; the delusion of Othello, a kind of inversion of pride, is at second remove from it. Like him, Hamlet is the victim of the will-to-power. But all these towering figures of free will are spiritually flawed, suffer the judgment or are redeemed, not necessarily into life but into "salvation." The "fall" of men of such nobility of spirit, so great that they seem "forms more real than living man," yet the more human for their very defects, gives full weight to the Aristotelean "pity and terror." Without free will and so internal conflict in tragic drama, there is virtually no tragedy at all. The translunary drama of good and evil in Shakespeare is of the very essence of tragedy. Hardy's "automatic sense Unweeting why or whence" and making human beings its puppets, takes the heart out of tragedy. Where would be the tragedy in *Macbeth* if the "Immanent Will" of Hardy had led Macbeth, a passive instrument, to the bedside of Duncan? Whether Shakespeare professed himself a Christian or not, his Tragedies conform, if more conspiciously in some than others, to the Christian conception of man and of the spiritual government of the universe. As such, they are less "enigmatic" than appears.

King Lear perfectly illustrates the triune Christian sin against reality, against nature and against God. The Christian recognition of the power of evil centred in the will of man but not derived from nature is written into the text with letters of fire. Lear brings the "judgment" upon his own white head by an infatuated pride whose folly is akin to Othello's. Stripped of his kingdom, his family, his all, and finding refuge in a hovel with his Fool and a madman, he is reduced to "the thing itself." He suffers martyrdom, he descends into the hell of humiliation, but finds therein the baptismal waters of compassion and so of redemption. In a double sense he is restored to his right mind. He reaches salvation through a perception of reality born of the extremity of his suffering. Aesthylean Lear is reborn into the heavenly grace. But he does not recover his earthly kingdom. His new kingdom is not of this world. His love for Cordelia is transfigured, but only to lose her once more and for ever. I use terms now strange to our

ears as a means of conveying how precisely and totally the
"soul-making" of Lear fits the Christian canon and the Christian
philosophy. Pagan Lear himself speaks such terms when,
waking to consciousness out of madness, he beholds Cordelia:—

> "Thou are a soul in bliss, but I am bound
> Upon a wheel of fire, that mine own tears
> Do scald like molten lead."

It is the same with the monsters and embodiments of evil
—Goneril, Regan, Cornwall, Edmund. We catch the terror
of the word "damnation." "Ancient damnation" Juliet calls
the Nurse when she counsels her to abandon Romeo. But in
King Lear we descend into the "sulphurous pit." We seem to
be witnessing a more than human drama of horror and
wickedness, a revolt of hell against earth. We are present at
a primeval collision between angelic and demonic powers,
shaking the solid globe to its foundations. We become vaguely
troubled that there may be some meaning and truth in the
Christian mythology of what was before time and place, so
huge and elemental are the contending forces. When Kent
says in tones like a tocsin, "Is this the promised end?" we
think of the end of a world. "We have seen the best of our
time," says Gloster, "machinations, hollowness, treachery
and all ruinous disorders follow us disquietly to our graves."
Antony and Cleopatra staged the downfall of Rome, "betrayed
by what is false within," into Cæsarism. But the theme of
King Lear is of the collapse of all values, truth and order. The
words of Albany fall on our ears with the dreadfulness of
prophecy:—

> "If that the heavens do not their visible spirits
> Send quickly down to tame these vile offenses,
> It will come,
> Humanity must perforce prey on itself
> Like monsters of the deep."

We think of our own world, a world of warring continents,
a world whose stabilities are in dissolution, the world of the
atomic bomb.

In the savage realm of Lear, Nature herself takes the stage. The storm is a natural projection of the storm raging in the breast of the outraged King. But though it beats upon his defenceless head, it is at one with him. He is no Ajax defying the lightning. "I tax not you, you elements, with unkindness." "Is there any cause in Nature that makes these hard hearts?" He calls upon nature to avenge him with "the judgment of the heavens." And in the storm to—

> "Strike flat the thick rotundity o' the world,
> Crack nature's moulds, all germens (seeds) split at once
> That make ingrateful man."

The guilt is in the spirit, not in nature.

> "This is the excellent foppery of the world," says Edmund— "that . . . we make guilty of our disasters the sun, the moon and the stars: as if we were villains by necessity; fools by heavenly compulsion; knaves, thieves and treachers by spherical predominance."

Had he been a contemporary of ours, he would have used different terms meaning the same thing: fools by the law of supply and demand; villains by dialectical materialism; knaves by the fatalism of the subconscious; evildoers by the force of determinism. So too, it is not economic policy nor finance nor bad farming methods nor an obsolete system of international trade which have been responsible for nature's breast of abundance running dry. The droughts that have desolated the world's crops are not man-made; they descend out of the blue to harry our innocent civilisation. Edmund has no such illusions about committing his own crimes. In declaring for the doctrine of free will and personal responsibility, he is echoing Brutus' "It is not in our stars but in ourselves that we are underlings."

With Shakespeare, nature is never a remote abstraction. Still less had he any conception of our own "apathetic fallacy" of regarding nature as the Great Machine. Even in this "global" drama, even in the violence of the storm, his native

Warwickshire is in his mind. One of the richest anachronisms even in Shakespeare is prehistoric Lear's:—

"You cataracts and hurricanoes spout
Till you have drench't our steeples, drown'd the cocks."

It is the storm that awakes his compassion for the sinner, more sinned against than sinning, for the poor whose "looped and windowed raggedness" is exposed to it, and for the still sad music of humanity. And it is during the storm that his vision is born of the first last and the last first:——

"Through tattered clothes small vices do appear,
Robes and furred gowns hide all."

When the blinded Gloster is feeling his way to Dover, it is the peasant, nature's husband, who succours him:—

"O, my good lord,
I have been your tenant and your father's tenant
These fourscore years."

The innocence of nature and the doctrine of free will are even more explicitly acknowledged in *Macbeth*. The various symbols of evil—the Three Witches, the floating dagger, the uncanny and disembodied Third Murderer—are not the ministers of nature. Macbeth absolves nature in his own words:—

"Thou sure and firm-set earth,
Hear not my steps, which way they walk, for fear
The very stones prate of my whereabout
And take the present horror from the time."

He has murdered sleep, nature's restorer, and the earth, recoiling from the murderer's violation of the natural law, "was feverous and did shake." Coleridge, in one of what Pearsall Smith calls flashes from his dark lantern, comments on Macbeth's distraction before the ghost of Banquo—"He has by guilt torn himself live asunder from nature." Lady Macbeth calls on the evil spirits to prevent the "compunctious visitings of nature" " to shake my fell purpose." The presence of Banquo, who resists the Witches' temptation on the blasted heath and so saves his "eternal jewel" that Macbeth lost, is proof positive that Macbeth chose the evil principle out of his own free will and reason; and so incurred the judgment.

Professor Curry, in some remarkable chapters from his *Shakespeare's Philosophical Patterns*, derives the thought of *Macbeth* directly from the mediæval scholastics. Its demonology exactly corresponds with their demonic metaphysics. He quotes lengthy passages from St. Thomas Aquinas as providing a precise analysis of Macbeth's inner state. The liberty of free choice is in mediæval theology " the supreme *bonum naturae*," and in defying the natural and eternal law Macbeth becomes more and more fatalistic, less and less able to exercise the divinely human principle of free choice. Macbeth is not only Macbeth, but essential man who has done evil and suffers the consequences to his soul defined in the moral philosophy of the scholastics. It is evident that the religious philosophy of the *Tragedies* is not the product of a vague theism. They repudiate the anthropocentric humanism born of the Renaissance. A purely secular society cannot understand them.

Hamlet's flaw is different in kind from that of the other tragic heroes, though, like Lear's, it is only redeemed and atoned for by his own death, simultaneously with the accomplishment of his task. But it is a flaw that circumstance fastened upon him and was a distortion of his normal nature. His mutability and morbidity, his frantic excitements and obsession with death, his folly and hastiness of action, his often macabre gloom and futility, his brutality to Ophelia (whom, however, he suspected of being Claudius' decoy), and his indifference to Polonius' death, are the weaknesses of a character subjected to abnormal strain from without. The "distemper" which causes him to act as he does and not to act as the Ghost and his own duty exacted upon him, was thrust upon him by a combination of horrors that unbalanced and split his whole nervous system. T. S. Eliot[1] regards his behaviour as "in excess of the facts," the facts being family

[1] *The Sacred Wood.*

murder, incest, adultery and usurpation. "What would he (the actor who weeps for Hecuba) do," Hamlet says:—

"had he the motive and the cue for passion
That I have? He would drown the stage with tears
And cleave the general ear with horrid speech . . . "

Dover Wilson[1] speaks of Hamlet as "a great, an almost super-human figure tottering beneath a tragic burden too heavy even for his mighty back." But too light for Mr. Eliot's judgment, which is perhaps why he calls the most convincing character in all drama an "artistic failure" and the play itself inferior to *Coriolanus*. A weaker man than Hamlet would have gone out of his mind; one far less sensitive and imaginative would, as Hamlet says himself after the Ghost had told his horrid tale, "with wings as swift as meditation" have swept to his revenge. But Hamlet, being the man he is, neither goes out of his mind nor sweeps to his revenge.

Shakespeare again and again makes it clear what manner of man he is. Hamlet has delineated himself in his own great words about man:—

"What piece of work is man! how noble in reason! how infinite in faculty! in form and moving how express and admirable! in action how like an angel! in apprehension how like a god! the beauty of the world! the paragon of animals!"

The disorder that falls upon him, plainly indicated in the text when the Ghost is hollowly muttering "Swear!" in the "cellarage," dislocates that noble nature "like sweet bells jangled, out of tune and harsh." It is because he is what he is that he suffers as he does and acts in every way but the way enjoined upon him. As Clutton Brock[2] has well said, "the discord in his nature reveals as nothing else could its underlying and implied harmony." Granville Barker[3] has acutely pointed out that this very discord causes Hamlet to condemn that artistry in words in which he was a master, so that "like

---

[1] *What Happens in Hamlet.*
[2] *Shakespeare's Hamlet.*
[3] *Prefaces to Shakespeare.*

a whore" "I must unpack my heart with words." The impoverishment of that nature is our enrichment by enabling us to see in its derangement how full and great it is. The richer the nature, the worse the outrage upon it; and the worse the outrage, the more discordant its effects.

In Hamlet there is a wholeness of faculty in "mind, body and estate." The artist and the thinker, the man of action and of conscience, of insight and imagination like Prospero's, of infinite jest like Mercutio's, of depth of feeling like no other man's in Shakespeare, these are parts of his nature that, before being thrown out of tune, all chimed together. That is one good reason why Shakespeare projected himself into Hamlet, and that he did suffer from some bitter disturbance of mind during the tragic period that opened with this play internal evidence is a speaking witness. There is, too, about Hamlet, as others have remarked, a mannerism of speech, a style, an address, that is extraordinarily intimate. Hamlet's wholeness can justly be called Shakespeare's own, and wholeness is impossible in man without deep organic roots. Those roots were the precious gift of his native Warwickshire, and the wholeness he drew from them he gave to Hamlet. Is not the action of the play exactly like the course of the Avon, with its leisurely reaches, quickening bends and final sweep into the sea of oblivion? And in Avon Ophelia sang her swan-song. It is not the least of Hamlet's tragedy that that wholeness in him is not only "jangled" but constricted into the odious specialism of dedicating itself to revenge. The reason why Hamlet has for three centuries won the love, the honour and the fascination of the whole world is not only the light of his genius but because it shone, if only in glimpses, out of a whole man.

The religious element in *Hamlet* is just as pervasive as the organic. The burden of the play is not the misuse of free will, as in *Macbeth*, but its frustration. The "ulcer" of procrastination that is Hamlet's undoing blunts not so much his power of action as what the Ghost in the Queen's chamber calls his "purpose"—namely his freedom to execute that will. Hamlet himself bears this out when he loses his last chance of despatching Claudius alone at prayer. "Now might I do it" confesses, as Bradley[1] noted, that his "desire" to do it is frozen at the

[1] *Shakespearean Tragedy.*

source. When Hamlet follows the Ghost on the ramparts, uncertain like Horatio and the others whether he is not a devil, and, as they try to restrain him, calls out, "I'll make a ghost of him that lets (stops) me," he has courage and resolution enough. The sentimental Hamlet of Coleridge, the poet-philosopher incapable of practice, is denied by his over-rapidity in killing Polonius and his promptitude on the ship making for England. But Denmark he cannot purge and Claudius he cannot kill, because the foulness has poisoned the springs of his will.

If *Hamlet* be both heard and read, its Christian thought is seen not only to govern it in principle but to be explicit in particulars. Half the play hinges upon Hamlet's doubt of the Ghost's authenticity as a Catholic one from Purgatory or a Protestant one disguising a devil. Hamlet forbears killing Claudius at prayer because he would kill him not saved but damned in some deed "that has no relish of salvation in't." This is plainly a pretext to himself for failing to kill him at all. But there can be no doubt that Hamlet believed in his own words, dreadful as they are. He himself was only prevented from killing himself because the Everlasting had "fixed his canon 'gainst self-slaughter" and for "the dread of something after death." When he is killed indeed, we do not feel it an incongruous archaism that Horatio says, "And flights of angels sing thee to thy rest." These examples are few chosen out of many, for to understand *Hamlet* it is impossible to avoid thinking theologically. Granville-Barker[1] insists upon Hamlet's religious doubts. But they are those of a religious man in conflict with himself. Only in despair does he feel or feign that indifference that brings him near to our own age. To think of this play in modern, especially psycho-analytical terms, is to miss it completely.

The most eloquent passage of the play's Christian atmosphere is when the Ghost intervenes to save Queen Gertrude from her son's maddened fury—"leave her to heaven," as he had said on his first appearance. As soon as the distressed Ghost fades from Hamlet's sight in Gertrude's chamber, Hamlet's whole demeanour changes. The transformation from the blood, hatred, anguish, scorn and shame that precede

[1] *Prefaces to Shakespeare.*

this change is like the peace of evening after the convulsion of storm:—

> "The holy time is quiet as a nun
> Breathless with adoration . . . "

Wordsworth's couplet is like a comment on this scene. Hamlet says:—

> "Confess yourself to heaven;
> Repent what's past; avoid what is to come;
> And do not spread the compost on the weeds
> To make them ranker . . . "

Once more the contrast between flower and weed, reiterated in this play.[1] A few lines later:—

> "Once more, good-night:
> And when you are desirous to be blest
> I'll blessing beg of you."

For a moment Hamlet is restored to his right mind but only for this moment. Shakespeare's acceptance in the Tragedies of the Christian philosophy was not only traditional. His profound insight into human nature squared with the Christian interpretation of that nature. He accepted free will not as a Gothic invention but as a fact of life. Only a culture in decay is fatalistic and accepts the loss of the person in the mass as " inevitable."

VI

Many writers in the long line of great Shakespeareans have recorded their delight in the haunted radiance suffusing the final trilogy of *Cymbeline*, *The Winter's Tale* and *The Tempest*. But it has not been so clearly recognised to what extent the various strands of past thought in the country-living and country-thinking Shakespeare have been gathered up and transmuted "into something rich and strange." The break from the Tragedies, though something like a conversion,

[1] See Page 15.

is not so abrupt as has been assumed. Just as Albany's vision
of humanity preying on itself is foreshadowed in Ulysses'
of "appetite, a universal wolf" making by "will and power"
"a universal prey," so the great theme of mercy issuing
from *The Merchant of Venice* and *Measure for Measure* becomes
the burden of all three. But it is transferred to and transfigured by its country setting. The old theme of the country
as opposed to the town is not only reaffirmed but invested
with new meanings. The sharpness of the contrast between
them is concentrated and intensified.

When Imogen escapes from the corrupt court of Cymbeline,
she is tenderly honoured and cherished by Belarius and his
two "sons." They are living swift and free and self-supporting
in the wilds, "gentle as zephyrs" from the "blazon" of nature
for all their roughness:—

"These are kind creatures," she says, "Gods! what lies
    I have heard,
Our courtiers say all's savage but at court."

What the courtiers say, ruffling in "their unpaid-for silk,"
our own journalists, professors and officials say about the small
farmer to-day. "Did you but know," Belarius adds, "the city's
usuries," anticipating what countrymen have been saying for
the past hundred years. "Would I were," Imogen exclaims,—

"A neatherd's daughter, and my Leonatus (Posthumus)
    Our neighbour shepherd's son!"

She echoes the very thought of Henry VI's longing for the
seasonal and tranquil shepherd's life. And Arviragus greets
her with nature's bounty on human lips—"The night to the
owl, the morn to the lark less welcome!"

The same pattern recurs in *The Winter's Tale*, *The Tempest*
and even in *Pericles*, all variations of the central motive in a
fugue. Cerimon foreshadows Prospero, and Marina is one of
the three Graces whose sisters are Perdita and Miranda. All
have their sources in Timon's refuge in his cave by the desolate
sea and in the banished Duke's Robin Hood adventure in Arden.
It is not an accident that Prospero, like Timon, finds refuge in

a cave of solitude, and Timon was a phase of Shakespeare's
experience as Prospero was the final epitome of it. But the cave
itself now gives forth blessings for curses. The immensity
of the change from *Timon* cannot but be the pointer to a spiritual
convalescence from the abysmal horror of and black preoccupation with evil that dogged Shakespeare's mind during
part at least of the period of the Tragedies. The parting of
the clouds, the last plays and the retirement to Stratford
synchronise too well for criticism to ignore their linked
significance.

But the development even from *As You Like It*, which tells
exactly the same story as that of the last plays, is likewise
a giant's stride. The caves and mountains of Wales, the
sheep-cotes of Bohemia and the enchanted Isle are new
translations of Arden. But they differ from sweet treble bells
as tones of richer harmonies. Arden is a perpetual spring like
the spring of the pastoralists. The trilogy at the end has
"a deep autumnal tone," chiming with the autumn of
Shakespeare's own life. He says good-bye in them to the
life of the town and in the last of them good-bye not only
to his art:—

> "Deeper than did ever plummet sound
> I'll drown my book"—
but to mortal life itself—"Our revels now are ended."

The fusion between the exquisite swan-song of *The Tempest*
and the closing years of his own life in Warwickshire is
luminously presented in *The Masque of Ceres* that immediately
precedes Prospero's farewell:—

> "Ye sunburned sicklemen, of August weary,
> Come hither from the furrow, and be merry:
> Make holiday: your rye-straw hats put on,
> And these fresh nymphs to encounter every one
> In country footing."

In his youth Shakespeare mixed up elves with village craftsmen.
Here farmers and fairies join the dance. Hellas and Warwick-
shire enter the Isle of Music and Magic, of "the remote
Bermudas" in the ocean's bosom. It is a yeoman's festival, a

harvest-home in his own home, a melody of blessing upon England's plenty and the husbandman's fulfilment. It is in song what the water-colourists have put into paint—the for ever England who rewards the sons of her soil with her maternal fruits. How Shakespeare loved that bounty is seen in Cleopatra's funeral praise of Antony's—"an autumn 'twas That grew the more by reaping."

In the woodland court of the banished Duke in *As You Like It*, there is an atmosphere of play-acting and a touch of self-conscious artifice in "the sermons in stones and books in the running brooks." A slightly bookish and Rousseauesque air surrounds the "return to nature" of the sparks and gallants of the town. This is entirely absent from the mountains of Belarius, the farmstead of Perdita and Prospero's land beyond the sunset. The pastoral convention is discarded. As Ariel, perhaps Shakespeare's supreme creation, is distant from Puck, the fantastic joker of the milk-pails, so Imogen, Perdita and Miranda have a gravity lacking in the sweet-and-twenty loves of Rosalind and Orlando.

The golden age carelessness of

> "Who doth ambition shun
> And loves to lie i' the sun,
> Seeking the food he eats
> And pleased with what he gets."

is a world away from the antiphonal chant of Guiderius and Arviragus. In measured responses they sing the ritual obsequies of Fidele, laying her head to the east. "Fear no more the heat o' the sun" has an archaic solemnity that seems the flower of that long pagan past when strange men, moving in stately dance round their funeral mounds, dwelt among our English Downs. Miranda, too, is clothed in a primeval if rather wooden innocence. But Perdita, the child of "great creating nature," the country "lass unparalleled" (truer of her than of Cleopatra) is something more as well. She is what Florizel says of her:—

> "no shepherdess but Flora
> Peering in April's front."

She personifies the English countryside itself. But also as "the queen of curds and cream." She is the presiding deity of the universal countryman's daily work. But also of those thanksgivings for it in rural dance and song that graced our English acres and consecrated them. It is from Shakespeare that we know what they were before the Puritan Revolution scotched and the Industrial Revolution killed them.

The meaning of the island, the mountains and Perdita's sheepwalks is that they are a sanctuary, not a holiday entertainment, the home of the English spirit, and, as Brandes says, of "spiritual health." They are not only a refuge from court and town but a natural setting for human nobility and affection. These three plays have about them a sense of timelessness. Drawn into their charmed circle, the reader or spectator becomes oblivious of or indifferent to their faulty and perfunctory dramatic technique,[1] for *The Tempest* alone fulfils all the dramatic "unities." In *The Tempest* there is the touch of the infinite. But in them all, we are transported beyond the world of mutability.

It is not at all a world of rarefied sentiment and pastoral poses. The shepherds and shepherdesses of the Shearing Feast in *The Winter's Tale* do not recline on banks of flowers, piping plaintive airs of love. They do not at all live up to the modern picturesque notion of them. They are independent countrymen who celebrate the peak of the year's seasonal rhythm. They drink English ale and eat English pies. They joke, romp and buy ribbons and trinkets. The lookers-on discuss the price of wool. The hostess serves them with a face "o'fire with labour and the thing she took to quench it." Their ballad-singer is no pale amorist but a jovial pick-purse. The disguised King discusses grafting with Perdita. Perdita herself, instead of a luxurious pastoral lament upon the discovery of her love for Florizel, goes off to milk her ewes. Play is rooted in work as the divine poetry of the lovers and the divinity of the feast herself are rooted in the wolds of Gloucestershire. Magic and homeliness are also blended in the *Midsummer Night's Dream*. But in *The Winter's Tale* the mysterious and yet wholly

---

[1] *Cymbeline*, like *Pericles*, cannot be Shakespeare entire. See Granville Barker's *Preface* to it. But the spirit of it can be no other than his.

feminine beauty of Perdita unites the spirit of the earth-
goddess and of an uncontaminated world with a rustic and
realistic feast-day.

Nor are the cosmic and Christian themes of the Tragedies
lost in Shakespeare's emergence from their underworld of evil.
On the contrary, the religious vision born of their spiritual
travail is now anchored to the unspoiled natural world. If
Macbeth had noticed the martlets under the eaves of his castle,
might he not have let Duncan go in peace? As nature's
revulsion from Macbeth's crime was vented in "lamentings in
the air . . . and prophecyings with accent terrible," so the
penitent Alonso describes to Prospero how the forces of nature
condemned him:—

> "O, it is monstrous, monstrous,
> Methought the billows spoke and told me of it,
> The winds did sing it to me, and the thunder,
> That deep and dreadful organ pipe pronounced
> The name of Prosper."

But the natural and the supernatural are "far more deeply
interfused" than in these lines.

These last plays belong, as it were, to the post-doom age.
They are bathed in the beatitudes of reconciliation and peace,
of charity and forgiveness, the cardinal Christian virtues.
Blake's "mercy, pity, peace" throws an evening light over all
three. "Pardon's the word to all," partly in sheer boredom
with villainy. A whole troop of scoundrels receives pardon for
punishment. Hermione forgives the jealous tyrant, Leontes.
Prospero forgives a whole shipload of schemers, traitors,
usurpers and would-be murderers. Imogen forgives her
contemptible husband, Posthumus, just after in her page's
dress he has struck her to the ground. The late Charles
Williams wrote—"The style of Imogen is the keynote of all;
the pardon of Imogen the pattern of all; and both style and
pardon, though so heavenly, are as realistic as anything in
Shakespeare." There is nothing lovelier even in Shakespeare
than the brief words which illustrate the mission of the
Gospels:—

Imogen: "Why did you throw your wedded lady from you?
　　Think that you are upon a lock;[1] and now
　　Throw me again!
Posthumus: Hang there like fruit, my soul,
　　Till the tree die!"

The natural image has a marvellous aptitude. Once more
it is the symbol of autumn and harvest. The forgiveness that
comes after injury and grief melts into the haze of the closing
year. Not that the vileness of self-willed man and the
worldliness of the world are left behind. Though they are in
a much lower key than Iago, Claudius, Edmund and Goneril,
they are a good pack of crooks in the last plays. But they
are confounded by forgiveness. This in unison with the
healing power of nature and the calm benediction of the
autumn scene sinks them into insignificance. In this way
Shakespeare interweaved nature with religion.

The Finis of *The Tempest* draws all these threads together.
It has been pointed out that nearly all the flowers mentioned
in it are of autumn. But the whole play is toned to the dying
fall, the mellow fruitfulness, the other-worldliness of the
season. Forgiveness is a kind of evocation from it:—

"The rarer action is
In virtue than in vengeance: they, being penitent,
The sole drift of my purpose doth extend
Not a frown further."

There is a touch of scorn, a sense of the vanity of things,
in Prospero's pardon. Of weariness too. He turns away from
the graceless crew of the ship into that contemplation of the
mysteries of life which accorded with the brooding temper of
nature, the enchantment of the Isle and his own self, Shakespeare's self at the end of his passage of discovery. His wealth
of wisdom is harvested, but even that takes on the autumn
hue of a dream. Prospero is not only Hamlet-Shakespeare
come to fruition—but also the Lear of prophetic vision who
has seen through the shows of the seeming world. In *King Lear*,
the only way out of an eruption of evil that rocks the world

[1] The *Shakespeare Head Press* edition prints "rock" for "lock," thereby making a
fool of Shakespeare. "Lock" is a wrestling term and so just right.

and wrecks its order is in an unearthly kingdom whose threshold is revealed to Lear and Cordelia. Cordelia marvellously discloses it in another of the great repetitions. "You have some cause" not to love me, Lear says, and she replies—"No cause, no cause." Prospero, almost as cruelly wronged (the refugees in *Cymbeline* and *The Winter's Tale* are also the victims of injustice and persecution), has overcome the world whose pomp and pride he sees dissolving into thin air. He apprehends a different order of reality by the agency of nature, the shadow of it. He has reached this detachment by the consummation of all his powers into a self-knowledge of which the anguished Lear saw only the beginning. Shakespeare's self-creation in Prospero gives full weight to Dryden's praise:—

"the man of all modern and perhaps ancient poets who had the largest and most comprehensive soul."

Shakespeare, like Prospero, had conquered the world. He returned home to that deepest England whose rural tradition had nourished his mighty strength. In *The Tempest* he saw his country home apparelled in the glory of a dream. And in Prospero he saw himself as his rich and tragic experience had made him. Prospero is no mere Merlin of the wand. His command over the forces of nature is reflected from his profound and ironic insight into men. He is the poet-philosopher whose imagination was at one with his knowledge. Self-knowledge had made possible his conquest of nature. Ariel, the projection of his lyrical genius into a bright spirit of nature, executes the will of that imagination which "bodies forth the forms of things unknown." He has become the master of nature by that ripeness ("the ripeness is all," as Edgar says) of imaginative understanding which Blake glorified in his Prophetic Books.

Professor Curry[1] has suggested that *The Tempest* is a classical myth interlarded with Christian concepts which is based on the Neo-Platonic idea of the human soul's possession of special powers over nature by virtue of its alliance with reality. Through it the human spirit approaches towards the final union with God. Be that as it may, this spiritual

[1] *Shakespeare's Philosophical Patterns* (1937).

conquest affords as great a contrast with the modern material
"conquest of nature" as Prospero himself contrasts with Caliban,
the sub-man or ape-man with his "very ancient and fish-like
smell." The modern conquest is an amoral and so irresponsible
mastery of the inorganic only. It can split the atom but no
longer knows how to cultivate the earth. Its conquest was
won by the intellect alone and has been turned to acquisitive
and therefore destructive purposes. Where it claims to super-
sede the values of the Natural Order as "the reflection upon
the minds of our ancestors of the agricultural rhythm in
which they lived,"[1] the modern intellect proves itself incapable of judging either Shakespeare or the first principles
his men and women violated or obeyed.

In the last chapter of his imaginative work, *On Reading
Shakespeare*, Pearsall Smith rejects the impeccable Shakespeare of Matthew Arnold's "Others abide our question, thou
art free," "the official all-British Shakespeare and Empire-
builder" and the modern Shakespeare, "a kind of monster who
turned out the sublimest poetry and the grossest ribaldry
merely in the way of business." What Shakespeare remains
when these successive coats of paint are removed? The imaginative, the musical, the magical Shakespeare is his verdict.
But this does not necessarily include the prophet, the realist, the
reader of the hearts of men and of "nature's infinite book of
secrecy." It may or may not leave out the ambassador of
cosmic truths. The organic Shakespeare is the least recognised
of all the Shakespeares. Yet this one, the Shakespeare of
Warwickshire, is the root of them all. The voice of enchantment speaks out of the depths of the true, the country England.

[1] *The Abolition of Man*, by C. S. Lewis (The Riddell Lectures, 1945).

CHAPTER II

"The best mixture of humane affairs that we can make are the employments of a Country life."

ABRAHAM COWLEY.

I

TO RE-READ Jane Austen again and again always discovers a multitude of novelties. The reader will have his favourite —Disraeli read *Pride and Prejudice* seventeen times—but he must test his allegiance by repeated experience. He may even transfer it. What will never waver will be his loyalty to her whole country.

In time, therefore, but still an explorer, he becomes familiar even with a world so crowded within a little space. It was this paradox which I found to be engaging me on my most recent expedition over each province of a nation so minute in area and incomparably rich in content Her characters are a nation and of so prodigal and intense a variety, so multiple a differentiation, that I myself put her second only to Shakespeare in this supremacy of otherness she has created. But it is a nation with only a governing class. Less, it is only a section of that class. Of its public affairs, its business, its work, its purposes and transactions, its ideas, its conflicts and even its ambitions, of its whole historical consequence, we hear just nothing at all.

But not only is it a governing class that is never seen to govern, but, most remarkable of all, there are no governed. Her early nineteenth century country gentry, just below the uppermost stratum and just above the rising tradesman who was to sweep it away, exists *in vacuo* so far as its national significance together with its philosophy of action is concerned. We are only allowed to see it after office hours or on the assumption that there are no such hours at all. We see the parson anywhere but in church, cottage or farm. It is like only knowing a horse when it is in stable, or a farmer only when he is having his tea, or an artist when he is not writing or painting. "Man in relation to God, to politics, to abstract ideas passed her by . . . She sees Mrs. Brown not as a soul or as a citizen but only as the wife of Mr. Brown."[1]

Nor is this aspect confined to the men whom we never see apart from the women. For, though the genius of Miss Austen is purely a domestic one, her women are certainly not domestic workers. They practise "accomplishments," or what Cobbett in *Advice to a Lover* called "showy and useless acquirements," but not the home-crafts. They are heretics to Cobbett's canons of the good housewife. Though "poor Miss Taylor" was once a governess and Jane Fairfax seemed doomed to become one, we see neither what was nor what might have been. Fanny's mother, toiling in slatternly confusion in a Portsmouth slum, and Fanny waiting upon Lady Bertram on her sofa are the exceptions that prove the rule. Miss Austen's women are women in their "hours of ease," and their playing, singing, sewing, drawing or reading are but embellishments of their "leisure state." They are drawing-room or parlour women. We know little more of their kitchens and their gardens than we do of their bedrooms.

In this charmed world we are continents away both from the modern one, in which women are ceasing to have any home at all, and the seventeenth century one, in which women of the same class and environment as Miss Austen's made of their homes little commonwealths in variety of resource, utility and self-supporting achievement. That Miss Austen herself should have achieved such inexhaustible variations of character and qualities in human nature in so uniform and circumscribed a setting, should have gathered such infinite riches within her little sitting-room, is perhaps the greatest miracle in our literature. Bounded in her nutshell, she became a queen over such dominions as Scott, who could do "the big Bow-Wow stuff," envied her.

There is even more in the paradox. In his Introduction to the Pocket Classics edition of *Emma*, Austin Dobson underlines these limitations. Her characters, he says, "are unperplexed by problems, social or political: if they are interested

[1] Lord David Cecil.

in riddles—transcribed upon hot-pressed paper and ornamented with beads and trophies—the riddle of the painful earth has plainly no place in that elegant anthology." Yet with convincing force both Saintsbury and Lord David Cecil have written of her universality:—

"Essential human nature," writes the last, " . . . this is always Jane Austen's preoccupation. Her characters are universal types. Miss Bates is the type of all bores. Mrs. Elton the type of all pushing vulgarians, Marianne Dashwood the type of all undisciplined romantics; when Mr. Woodhouse tells us that his grandchildren are all remarkably clever, '. . . They will come and stand by my chair and say "Grandpapa, can you give me a bit of string?"'he sums up the fatuous fondness of all grandparents; when Mr. Darcy says, 'I have been selfish all my life in practice but not in principle,' he exposes the weakness of high-minded domineering males in every age and climate."

Jane Austen was as universal as Shakespeare.

Saintsbury, who considered her not inferior to Swift as a satirist, wrote of her cosmic capacity, as one whose art and humanity were in what she actually attempted supreme. Yet she deliberately avoided the fantastic, the sensational, the grandiose, even the highly coloured, whether in incident or person. Her extreme delicacy of touch relied upon psychological undertones for conveying her impression. She chose the drab, the trivial and the commonplace to manifest her revelations of being. Her villages are without villagers, and country house servants, if they appear at all, automata. Her universality, however mysterious, must therefore have been nurtured within a framework or matrix that favoured its freedom of growth. To account for it is impossible. Genius has no causation nor measurements—but we may discern in what kind of soil its root-system flourished.

Jane Austen was, in fact, a country writer, fertilised by the great rural tradition which in her day had passed its meridian, and after her death was to sink below the horizon of the national culture. Her unique art was the last exquisite flower of the eighteenth century. But no critic, so far as I am aware, has regarded her as the autumnal bloom whose stock was rooted in a subsoil that underlay the era of her birth. Besides, the eighteenth century was, or rather was in process of, becoming an urban culture. The ruralism of Miss Austen was of her very bone and grain. The country aristocracy was her theme; the village the home both of herself and the children of her imagination. Her ideas, her proclivities, her ancestry were almost entirely rural. The man of all her contemporaries she would have chosen to marry was the country poet, George Crabbe. How are these phenomena related to her novels, and what inferences, historical and otherwise, can be drawn from them? I will begin with her own personal life.

Miss Austen was a countrywoman born and bred. All her novels were sited from the country house and the village. Even her scenes of town-life—Bath in *Northanger Abbey* and *Persuasion*, London in *Sense and Sensibility*—were holiday and visiting ones. Her social groups "in town" have all come from their homes in the country. "Three or four families in a country village to work on" was her advice to a budding novelist. It seems likely that she shared Anne Elliot's dislike of Bath. Anne, doomed to residence with her popinjay and Debrett-ridden father and eldest sister, might indeed be expected to shrink from the prospect of leaving Uppercross for the stilted bloodless "private parties" of Camden Place, "a highly dignified situation, such as becomes a man of consequence." But when Anne, after the prison doors had closed on her, exclaims, "Oh, when shall I leave you again?" it is not unlikely that she was echoing her creator. There is only one good moment in Bath, when Anne and Captain Wentworth walk up Union Street after dropping Charles Musgrove behind them. The rest of the town-times for her creations both in Bath and London is nearly all spent in pain, anxiety, boredom or disillusion. Even the gaieties of the Allens, Thorpes and Tilneys in the first part of *Northanger Abbey* are presented with a gusto never other than satirical. These gropings after Miss Austen's own feelings about town life are in the dark. But the tradition is that, when her mother told her the family was to leave Steventon for Bath, she fainted. Emma Austen-Leigh in her Memoir, *Jane Austen and Bath*, says, " there is little doubt that for a time she was very unhappy" there. Like Elizabeth Bennet and the Dashwood girls, she was a great walker. To walk in the neighbourhood of Bath (as it once was), that little Rome of the limestone hills, would have been one of the glories of existence.

If she disliked Bath, she probably hated Southampton, though Southampton must have been an enchanting little town in 1810, half-married to the sea and half to the soil. No reflection of her four years' residence there appears in her books. But her prevalent feeling in both must have been the longing for her country parsonage. This nostalgia explains the chronological data of her creative periods. At Steventon, the first draughts of *Pride and Prejudice, Sense and Sensibility* and *Northanger Abbey* were all written between the ages of twenty-one and twenty-three. At Chawton they were revised, and *Emma, Mansfield Park* and *Persuasion* written between the ages of thirty-six and forty-one. During the eight years of her life in Bath and Southampton she wrote only the fragment of *The Watsons*. The life of the town was alien to the flowering of her genius. Only in its native soil was it capable of brilliance of colour, exuberance of growth and its ultimate perfection. Not only her natural and rural environment were indispensable for the full development of her powers, but she also needed to be at home in her own place.

Jane Austen created a universe of characters in the round, intimately known by us and particularised by her. Yet they are representative, and all out of the most conventional experience. She is the sovran example of the universal contained in the particular, in her two inch "square of ivory." Nor were these masterpieces won by conflict with, emergence from, triumph over the littleness of her environment. They were the result of accepting and so transcending her limitations. It is impossible to imagine a less revolutionary, less ideological and more conservative writer than Jane Austen. Just as the Midas fortune of rural allusion, painting and imagery in Shakespeare was made out of Stratford, so her multitudinous character-drawing was born of Steventon and Chawton. This transcendance of the local and the particular would seem to be a universal law of life: the august prototype of this principle of creation is seen in the Manger at Bethlehem. The para-

doxical relation of greatness to humility is part of it. It is a
peculiar property of country life, the distinguishing mark of
the countryman. No farmer could farm, no gardener garden,
no craftsman labour without it. They are always accepting,
transforming and transcending the conditions imposed by
nature. Thus all rural occupations are a kind of art. The
universalism of Miss Austen accepts a confined space. We fail
to understand her if we say "in spite of" instead of "because of."

The other supreme quality of the novels and to be paired
with the cosmic is their realism. Jane Austen was actually far
more of a realistic writer even than Defoe, who was first and
foremost a great journalist. Her realism explains more than
the extraordinary reality of the very least of her characters
and the extraordinary solidity of her pictures of the life of the
English country gentry. It explains why she forebore to step
outside the range of her own intimate knowledge. Her
observation was so acute, so subtle and precise that it makes
for her "infinite variety," especially in the satirical portrait.
But all her heroines are sharply differentiated. Her detail is
of the minutest, without ever ceasing to be representative;
her strokes of perception are endless, and yet everything is
expressed in the most concentrated form. And it is a realism
closely allied to an exquisite justice. Miss Austen was the
justest of writers, and justice is not a woman's virtue.

Even those immortals she best loves are never too good
to live on earth. They are of mixed composition. This is as
true of her villains as of the figures of a never too heroic
stature. Such realism is symbolic and universal; but it is the
reverse of abstract. The fundamental difference between the
rural and the urban outlooks is that the one is abstract, the
other realistic. There have been many romantic poets who
have written about nature; no countryman who has worked
with nature is other than a realist. Realism does not, of course,
exclude poetry; its poetry rises from the earth like a flower
rather than is detached from it like a tinted cloud. The chief
cause for the dominance of abstract thinking in modern life
has been urbanism.

II

Northanger Abbey, being a burlesque upon a certain type of outmoded romanticism, needs no separate treatment. *Mansfield Park* illustrates rather more clearly than the others a conflict, symbolically presented, between rural and urban values. It is not headlined by the author, because rural values and the rural attitude were part of her inward consciousness. But the conflict is there for the reader to perceive.

The principals in the contest are, of course, Fanny and Edmund on the one hand and the Craufords on the other, with the two Miss Bertrams as their auxiliaries. In a character-drama of such fixed opposition it is much to be regretted that nearly all the charm and attraction go with the losing side. Though virtue triumphs, it is nothing but virtue. Fanny, who at the ball is like a willow in spring, is too often as heavy as mahogany. A priggish solemnity and at times downright dullness cloud the hero and heroine. The air of copybook sententiousness is foggier in Fanny because she has so many exquisite moments. This is not the only uncertain touch in a book which does tend to sacrifice an artistic to a moral propriety. Yet, as the champions of virtue, Fanny and Edmund are also upholding the settled excellences of a country life as opposed to the restless, uprooted, nomadic, urban worldliness of the Craufords. So strongly is their creator committed to the former, so manifest and urgent are her sympathies, that she ends by upsetting the plot. This plot is so loosely woven or architecturally rambling in structure—very much unlike the beautiful proportions and inevitable formation of that of *Pride and Prejudice*—that it virtually collapses under the strain.

Quite apart from the plot, Henry Crauford, the last of the quartet of Miss Austen's playboys, is shown as the volatile man of pleasure and fashion whose true habitat is the town. Of his estate at Everingham he is the absentee landlord. He flits to and from Mansfield Park, and can only be kept there for any length of time by the sport of flirting with the Bertram sisters. He is drawn by the novelty of "improving" the Rushworths' Sotherton, and the play-acting of "Lovers' Vows" is a double stimulus. He is an epicure in new sensations and emotional experiments. His pursuit of Fanny (when the Bertram girls are away) is one of them. But the trapper is caught in his own snare.

The subtlety of Mary Crauford's counterpoint to him is full of beauties and varieties in the telling. She is as unprincipled as he, but in a cooler, more detached and speculative hedonism. She abets him in his designs of captivation but as the spectator of a play, and her self-interest is more calculating than his. She is something of an iconoclast of the family strength, the home allegiance, the rural solidarity and integrity embodied by Fanny and Edmund. She is, in fact, an eighteenth century sceptic and rationalist. One of her mental amusements (the edge on her mind is one of her greatest charms) is her wonder at herself that she had spent " the quietest five months I have ever passed" in the country. She boldly challenges Edmund's resolve to take orders. The debate between them on the difference between the town and country clergy ("we do not look to great cities for our best morality," says Edmund) unveils Miss Austen's private views. In the country clergy, says Edmund, the personal element is dominant, and personal relations were everything to her, both as a woman and a novelist. Mary comes nearer to being a free-thinker (country people are very rarely such) than any other portrait in the whole long gallery.

The contrast between her and Fanny, between (one might well say) the modernist and the ruralist, is accented, even laboured. On the famous drive to Sotherton Park, Mary "saw Nature, inanimate Nature, with little admiration; her attention was all for men and women, her talents for the light and lively." How indignant she was when at haysel time she could not hire a cart to fetch her harp! "Guess my surprise when I found that I had been asking the most unanswerable, most impossible thing in the world; had offended all the farmers, all the labourers, all the hay in the parish!" Fanny's attention was very different as they drove along:—

"Her own thoughts and reflections were habitually her best companions; and, in observing the appearance of

the country, the bearings of the roads, the difference of
soil, the state of the harvest, the cottages, the cattle, the
children, she found entertainment that could only have
been heightened by having Edmund to speak of what she
felt. That was the only point of resemblance between her
and the lady (Mary) who sat by her; in everything but
a value for Edmund, Miss Crauford was very unlike
her."

It is astonishing to reflect that Fanny here might change
partners with Cobbett. She was observing exactly what
Cobbett habitually did on his rides. Yet what worlds away
were Cobbett and Miss Austen! It was a theme for Landor to
bring them into an imaginary conversation. At one time they
were actually together at the same time in the same village
(Uphusband or Hurstbourne Tarrant). About Cobbett's noble
passions and preoccupations Miss Austen never said a word;
about *her* county *élite* Cobbett was often decidedly rough and
even libellous. Yet they were both ruralists. G. K. C. in his
Cobbett wrote of them both: "They were the four sharpest
eyes that God had given to the England of that time; but two
of them were turned inward into the home, and two were
looking out of the window. I wish I could think that they
ever met."

What is even more astonishing, we discover Fanny talking
about nature not only like Cobbett but like the Byronic
Marianne Dashwood, her creator fully approving. In one of
those shrubberies that no well-appointed house of Miss Austen's
frequentation was without, she exclaims, "The evergreen, how
beautiful, how welcome, how wonderful the evergreen!" Her
ecstasy on the sublimity of nature as seen through a twilit
window at Mansfield Park is Marianne to the life, with a
touch of truer poetry:—

"Here's harmony! here's repose! Here's what may leave all
painting and all music behind, and what poetry only can
attempt to describe! Here's what may tranquillize every care,
and lift the heart to rapture! When I look out on such a
night as this, I feel as though there could be neither wickedness nor sorrow in the world."

On such a night! How curious the echo from Belmont to the
Bertrams' drawing-room! An echo passes through my own
ears from *Midsummer Night's Dream* to the scene at Sotherton,
where Fanny sits alone on the seat while Henry Crauford
wanders about with Maria Bertram and Edmund with Mary,
an echo not only in situation but also in a subdued and polite
magic.

In the evergreen passage, Fanny goes on:—

"When one thinks of it, how astonishing a variety of
nature! In some countries we know the tree that sheds its
leaves is the variety, but that does not make it less amazing,
that the same soil and the same sun should nurture plants
differing in the great rule and law of their existence. You
will think me rhapsodizing, but when I am out of doors,
especially when I am sitting out of doors, I am very apt
to get into this sort of wondering strain."

This "rambling fancy" is, again, most significantly, brought
up sharp against Mary's attitude beside her: "Miss Crauford,
untouched and inattentive, had nothing to say." If Fanny had
actually been Marianne "rhapsodizing," Miss Austen could
hardly have blamed Mary for her inattentiveness. But it is
Fanny, the one heroine who is not quite what Miss Austen
intended her to be. What she intends her to be in part is the
votaress of country felicity and the moralist of country truth
against the hard-boiled urbanism of Mary Crauford. Whether
Fanny is being ridiculous or touched with grace as in the
window passage, we are not left in confusion as to where
Miss Austen's sympathies lay.

The "zeal after poachers" of the loutish Mr. Rushworth
also brings into distant view the dynamic world of Cobbett.
Dr. Grant is a minor Parson Woodforde—"'Dr. Grant is ill,'
said she (Mrs. Grant) with mock solemnity, He has been ill
ever since he did not eat any of the pheasant to-day. He fancied
it tough, sent away his plate, and has been suffering ever
since.'" But the minor figures are forgotten in the strange
climax of the book. It must be disconcerting to the select
company of the criers-up above the rest of *Mansfield Park*.
This is Henry Crauford's elopement with Maria. I feel it a

violent wrenching of the plot off its axis, a horrid intervention of the goddess out of the machine, a grisly sacrifice of art and truth to morality. It makes me wonder whether there is any basis of fact in Miss Austen's reputed evangelical leanings in her latter days.

How sad it is to see the subtle complexity of Henry Crauford's character thus standardised and conventionalised! For if he is the playboy he is also the man of parts. His sensibility and grace of mind and personality are clearly presented. How charged with feeling, insight and eloquence are his famous words on Shakespeare! The love of Shakespeare "is part of an Englishman's constitution: one is intimate with him by instinct." What is more to the point, his devotion to Fanny is unquestionably genuine; it is felt along the heart. We are witness to a conversion. Henry's by the power of love is, allowing for differences of temper between the two men, precisely the same both in cause and effect as Darcy's. If we do not discredit the fall of pride in the one, I see no reason why we should discredit the fall of play-acting and hedonism in the other. Henry's very elasticity shows him capable of change.

How improbable and irrational, how *unrealistic*, appears the news of the elopement almost immediately after his visit to Fanny at Portsmouth! I cannot understand how any reader can receive this intelligence without a shock of incredulity and distaste. The visit is very pertinent to my theme. One of Henry's reasons for it, endearing itself to Fanny's down-at-heels family by his solicitude, considerateness and humility, was to give Fanny report of what had happened as a consequence through her of his change of attitude to his estate at Everingham. "He had introduced himself to some tenants whom he had never seen before; he had begun making acquaintance with cottages whose very existence, though on his estate, had been hitherto unknown to him." He had renewed the lease of an industrious family in contravention of his agent's threatened eviction of it. "Your judgment," he says to Fanny, "is my rule of right."

How could so earnest a redemption have lasted but for a few days after so self-committing a pledge of it? In a letter to Fanny, Edmund writes: "I am more and more satisfied with all that I hear and see of him. There is not a shadow of

wavering. He thoroughly knows his own mind and acts up
to his resolutions: an inestimable quality." Not to believe
that "he had rationally as well as passionately loved" is not
only to distrust all values but even Miss Austen's own.

That one of these was a conviction of the virtue of
responsibility in ownership others of her books reveal. She
could not have meant us to regard Crauford's perception of
the need for a personal administration of his estate as nothing
but an idle gesture, a new weapon of his wooing. For personal
responsibility in all country callings is the key to its moral
philosophy, whether in peasant, squire or yeoman. The
Enclosures that finally dispossessed the peasantry in Jane
Austen's own lifetime were the grand heresy against that
doctrine, and the Enclosures were the consequence of an
absentee landlordism. Of the desperation and persecution of
the labourers in the early nineteenth century we hear not a
word in her books, though it should be said that its climax of
penal virulence occurred after her time. It was fourteen years
after her death that Henry Cook of Micheldever (four miles
from her home at Steventon) was hanged for striking Bing-
ham Baring, the grandson of the "loan-jobber" who made
seven millions. Crauford's conversation with Fanny in the
squalid and uproarious house at Portsmouth, contrasted with
the order and serenity of Mansfield Park, catches a reflection
of events that were to disintegrate the pattern of English life.
We do gather here an oblique impression of her own views
upon their meaning. For if the landlords had lived up to the
personal obligation which was the traditional basis for the
holding of land, the Enclosures would not have been the social
and economic tragedy they were. Miss Austen's mind is read
in Henry Crauford's conversion through Fanny to responsibility both for his love and his land. There would seem to be
good warrant for the suspicion that she changed it and so was
too severe with the Craufords.

What can have possessed her to stage that fantastic elopement? One reason may have been her desire to underline the
division and incompatibility between the country party as
represented by Fanny and Edmund and the opposite party as
represented by the Craufords. But it overran her discretion,
and forced her to substitute mechanics for art, a trick for

truth. The penalty is heavy. The marriage of Fanny with Crauford and even of Edmund with his sister might well have been an almost ideal balance and poise, each correcting the weaknesses and enhancing the excellences of the other. But the marriage of Edmund with Fanny, simply because, as Saintsbury says, Mary shocked him, makes us glad to close the book and vacate their company. The country party won the war but lost the peace.

Before leaving *Mansfield Park*, I should say something more from a different angle about the expedition to Sotherton. It takes place not merely as a *parti de plaisir* but with the definite object of suggesting "improvements" to the Park. The company actually mentions calling in Repton to effect them. This is almost the only mention of an historical personage in all Jane Austen. The idea evidently was for Sotherton to be landscape gardened. Repton was one of the disciples of Capability Brown, though a great deal more judicious and less of a destroyer than his master. Among his celebrated Ten Principles were vetoes against the uprooting of hedges, against sham ruins, against the practice of dumping water on hills and leaving the immediate area round the house as bare and naked as a ballroom. Capability Brown himself, in his frigid and tasteless "imitation of Nature" by which he constantly violated Nature, had no such reticences and reservations. As for the imitators of his imitations, they went to every kind of mechanical excess. The Mawsons have justly pointed out in their monumental *Art and Craft of Garden Making* that the traditional designs of English gardening were swept away with nothing to take their place but clumps of trees, single trees, undulating lawns and stock sheets of water. What Cobbett (*Rural Rides*) called these "improvements" was "a parcel of divers-shaped cockney-clumps, planted according to the strictest rules of artificial and refined vulgarity." The party to Sotherton, therefore, may be considered as a party of modern planners.

Though the given details of Sotherton are scanty, they represent the architectural school of garden design. This was the rural and traditional one affronted and partly devastated by Efficiency Brown and his naturalistic following. There was a lawn bounded by a high wall, a bowling green, a terrace wall backed by iron palisades with a view of "the wilderness" ("a good spot for fault-finding"), entrance to which was by a flight of steps and through a door. There was also the avenue, lamenting whose proposed felling Fanny quotes Cowper, "ye fallen avenues, once more I mourn your fate unmerited." The Mawsons' folio and Loudon's *Encyclopedia of Gardening* leave it in no doubt that these features illustrate the authentically English style, reaching far back into the Middle Ages. The metrical romances and illuminated manuscripts reveal the formal, or rather architectural, lay-out of the monastic gardens and estates. They were rich in parterres (Cobbett had a special love for the parterre), pleached alleys, topiary work, fountains, arbours, flowered trellises, alley-walks, hedges and patterned flower-beds. Especially so with the Cistercians, who chose their sites with an unerring taste for the natural beauty of their environment. They studied to render into terms of planting and building their conceptions of the mutual relations and harmonies between God, Man and Nature. Therefore, they sought a contrast and interplay between the natural and the artificial, between Gothic architecture and its chosen setting of wood, hill, valley and stream.

Tudor innovations made no revolutionary change. But they admitted the moulding influences of the Italian, French and Dutch styles, whose pomps, displays and extravagances were constantly liable to overbear the less pretentious and more homely formalism of the English tradition. Andrew Boorde[1] and Thomas Hill,[2] however, succeeded in restoring it from too ambitious a foreign conquest. They were supported by Gervase Markham and William Lawson,[3] whose enclosing walls, clipped hedges, knot gardens, grass courts, straight paths, founts, sundials and pyramids were perfectly compatible with the most sensuous love of nature. Lawson wrote:—

"What more delightsome than an infinite varietie of sweet-smelling flowers? decking with sundrie colours the greene mantle of the Earth, the universall Mother of us all, so by them bespotted, so dyed, that all the world cannot sample

[1] *The Boke for to lerne a Man to be Wyse in Buildying of his House for the Helth of his Body* (1540).
[2] *The Proffitable Arte of Gardening, etc* . . . (1672).
[3] *A New Orchard and Garden* (1618).

them and wherein is it more fit to admire the Dyer, than imitate his workmanship, colouring not only the Earth, but decking the ayre, and sweetning every breath and spirit?"

This is thoroughly traditional and mediæval in tone: to "imitate his workmanship" bears a very different meaning from Capability Brown's academic imitation of nature. But when the salutary principles of these true native interpreters waned, the museum piece excesses of the French and later the Dutch importers, grandiose in the one, conceited in the other, and ridiculed by Pope, Addison and Walpole, were imposed upon the English idiom. They opened the way for the apish naturalism of the Brownites.

Capability Brown "improved" our traditional garden designs. So the Enclosures "improved" the holdings of our peasantry. So the hedge-grubbers are now improving our native landscape and husbandry in the interests of factory-farming. When these improvers get busy, they regard the past, of which they know nothing and care less, as their legitimate prey. The loving, mature and seemly work of centuries is undone. As Gerard Manley Hopkins wrote:—

> "When we hew or delve:
> After-comers cannot guess the beauty been.
> Ten or twelve, only ten or twelve
> Strokes of havoc unselve
> The sweet especial scene,
> Rural scene, a rural scene,
> Sweet especial rural scene."

So in our own days our gardened countryside and the patterns of living evolved from it are being eclipsed. Modern civilisation is expert in destruction. Its performances in improvement are much the same thing.

Miss Austen was herself critical of the Brownesque "improvements" with which Sotherton was threatened. The whole episode is a kind of marginal comment upon the dramatic conflict in the book. The oafish Rushworth, the owner of Sotherton, is a pawn in the hands of the nimble-minded Henry Crauford. In this, his unregenerate period, he is picked out as the chief "improver" in landscaping Sotherton out of the true.

He and sister Mary are seen playing exactly the same part when the former discovers Thornton Lacey, the scene of Edmund's future incumbency. From the parsonage the farmyard is to be cleared away and the blacksmith's shop shut out. The meadows at the back of the house are to be "laid together." It is to be raised into a "place," "the residence of a man of education, taste, modern manners, good connections." Crauford asks Fanny whether she agrees with him and "Fanny gave a quick negative." Mary, dispirited at the idea of Edmund becoming a *bona fides* parson, saw "only the respectable, elegant, modernised and occasional residence of a man of independent fortune." What a contrast with the views of the Craufords that of Squire Dale in Trollope's *The Small House of Allingham*:—

"I fancy that our ideas of rural grandeur have altered since many of our older country seats were built. To be near the village . . . seem'd to be the spirit of a gentleman when building his house in the old days. A solitude in the centre of a wide park is now the only site that can be recognised as eligible. No cottage must be seen, unless the cottage *orné* of the gardener. The village, if it cannot be abolished, must get out of sight . . . When some old Dale of Allingham built his house, he thought differently. There stood the church and there the village, and, pleased with such vicinity, he sat himself down close to his God and to his tenants."

It was the new Dales who represented the spirit of the Enclosures, the "improvers" and the Craufords. *Mansfield Park* shows its author to ally herself implicitly with the old Dales.

III

Squire Knightley, the real hero of *Emma*, was of that tradition and conviction. To begin with, Donwell Abbey, his home, is on a smaller scale, and with "the old neglect of prospect" a kind of unimproved Sotherton. It was "low and sheltered," with ample gardens stretching to meadows washed by the stream. "Rambling and irregular" but comfortable, it was "just what it ought to be and looked what it was—the residence of a family of true gentility, untainted in blood and understanding." Like Sotherton and most of the traditional mansions (Tennyson's "stately homes" suggests Italian or French "nouveau art"), it had its avenue, this time of limes instead of Sotherton's oaks. The view at the end was over a low stone wall with high pillars. They seemed but were not an approach to the house, to the clover meadows and fishponds.

The Abbey itself stood at the foot of a slope (like Tintern); Abbey Mill Farm close by, where Mr. Martin lived, was backed by "the grandeur and abruptness of a wooded bank," with meadows in front and the river making a close and noble sweep about it (still more like Tintern). "With all its appendages of prosperity and beauty, its rich pastures, spreading flocks, orchard in blossom and light column of smoke ascending," farm, manor and estate appeared "a sweet view, sweet to the eye and the mind. English verdure, English culture, English comfort, seen under a sun bright, without being oppressive." In this generous home of dignity, peace and richly matured associations, Mr. Knightley walked with Harriet Smith on the occasion of the famous strawberry party, "giving her information about the modes of agriculture." Emma, passing by, "received a smile which seemed to say, 'These are my concerns. I have a right to talk on such subjects without being suspected of introducing Robert Martin.'"

This gracious picture is full of revealing touches and intimations. The personal integrity of Mr. Knightley went with his largeness and generosity of temper. He was courtly and magnanimous, tolerant and humane, simple and downright. He hated subterfuge and intrigue. His gravity is never ponderous nor unsuited to a mellow humour and irony. His kindness was steward to the kind earth and its kindly fruits. These and his wisdom and soundness of judgment, his very air and walk and stature, accord to perfection with the ancient house where he lives. They are as nobly matched as a jewel of antique cut to its setting. There is a distinct grace of the archaic about him which makes his very name a symbol. He lived by *noblesse oblige*. He is one of the few living and primary characters in Jane Austen whose nature is not a mixture and subject to change. It remains at the end exactly what it was in the beginning. He is thus representative, an ideal type, yet every bit as warm with breathing life as Emma, who does change. He is certainly not nobility on a monument. This combination of a greatness emanating from the past with a reality in the present puts him a cubit higher than all the other characters in the book, as Donwell is the queen of the neighbourhood. Miss Austen was seeing in him the pattern and exemplar of the landed gentry, of the true English gentleman—the *gentil homme*. Did she, then, care only for personal behaviour and nothing for the maladies of the world?

In the first place, Mr. Knightley, with all his culture, his high principles and his easy social affability, is a farmer. He is the only farmer in all the aristocratic gallery of the novels who is singled out as such. There was no need for others; Mr. Knightley is a kingdom in himself. He is the resident squire who farms his own land. He is constantly closeted with his bailiff, William Larkins, consulting agricultural books, attending in person to the details of estate management. He is *adscriptus glebae*—the worker, the husbandman, the home-keeper. He represents the English squirearchy—as it might have been if it had not by the Enclosures abrogated its personal leadership. But it betrayed the canon of the country gentry, that of a moral and individual responsibility, a responsibility both of place and person, handed down by feudalism for all its failures to the squires and landowners. "The fundamental character of feudalism," wrote the Carlyles in *Mediæval Political Theory*, "is to be found in the principle that it was a system of mutual and fixed obligation." Mr. Knightley received that tradition and tended it into a finer growth. His last bag of apples he sent to Miss Bates.

It is to be particularly observed in his relations with his tenant farmer and Harriet's lover, Mr. Martin. The latter is unique in himself as almost the sole being below the rank of the gentry who plays any kind of a figure in all Jane Austen. A very worthy man he is, constant to his feather-headed Harriet in spite of her flightiness towards him and Emma's learned airs of a spurious superiority, a lover of books, a good letter-writer, a man of honour and feeling. He illustrates the old yeomanly relations of the farmer to his men in Harriet's remark that he "had had his shepherd's son into the parlour one night on purpose to sing to her."

But even more significant are Mr. Knightley's attitude and conduct towards him. He speaks of Martin's "good sense, warm attachment, liberality, propriety (an important quality in Jane Austen), and delicacy of feeling;" he attributes to him elsewhere "sense, sanity and good humour," together with "a true gentility." They are always consulting one another (as Emma says) "of business, shows of cattle or new drills . . . or the dimensions of some famous ox." He calls Martin his friend, treats him rather as a father and is deeply mortified at Emma tempting Harriet away from him. He is in no doubt how much she was his inferior. He is enchanted when in the end Emma is reconciled to Martin's marriage with Harriet. The whole story portrays the ideal relationship between squire and farmer. Cobbett supplies a marginal comment. Mr. Knightley, though he is something more as well, is

"the resident native gentry, attached to the soil, known to every farmer and labourer from their childhood, frequently mixing with them in those pursuits where all artificial distinctions are lost, practising hospitality without ceremony, from habit and not in calculation."

And Mr. Martin represents Cobbett's cottagers:

"of an honest and independent character, while at the same time they held the neighbouring gentry in the greatest estimations and respect, and these again, in return, did not overlook them, but were interested in knowing that they were happy and well."

The underground stream of Miss Austen's country convictions and principles comes to the surface again in Mrs Elton. Emma's view of her after her first visit to Hartfield epitomises her:—

"A little upstart, vulgar being, with her Mr. E. and her *caro sposo*, and her resources, and all her airs of pert pretension and underbred finery. Actually to discover that Mr. Knightley was a gentleman! I doubt whether he will return the compliment, and discover her to be a lady."

Upstart is the key-word. Mrs. Elton was the daughter of a Bristol merchant, and so the representative of a rising commerce. It was ultimately to displace the landed gentry in the struggle for power and to make England a plutocracy. It was not a snobbery like her own treatment of Harriet which made Emma regard her as of a lower social status than herself. She was right to find odious the comparison of the shrubberies and laurels and "barouche-landau" of Maple Grove with the shrubberies and laurels and carriage of Hartfield.

Maple Grove, there is history in the name. Its sham gentility prefaced Suburbia and the garden city, remorselessly washing away the old landmarks and boundary-stakes, dragging out the old anchorages that time had cemented, obliterating into its muddy uniformity the old regional distinctions and hierarchical varieties of English rural life. Ideologues who placard the age with their headlines of equality are actuated from beneath with the desire for power. This is the real motive of Mrs. Elton. Maple Grove was not flung out in complacence as the equal of Hartfield but in defiance as its competitor and would-be usurper. So it was to become. The society painted by Miss Austen had its faults. But its crime was in not preserving its hierarchical structure. It violated it by striking down the peasantry and allowing its ethics to be overwhelmed by the money-power. Its nemesis was, that Maple Grove entered the breach its own hands had made.

The characters of Jane Austen seem indolent. The population of them is mostly seen in family intimacy or social congregation. But Emma is as busy about the village as Lady Catherine de Bourgh, though, as Miss Kaye-Smith has pointed out, with "a different technique." Miss Austen wrote *Emma* nearly half a century before the General Enclosure Act. Many of the villagers she knew must still have been men of property *and so of independence and economic liberty*. Personal charity, therefore, had not yet been degraded from its Scriptural purity, though it was in process of becoming so. Mrs. Elton was the van of the host that overthrew the old culture (partly through its own weakness) and replaced it with much in its social aspects of envy and ostentation. When Maple Grove moved into Hartfield, it came as an invader.

IV

Pride and Prejudice was Saintsbury's favourite. One reason he gives for his choice is that its structural mastery is matched by its fertility in character-drawing. The elopement of Lydia with Wickham, for instance, is one of the hinges of the action and centre-pieces of the composition. It is free from the arbitrariness of Maria Rushworth's with Crauford. Lydia's pert wildness is definitely not a country one. She is hard, dashing, shameless, what Dr. Johnson called "unidea'd," and as slangy as maidens in gentle circumstances could be in the pages of Jane Austen. All her delights are in the town, Meryton, Brighton, London. She abhors the country for its dullness, and is always scampering off to the "amenities" of town life. "Untamed, unabashed, wild, noisy and fearless," she has a distinct flavour about her of our own nineteen twenties, a kind of slickness and the shininess of metal polish. How exquisitely her townish glitter is contrasted but also compared with the gaiety like Rosalind's, and the astringent mettlesome quickness like Beatrice's, of her country sister, Elizabeth! Both are "fearless," both "unabashed," both quick, but the one in the vulgar, the other in the older sense of aliveness and responsiveness. "A quickness which my God hath kissed," as Henry Vaughan wrote of life.

Mrs. Bennet has the same longing for town joys as Lydia. Her peevishness at being denied the joys of Brighton is mocked by a husband whose subacid entertainment at her follies are his compensation with his library for his own folly in marriage. Miss Bingley and Mrs. Hurst are rather betwixt and between; they are fashionables, but also, like Elizabeth Elliot of Kellynch Hall, leaders of county society of a familiar type. The whole Bingley family gives an impression of being uprooted, homeless, restlessly flitting from the flowers in the urban window-

box to the flowers in the country conservatory. How superci-
lious these spuriously elegant sisters are at Elizabeth getting her
petticoat splashed with mud when she walked over to Nether-
field to nurse Jane! If they rarely missed the London season,
they were also intimate with the respective Prides of Pemberley
and Rosings. Lady Catherine de Bourgh for her part never
shirked the onus of rural responsibility :—

> "She was a most active magistrate in her own parish, the
> minutest concerns of which were carried to her by Mr.
> Collins; and whenever any of the cottagers were disposed
> to be quarrelsome, discontented or too poor, she sallied
> forth into the village to settle their differences, silence their
> complaints, and scold them into harmony and plenty."

This Lady Bountiful is not a caricature. But for the
relentless malice of her presentation and the spare strokes of
her portraiture, she might have been found in the pages of
Trollope. She might easily be a distinguished member of
his De Courcy family. The landed aristocracy in Trollope is
very definitely one still in power but run to seed. It has been
said of Miss Austen, with gross injustice, that "her plots and
characters are dominated by questions of money." But this
libel ceases to be so if it be transferred to the world of Trollope,
which is sodden in money. In Trollope, the new money-values
of an England becoming rapidly commercialised are seen in
conjunction with a landed gentry that had become corrupted
with power, and was in nemesis soon to lose it to the lords of
money alone.

Lady Catherine de Bourgh is a foretaste of the Trollopian
squirearchy, but with a vitality of her own that the Trollope
squires mostly lack. Both she and her sycophant, Mr. Collins,
one of the most brilliant characters ever drawn in any fiction,
are Miss Austen's reflection, as a traditional ruralist, upon a
process of disintegration that culminated in the Enclosures.
The part played in them by the country clergy was in historical
truth the greatest scandal in the entire annals of the Church
of England. I feel rather rueful that Mr. Collins, that
master in the pomps and periods of toadying to the Great
House, should have been depicted as a gardener. "To work in

his garden was one of his most respectable pleasures." But there it is. I should have liked to have known his views on Capability Brown. For Mr. Collins was an admirer of prospects, pointing them out "with a minuteness which left beauty entirely behind."

The whole of *Pride and Prejudice* is a parable in the form of dramatic comedy upon its title. To this it is consistently faithful. It is, therefore, one of the greatest briefs for a Christian humility ever written. I cannot myself understand those critics who have found the conversion of Darcy to it unconvincing. It is, like Crauford's, a redemption of love, and for what a love! If Darcy accomplished a great feat in self-discipline, to how bright a star he hitched it! Who, granted Darcy's powers of understanding, would not be steadfast in self-government to win such a one? Redemption is a word of very little meaning nowadays, for the modern world does not admit the validity of sinfulness. But Miss Austen came in the evening of a very long day when such beliefs were universally held. To her and to these believers and to some moderns still, such an inner conquest was and would have been and is the most reasonable of phenomena. Besides, Darcy's change of heart is as natural and realistic as the incentive to it was all-compelling. Far more natural than the excessive hauteur and incivility of his first meetings with Elizabeth. They showed a lack of breeding on which his very pride was founded. There was not a trace of such consequential airs in Mr. Knightley, who was a paladin of good breeding. Darcy's opening arrogance is almost inhuman. His proposal to Elizabeth in Mr. Collins's parlour goes to the length of such crassness as allies him with fools in pasteboard like General Tilney and Sir Walter Elliot.

When the change bursts upon us like the parting of the clouds, it was made visible in the grounds of Pemberley. Graciousness of place is made at one with graciousness of person. No judicious reader can doubt that Elizabeth would have had him without any Pemberley, than which "she had never seen a place for which Nature had done more, or where natural beauty had been so little counteracted by an awkward taste." Pemberley and Darcy are seen in a bond of mutual interpretation. When Elizabeth catches sight of him along

the walk by the stream where " every step was bringing forward
a nobler fall of ground or a finer reach of the woods," the
fitness between the man and his setting reminds us, if a trifle
less warmly, of Mr. Knightley at Donwell. And it is stressed
what a conscientious and solicitous personal owner he was,
" the best landlord and the best master that ever lived," as his
housekeeper says. It is to be hoped that Elizabeth kept him
more at home.

A word must be said about Mr. and Mrs. Gardiner, the only
entirely sympathetic portraits of an urban business man and
his wife in all the novels. But Mr. Gardiner, besides being a
country-lover and a fisherman, lived in sight of his own
warehouse. The impersonality of big business and finance
was yet to appear, and its utter remoteness from the sources of
their wealth and of the workmen who made it. The holding of
property had not yet progressed into complete irresponsibility,
because the traditional links between town and country had
not yet been severed. Once the country had ceased to be the
stronghold of responsible property, whether in peasant, squire
or yeoman, there was nothing to restrain the rapid dissolution
of the social organism into proletarianism, the combine and
the total power of an autocratic State.

v

In the province of housing *Sense and Sensibility* is as revealing
as *Emma* and *Mansfield Park.* This is Colonel Brandon's
Delaford as seen through the Cockney eyes of Mrs. Jennings:—

" Delaford is a nice place, I can tell you; exactly what I call
a nice old-fashioned place, full of comforts and conveniences;
quite shut in with great garden walls that are covered with
the best fruit trees in the county; and such a mulberry tree
in one corner! . . . Then there is a dovecot, some delightful
stewponds and a very pretty canal."

We also hear of an old yew arbour behind the house. Plainly,
Delaford had been no more improved by Capability Brown
than Donwell Abbey. There were still breakwaters in the home

style that stood up against the salt estranging seas of "improvement." Both Donwell and Delaford are regarded as comfortable, a word that may be extended to cover grounds as well as rooms. The comfortless starkness and nakedness of the environs of a country house when the experts of naturalism had done with them must have been a main characteristic of them.

Contrast Delaford with Norland Park, into whose possession John and Fanny Dashwood had crept by a good fortune unattended by any other form of goodness. In Chapter II, that satirical masterpiece of the arts of meanness, this pair succeeded in disembarrassing themselves of any obligation to Mrs. Dashwood and her three daughters except in helping them to remove their furniture to Barton Cottage. They proceeded to the enclosure of Norland Common. This is Miss Austen's sole reference to the Enclosures that changed and soured and aged the face of English country life. But it is enough, and it is not the view of the modern progressive. The next step was to fell all the walnut trees on "the knoll," to clear away "all the old thorns that grew in patches over the brow" and erect upon it—a greenhouse. So was to perish the old English comeliness that was the flower of an ideal match between nature and man. With the loss of that secret beyond price, price became the sole consideration in all things that had nothing else to recommend them.

As an appendix to the advanced views of the John Dashwoods are to be seen those of another pioneer, Mr. Robert Ferrars, the proper husband for that Becky Sharp in a minor key, Lucy Steele. Mr. Robert Ferrars was the first, at least to my knowledge, of the cottage week-enders:—

"For my own part I am excessively fond of a cottage; there is always so much comfort, so much elegance about them. And I protest, if I had any money to spare, I should buy a little land and build one myself, within a short distance of London, where I might drive myself down at any time, and collect a few friends about me and be happy."

The "cottage" of one of these friends, Lady Elliott, had a dining parlour, with room for eighteen couples at a dance, card-tables in the drawing-room, tea for all in the library and supper in the saloon. We also seem to catch a faint ironic murmuration upon the even then loudly advertised London school of the picturesque in the description of Barton Cottage —"The building was regular, the roof was tiled, the windows were not painted green nor were the walls covered with honeysuckle "

But the kernel of Miss Austen's attitude to the romantic-picturesque is contained in the comedy, carried to the most delicate point of craftsmanly finesse, of the conversation between Marianne, Elinor and Edward Ferrars in the rich Devonshire valley at whose head the cottage stood.

" ' Oh!' cried Marianne, ' with what transporting sensations have I formerly seen them fall (the autumn leaves at Norland)! How have I delighted, as I walked, to see them driven in showers about me by the wind! What feelings have they, the season, the air, altogether inspired! Now there is no one to regard them, they are seen only as a nuisance, swept hastily off, and driven as much as possible from sight.' 'It is not every one,' said Elinor, ' who has your passion for dead leaves.'"

Marianne calls Edward's attention to the "prospect" of the valley, and he replies, "It is a beautiful country, but these bottoms must be dirty in winter." When they talk of books, Cowper, Scott, Byron, he remarks tartly enough for Edward, "She would love every book that tells her how to admire an old twisted tree." Again, when Marianne, with whom Shelley might easily have fallen in love, is what Fanny in *Mansfield Park* would call "rhapsodising" on the scenes in the neighbourhood of the cottage and questioning him, Edward bluntly replies:—

"You must not inquire too far, Marianne—remember, I have no knowledge in the picturesque, and I shall offend you by my ignorance and want of taste, if we come to particulars. I shall call hills steep, which ought to be bold; surfaces strange and uncouth, which ought to be irregular and rugged; and distant objects out of sight, which ought to be indistinct through the soft medium of a hazy atmosphere. You must be satisfied with such admiration as I can honestly give. I call it a very fine country—the hills are steep, the woods seem full of fine timber, and the valley looks comfortable and snug—with rich meadows and several neat farm-houses scattered here and there. It exactly answers my idea of a fine country because it unites beauty with utility—and I dare say it is a picturesque one too, because you admire it; I can easily believe it to be full of rocks and promontories, grey moss and brushwood, but these are all lost on me. I know nothing of the picturesque."

I am afraid so, says Marianne, but why boast of it?

Elinor here interposes in a balance between the two extremes, and suggests that Edward "is fastidious and will have an affectation of his own" because of the pretentiousness of many of the nature-lovers. Edward again takes up the tale:—

"'I like a fine prospect, but not on picturesque principles. I do not like crooked, twisted, blasted trees. I admire them much more if they are tall, straight and flourishing. I do not like ruined, tattered cottages. I am not fond of nettles or thistles, or heath blossoms. I have more pleasure in a snug farm-house than a watch-tower—and a troop of tidy happy villagers please me better than the finest banditti in the world.' Marianne looked with amazement at Edward, with compassion at her sister. Elinor only laughed."

This admirable epitome of the authentic countryman's point of view (allowing for the term "uncouth" as applied to mountainous or rocky country, which is pure eighteenth century) is one of the most significant passages of self-disclosure in all the works of Jane Austen the countrywoman. It is the very voice of Cobbett, whose countryman's eye loved a clean, well-grown, upstanding tree as much as it hated a twisted one. And though Marianne's origins were actually more rural than Edward's, she is expressing to comic perfection the attitude of the sentimental townsman.

The word "picturesque" appears to be derived from the Rev. William Gilpin's *Picturesque Remarks on the Wye, Observations on the Coasts of Hampshire, Sussex and Kent, relative chiefly* to *Picturesque Beauty*, and similar guide-books written towards the close of the eighteenth century. They were best-sellers because they caught and directed the reaction to the country of a nation at the beginning of its process of becoming urbanised. The real power was being transferred from the country to the town. Marianne's picturesque enthusiasms were also, of course, compatibly allied with Capability Brown's naturalistic iconoclasm and the "neo-Gothick" fashions that loved to erect sham ruins and plant ivy round pillars and up walls and façades.

The normal and timeless rural mentality never dreamed of separating beauty from utility. Their divorce thus reveals a profound split in the national consciousness. It became a definite cleavage as soon as the Industrial Revolution had got well into its stride. The building of the new industrial towns came to represent one side of the partnership—utility —from which the other was wholly excluded. Since beauty was thus ostracised from the practical business of men's lives, that was to become the acquisition of wealth for its own sake or the struggle to avoid destitution, beauty was left in the air. It became segregated and specialised. Art acquired a capital letter. Sensibility was cultivated as a desirable æsthetic emotion. The picturesque in nature became the antidote to the squalor and misery of the new industrialism. Ornamentalism became a cult, sufficiently lavish in the decoration of Victorian living-rooms. Marianne's romanticism came from the same root-stock as the heavy draperies and excess of furnishings in these rooms. Her creator's realism revealed in Marianne's suffering how insecure was its hold on truth. "We are betrayed by what is false within."

Towards our own times, the landslide of the dispossessed poor from a decaying countryside into the new towns was followed by a counter-migration of the dissatisfied upper and lower middle classes from the towns into the country. All, whether colonisers of the suburb or week-enders of the reconditioned cottage or farmhouse, were rallied under the banner of the picturesque. The suburban villa, with Tudor-esque half-timbering nailed on, ye olde hostelrie, the hobby of antiquarianism, the Arts and Crafts movement founded on the condition that it should not "interfere with trade," lawn and drawing-room folk-dancing, the exploitation of the beauty spot, the preservation of craftsmanship as a museum-piece exhibition, the half-contemptuous appraisal of the countryman as "quaint" and of his tools as "bygones," the "gone rustic" type of literature—these and other manifestations were so many different facets of the picturesque. The town took notice of the country as a show-place. The country had become the playground of the town.

For the picturesque means beauty divorced from the service of men's needs: its quintessence is and was that natural beauty has nothing whatever to do with utility. This is the fundamental reason why the love of the country has become skin-deep rather than bone-deep. Wild natural beauty stirs the heart and refreshes the spirit. But for more than a century these emotions have been falsely extended to a nature *gone wild*, which is a very different thing. And history has shown that the picturesque has co-existed with a derelict countryside—a countryside, that is to say, no longer occupied with supplying human needs. A countryside which is no longer useful in producing food and clothing, in supporting a multitude of small trades dependent on agriculture and replenishing the towns with both raw material for industry and a healthy human stock, becomes the arena of sentiment only. It becomes the recreation of the townsman in his leisure. Its fields, as Edward says, become a wilderness of thistles and "brushwood," and its former activities are covered with "grey moss."

But a busy and thriving countryside cannot do other than associate, as Edward also says, beauty with utility. Country craftsmanship in every age and every clime has created beauty as a by-product of utility and so made it a common grace and possession. All of our deeper "nature poets"—Milton, Chaucer, Langland, Drayton, Shakespeare, George Herbert, Wordsworth, Cowper, John Clare, Hardy, William Barnes—have defined the rural scene as a way of life. The same is clearly true of our great schools of water-colour painters —Constable, David Cox, Wilson, de Wynt, Girtin, Cotman, the Cosenses and the Chromes. All of them humanised the natural scene. Before the word "picturesque" was invented, there was no difference in kind between the cathedral and the homeliest cottage, while Michelangelo became the greatest of sculptors as the master-man of a workshop. The great Gothic building was as useful for men's salvation as the shape of a scythe-snathe cut from the underwood was beautiful. Straight, sound timber is an object of beauty to all countrymen no less than it was to Edward, whereas the crooked and twisted tree is an advertisement of decay. To him for the same reason a tidy farmhouse was more beautiful than a ruined cottage. An organic sense of beauty looks below the surface, never dissociating it from health, from fitness to environment and from a right relation between man and the earth. A thistle is a thing of beauty in its right place; in a cornfield it is an excrescence.

Beauty to the countryman is the part, an indispensable part, of the whole. Marianne so little belonged to the whole that her "competence" is Elinor's "wealth." Even with Willoughby, whom she loved so romantically, she would not, in spite of the claims of romance, have been satisfied with less than two carriages, hunters and a "proper establishment of servants." But Elinor, like Miss Austen herself, did belong to the countryside in heart as well as birth, and saw beauty, "sense," prudence, utility and moral values all in their true places as parts of the whole. It is just as significant that both Marianne and Willoughby repent of their false attitudes, the one of the deceitfulness of pure romance, the other of the deceitfulness of riches. Though a reader should be chary enough of identifying a great writer's own philosophy of life with any section of the world he or she creates, yet the artist will always project the essence of himself into it.

VI

Realism in art finds its metaphysical content in symbolism. This is eminently true of Jane Austen, every one of whose novels is an intellectual whole and illustrates a coherent "scheme of values."[1] Throughout, it is the same vision, but astonishingly varied within the small compass of its environment both in stress and in mood. Lest we should be rashly inclined to affix a too prudential and rational cast of thought

[1] Lord David Cecil.

to the author of *Sense and Sensibility*, *Persuasion* is a divinely gentle reproof to an excess of zeal in prudence. Lest we should be disposed to feel the patience and self-discipline of Elinor as too victorious over the impetuous fervours and subjective illusions of Marianne, *Persuasion* is richly dyed in the poetry of nature.

It is by far the most lyrical of all the novels, not in the quality of spring, but, as has been often remarked, of autumn. Shakespeare's *The Tempest* and Jane Austen's *Persuasion* match one another as symbolic masterpieces of autumn. It is not the finery of autumn, when every leaf becomes a flower, that is symbolised. It is something more subtle and elusive, a mild elegiac radiance that suffuses both recollection and promise, both loss and fulfilment. Autumn is not only the full maternity and maturity of the year; it is at once summer in memory and spring in hope. Underneath the dangling fruits the apple-buds are forming and the earth is dense with shoots and seedlings. So Anne Elliot's year looks before and after. Memory is blended with hope. Desolation moves by hardly perceptible steps into renewal. Her life's consummation could never have been what it was but for the extinction of that promise which preceeded it The first shoots of a new flowering for her, the early streaks of a new day would have lacked the poignancy they have if the moulding power of continuity with a past at once brighter and more shadowed had been absent. The theme is the constancy of love rather than love itself, and it is clothed in all the reverie and ripeness of autumn, its tenderness and mournfulness.

As the narrative unfolds, a seasonal rhythm in Anne's emotional development is still more closely followed. The reawakening of her hopes and physical beauty at Lyme Regis times with the very last days of autumn in its retrospection, its sense of an irrevocable parting and the fading of her youthful bloom. At Christmas the action is in suspense. Captain Wentworth's arrival in Bath with all its presages of a final reconciliation takes place at the very earliest dawn of spring. Yet we must not over-simplify the parallelism and make these emotional sequences a pedantic imitation of the natural. Though Anne enters upon a second spring, it is one dyed in autumnal experience. The autumn estrangement is also one of spiritual growth which absorbs and makes use of pain and loss.

In yet another direction *Persuasion* is profoundly ruralised. It is marked how interpenetrated great events of the spirit are with the open air, the natural scene and the act of walking. We know, as I have said, that Miss Austen herself was a great walker. Elizabeth Bennet was a lover of solitary walks, and walked for miles with Darcy after their engagement. Mr. Knightley spoke his heart to Emma upon a walk, and Catherine Morland was initiated into the appreciation of landscape on a walk with the young Tilneys. But the walks in *Persuasion* are even more organic with inward psychological implications. There is the famous walk from Uppercross to the brow of the hill overlooking Winthorp:—

> " Her (Anne's) pleasure in the walk must arise from the view of the last smiles of the year upon the tawny leaves and withered hedges, and from repeating to herself some few of the thousand poetical descriptions extant of autumn, that season of peculiar and inexhaustible influence on the mind of taste and tenderness, that season which has drawn from every poet, worthy of being read, some attempt at description, or some lines of feeling."

Arrived on the hill-top, Anne hears Captain Wentworth on the other side of the hedge praising firmness and decision of character to Louisa Musgrave in their " gleaning of nuts." She understands her own finality of separation from him to be sealed. There are the yet more famous walks along the Cob at Lyme, when her being takes on a new life and enlargement from wind and sea and cliff. It is on a walk that Mr. Elliot's acknowledgment of her new-found beauty rouses Captain Wentworth's perception of it. The immediate consequence, again, of Louisa's fall is his realisation of her promptitude, good sense and practical judgment in emergency. And there is the supreme walk with Captain Wentworth up Union Street in Bath when her way of resignation and renunciation is changed to the way of abundance of life.

It is noticeable, too, that country reference and imagery are more frequent in *Persuasion* even than in *Mansfield Park*. The principle street of Lyme is delicately caught "almost hurrying into the water." Captain Wentworth, in describing

Louisa's loss of high spirits and nervous reactions after her accident and engagement to Captain Benwick, says—"If one only happens to shut the door a little loud, she starts and wriggles like a young dab-chick." Captain Wentworth, again, moralises in the Jacques manner on the hazel-nut during his walk and talk with Louisa:—

" 'Here is a nut to exemplify: a beautiful glossy nut, which, blessed with original strength, has outlived all the storms of autumn. Not a puncture, not a weak spot anywhere. This nut,' he continued with playful solemnity, ' while so many of its brethren have fallen and been trodden under foot, is still in possession of all the happiness that a hazel nut can be supposed capable of.' "

The warm colours in which Lyme and its liassic cliffs are praised, the many touches about the Somerset country between Kellynch Hall and Uppercross are a kind of thanksgiving for a country-side whose harmonies permeate the book. They lend to its peculiar moral and emotional tone a music not to be forgotten.

The grace and charm of the naval officers can escape no reader of *Persuasion*. All are depicted as the most warm-hearted, good-humoured and considerate of family men. They have deep affections and great integrity of character, while the little group at Lyme is given to pondering on the mysteries of human nature. And how vastly superior in responsibility were Admiral Croft and his good wife in their charge of Kellynch Hall than was its owner! Captain Benwick is of a studious bent, and the open, free, robust and yet delicate nature of Captain Wentworth makes Anne's devotion completely intelligible, even if she were not Anne. The naval officers also play an indispensable part not only in the structure and significance of the narrative but in its spiritual truth. They introduce variations upon the central motive of constancy and on the action of Lady Russel in separating Anne from her lover. Captain Harville's discourse to Anne while Captain Wentworth writes his letter, Captain Benwick's inconstancy to Harville's sister, Admiral Croft's early marriage to his wife, all are threaded integrally into the pattern.

It is, of course, easy to account for this partiality in Miss

Austen by her own family circumstances. Her brothers were sailors in Nelson's Navy and she herself is reputed to have been engaged to a naval officer. But I believe there is also a wider and more general reason for the affinity in her works between a rural society and the Navy, that only twice, at Portsmouth and Lyme, visits the Britannic coasts. A reason allied to, but other than that of our native tradition both of the sea and of the land, now broken so artificially in respect of the land. The affinity was an organic one. A ship, whether of war or peace, is a self-contained, self-supporting unit, just as the English village once was. A ship is a co-operative organism, and so once was the village. A ship is a hive of craftsmanship, and so was the village. A ship's society is hierarchical, like that of the manorial village. A ship floats among the elemental forces of nature; a village rests upon the earth. Jane Austen's intuitive feeling in drawing them together in *Persuasion* and to a lesser degree in *Mansfield Park*, was thus an aspect of objective reality that demonstrates her country sense as well as any other.

The spirit, the mentality and the genius of Jane Austen were as deeply rooted in English soil as Shakespeare's. Her moral values, her sense of home and family, her conviction of the importance of the person, the realism of her art and the serenity of her mind, her comedy, her sanity, her poetry and her justice, her individual vision and her very creativeness, were the autumnal fruits of the English rural tradition. Her apprehension of the moral order, her *Tao*, was conspicuously so, both Christian and rural. Not the least of the reasons why some modern criticism is unduly concerned with the "narrowness" of her outlook is the rootless belief in the relativity of ethics and an urbanism that has ceased to be fertilised from the humus of its own past.

CHAPTER III

IRESON OF STAMFORD

The angels keep their ancient places;—
Turn but a stone and start a wing!
'Tis ye, 'tis your estrangèd faces,
That miss the many-splendoured thing.
                              FRANCIS THOMPSON

I

STAMFORD is the very individual and dignified old market-town
on the Welland where Lincolnshire meets Northamptonshire.
There the limestone houses climb the slope from the bridge as
they do at Bruton, Burford and Bradford-on-Avon. The spires
and towers of her five churches are clustered about with inns,
grammar school, hospitals, burghers' residences and bits of
walls and halls. All are not only in stone, but faithful to the
architectural idiom of the oolite limestone whose local
variations can be witnessed along the winding ridge from
Burton Bradstock on the Dorset coast to the Yorkshire border.
Though the Great North Road runs through the middle of
Stamford, her true identity and integrity as a local market-
town have not yet been compromised or destroyed by red-brick
villas, by the chain store, office buildings and the like in the
"paladin" style and cinemas in Gorgonzola marble.

First and indirectly by his letters to me and later by
meeting him in person and in his own place, I have been so
fortunate as to form a friendship with a contemporary
master-builder of Stamford. Through A. S. Ireson, the
director of a Stamford building firm, I was enabled to see
something of the inward spirit of the English market-town
and to bridge the gap between past and present. I had no need
for a laborious *recherche du temps perdu* when this man, who
maintains the English tradition in stone, still lives and works
in his native town. I had no need to look for the kind of life
he embodies in what is left to-day of this place or that. An old

town is the expression of a way of life. Ireson is its living representative. A true architecture is an organic growth, and through him I became acquainted with the workings of the organism responsible for it.

The engravings of old devotional books show the pilgrim making his way through a grisly land of sin and suffering towards heaven. Approaching the great stone country of the northern oolite ridge from the south, the traveller recapitulates the story John Bunyan has told. Years ago, when I traversed this stone-jewelled ridge from the Dorset coast to Grantham, I met Apollyon straddling across it, as Shakespeare's Antony did the ocean. "His legs bestrid" the whole triangular block of country between Northampton, Wellingborough, Higham Ferrars and Kettering. I was not anxious to repeat the experience. So I edged east of his giant body of iron, setting my course for Kimbolton, the multicoloured little town in Huntingdonshire, with the chilly Vanbrugh pile in the south looking up its gay winding high street.

But I did not escape. Descending from the high ground, whose ornaments are Woburn and Ampthill, seemly in the rose-red brick of this minor Dukeries, I ran straight into another giant. He is not of iron but of brick, and not rose-red, but of that Fletton and Phorpres' (pressed four times) pink which has desolated miles of the Soke of Peterborough. In the Bedfordshire plain, this giant looks of a milder disposition than Apollyon. The huge gaunt stacks of the Company have a certain heathen dignity unlike the sordid grimness of Apollyon's realm. But I doubt whether he has not done as much hurt to the great culture of stone in the north as Apollyon himself. The bilious pink of Fletton brick[1] is not deliberate. It is a by-blow of that monetary cheapness which has nourished these two monsters into their modern stature. The vast brick-deserts of Peterborough have eroded the land because Fletton and Phorpres can be baked by a process that consumes a minimum of fuel. It has been so triumphant that the kingdom of stone has been invaded by brick as well

[1] The new sand-faced brick of this Combine is a great improvement on the pink horror.

as iron. They have not yet laid it waste. But they have almost stifled those creative powers active for a thousand years from Saxon Barnack to the contemporary works of the Iresons I was on my way to see.

I stopped at Warmington Church—a decade ago I had made a special journey of 150 miles to see it. It is a masterpiece of the Early English, profuse in refinement of detail, especially in dogtooth ornament, corbel-heads, the oaken arches springing from the stiff-leaf foliage of the nave-capitals, the lancets and the exquisite crosses surmounting the spire-lights of the broach-spire. But the purity and wholeness of this architecture, whose multiplicity of beauties is all disciplined to the simplicity of the structural conception, had not yet captured me. Nor yet was my inward eye kindled by the broach-spire dominating the landscape of three counties—Northamptonshire, Lincoln-shire and Rutland. I could see them already—the spire of Warmington looking across to the double octagonal lantern of Fotheringay, the spire of Oundle, the spire of Wansford, and at last the spire of St. Mary's, Stamford. Apart from the parapeted spire, less common, there are two types of these broach-spires, the squat and the soaring, and all have spire-lights. Yet none is like another of either type, and few there be among the scores of them that are not the masters of the earth far and wide from where they stand. This great Stone Age courted the eye of heaven. But I had been so long absent from so strange a culture that as yet they were only a spectacle.

When I first met Ireson on Barn Hill in his modest seven-teenth century house with an eighteenth century pediment over the front door, I got something of a shock. Was this the man who had written me those extraordinary letters? But whom had I expected to see? Perhaps somebody after the style of the self-portrait in stone of Henry Yevele, the master-mason of Westminster Abbey and Hall? I was now delivered from this romantic folly: the man who opened the front door looked like the neatly dressed director of an engineering firm. What was even more surprising, he was a young man somewhere in the thirties. The depth of local knowledge in the letters had perhaps conjured up a broad gnarled face with a grizzled beard. This quiet-spoken undemonstrative man was at any rate master of himself as well as of his craft and of nearly forty men who worked for him. But there was one thing my baffled look sensed at once through these uncommunicative externals—here was a man with deep roots. How deep even his letters had not discovered to me. Now, after less than two days in his company, I do know.

At the end of our first evening together, we went into his office opposite the sitting-room. It is like any other sitting-room of a fairly well-to-do man of business in a small town. Except for one thing—the books. Not books in shelves: there were none. But lying on a table among some copies of *Country Life* and a technical journal was the book written this same year about Henry Yevele. It has a sub-title on the cover —"The Life of an English Architect." I spoke to him about the book and he said at once, pointing to the caption, "That's quite wrong. Yevele was a master-mason, not an architect in our sense at all." It was only at the end of my visit that the full implication of his words came home to me.

He then produced from some recess two other books. One was the plump uncut quarto of a nineteenth century local history of Stamford, finely bound by himself. It contained a number of good prints of Stamford, but its companion was of even more interest to me. This was an ordinary pocket-book of a master-mason of Stamford, Thomas C. Halliday, who died in 1842. In it were a number of architectural pencil drawings, interiors of churches, elevations of buildings, shop-fronts and the like. All were of exemplary precision and delicate feeling. But the Georgian shop-fronts and one drawing of an elaborate cross were superb.

This Halliday belonged to a Stamford family of quarry-owners and builders, distinguished for their work in the nineteenth century. The most celebrated of them was Samuel Halliday, who became an alderman and mayor of the town. He owned a pair of quarries, one of them the Casterton pit north of Stamford, where the Romans had a station. This, with the exception of Ketton stone, provided the best quality of free-stone in the neighbourhood, and Halliday made good use of it. He restored churches and country houses and built rectories, gate lodges, stables, estate cottages and other buildings over a wide radius of the three counties whose borders meet at Stamford. But not in the manner of the Gothic revivalists of the last century. He built as a son of Stamford and so in the manner of his fathers. In such circumstances, there was no possibility of the academic imitation of an old style from without. The Halliday family had been masons for generations in Rutland. As a quarry-owner, Samuel Halliday was enabled to maintain a number of other masons both in the pit and on his buildings. Ireson's grandfather was one of his foremen, and Ireson's father served his apprenticeship in the dressing of stones under him until in 1903 he founded the present Ireson family business. Ireson told me that Halliday followed the true tradition in another way—by often sinking trial holes and opening up new pits. Holding in my hands the beautiful drawings of a Halliday pocket-book in Ireson's sitting-room, I was seeing as in a precious manuscript the history of Stamford through the ages.

The very last of this society of master-builders who were also quarry-workers and quarry-owners of the Halliday type was John Woolston. He also became alderman and mayor of Stamford. His principal works were the restoration of St. Michael's Church, the Crown Hotel and the Town Bridge. The quarry he owned by the Great North Road a mile from Stamford produced good ashlar. When he died in 1917, his craftsmen, instead of being dispersed and in the end drifting into the industrial towns, were absorbed by the Ireson firm. They changed masters but kept their proper jobs, and so the continuity of the great tradition. Woolston was also a farmer who combined quarrying on his own ground with cultivating his own fields by a famous team of horses beside it, and experimenting with sugar-beet, now grown all over Lincolnshire.

One of the most interesting of these glimpses into an ageless Stamford was that John Woolston was called "Old Johnny," but Samuel Halliday always "Mr. Halliday." Both mayors, both owners, both master-builders, and yet there was a social distinction between them. I seemed to touch here the very essence of that mediæval society to which Cobbett and Disraeli after him appealed as against the two classes and "two nations" of employers and employed, or, as Cobbett called them, masters and slaves. Between Woolston and Halliday there was a social difference in a hierarchy of long and subtle gradations. It was the same kind of society Shakespeare had known in Stratford. Through Ireson's letters and talks and the personal contacts I made through him, I was introduced to other rungs of the ladder.

I was enabled, too, to observe the closely knit mesh of relationships falling apart. One of Old Johnny's craftsmen to come to Ireson was Roberts, a joiner. His family of master-builders owned another Stamford quarry whose limestone was used for burning and dry-walling. But it has gone derelict, and so the link between ownership and craftsmanship has snapped. George Medwell, another farmer, owned a quarry that produced the fine Clipsham stone of which the House of Commons was partly built. The Molesworths owned a quarry whose clay "overburden" (the deposits overlaying the stone beds), they used for setting up a small local brickworks. Both pits that once made fertile work for a minutely graded society have become mere holes in the ground.

In the top-layers of this society were squires like the Davenport-Handleys of the Clipsham quarries. They extracted large quantities of building stone, together with thousands of tons of "overburden," and, like prospectors, opened up many little quarries. In the same way, the Earls of Ancaster fostered a rich school of building craftsmen, mostly for work on farmsteads and farm buildings, by means of the Ancaster freestone in their quarries. But either the quarry-squires have died and the sons gone to the wars or the wens, or, impoverished by Death Duties and other taxation, have seen their estates carved up or sold, or the grass now grows over the quarries themselves. With the village owner-masons, who represented the lower strata in the series of active and responsible ownership, I came later into touch. But in Thomas Halliday's pocket-book and its near or far associations I had seen enough to be no longer surprised at the tenacity and durability of this social network based on a Gothic past. It had outlived three centuries of social change, each one becoming increasingly hostile to that past, and the last, our own, its total enemy. But its anchorage lay in the fusion between ownership and vocation and in the co-operation between every grade of local society in

handling, dressing, constructing and managing the grey stone
to preserve and enrich the continuity of Stamford.

How, then, had this culture in stone come so near to its
end? Ireson had written to me—"I quite agree with you that
when men cease to build in stone their culture is virtually at
an end." The æsthetic qualities indispensable for building in
stone are a by-product of other qualities in a man himself.
Thomas Halliday had died in 1842, just after the close of the
last of the great architectural periods of England. In general
terms, it is easy to assign causes for the decline in stone-
building. The loss of local self-government in commercial and
bureaucratic centralisation, of the workshop in the factory,
of craftsmen in mass unskilled labour, of the rural community
in industrialism, of vocation in the money motive, are some
of the more obvious. But what had been the local reasons
in so stable and closely geared a community as Stamford's?

One of these, as Ireson told me, was the disuse of the smaller
quarries. The growth of motor transport and so the breakdown
of local self-sufficiency made them commercially unprofitable.
This in its turn loosened the inter-relation between quarryman,
mason, builder and owner. They tended to become separate
entities. For instance, Ireson's own dealings with the owners,
managers and workers of the quarries is now confined to
selecting blocks, arranging for them to be sawn, collecting the
stone and paying the bill.

Another reason, according to Ireson, is that the Rent
Restriction Acts, by pegging down rents to a low artificial
level, have had the curious effect of preventing old houses
from being repaired. But I think there is a more fundamental
reason why the old properties, part of the national culture,
either deteriorate until they crumble into ruin or are pulled
down to make way for something slick in the modern style,
or, if propped up by repairs, are botched for cheapness' sake.
The real villain of the piece is a financial system based on debt
and cut-price competition against the world and once more
tied down to gold. It moves by inflation and deflation, and
artificially restricts purchasing power. Tight money has
allowed, and will again allow, such properties, ninety per cent
of them structurally sound, to tumble down. If money were
equated to production, old houses could be restored or turned

into new houses by reconditioning. If goodness, not cheapness, were our aim, the housing shortage itself would quickly disappear.

Yet the tradition of responsible ownership in Stamford is so strong that Ireson gave me several instances of houseowners sinking their capital on old cottages purely for love and with no hope of return. One of them spent £300, another £200. But few have the means, if they feel the inclination, to spend their money out of a disinterested desire to preserve from ruin the villages and towns of the stone belt. Still less so when the houses are more than cottages or need to be fitted up with modern sanitation, electric light, a bathroom and hot and cold water.

A third and more crucial cause (or effect) of the decline in stone-building concerns apprenticeship. The fact that there are still fifteen apprentices left in Stamford is one explanation of why I was able to catch the last sunset streaks of its building tradition. Unhappily, none are apprenticed to banker-masons, the last two having left Stamford between 1915 and 1945. The Ireson firm employs nine of these apprentices—a slater, a joiner, four carpenters, two bricklayers and a painter. Most of these have or had fathers and grandfathers in the trade. The joiner has a family memory of a great grandfather on his mother's side, and a great-great-grandfather on his father's who were Stamford joiners. He, Ireson told me, "is the most promising boy of the lot." He would be.

Why have these apprentices so fallen off during our century? Because stone-building itself is ceasing to be continuous. Apprentices to banker-masons served a five-year term, but bits of those years took the heart out of them. The "melancholy long withdrawing" ebb of apprenticeship, again, is speeded by so many sons of existing craftsmen becoming school teachers, political agents, shopmen and clerks. Not because they necessarily make more money nor are better suited to work at the desk of school or office, but simply, as Ireson said, because of "false values." Ireson tries to save apprenticeship—this best of all systems for holding the fabric of continuity together—by switching over his bricklayer apprentices to the monumental masons. Government schemes for instructors and mechanical school training for two half-days a week he regards as a futile substitute for a long-term apprenticeship that in the days of the Trade Guilds was the background to the building of the cathedrals. And even this tinkering with the issue defeats its own ends by the boys becoming conscripts at their most impressionable age. Upon this thread of apprenticeship hangs to-day the whole culture of the stone age of the Midlands.

These "false values" are not, of course, confined to the building trade. Any trade in which a man works with his hands has sunk into a stagnant malodorous marsh of fallacy. It not only depresses the craftsman but exalts the man at the desk to a superior being. The shop-walker who shows potential buyers round, the cashier who makes a note of what they spend, belong to a higher caste than the maker of fine and useful things which are not even sold in the shop. Fine and useful things are "uneconomic." The degradation of work for which this attitude is responsible has on the concrete side condemned "the workers" to the virtual slavery of the conveyor belt. On the abstract, it has diffused a false philosophy of values which eats into the very core of humanity. An example came my way soon after I had left Stamford. A friend of mine, a distinguished man of letters, has a nephew who is a magician in wood and whose one ambition is to become a working craftsman. My friend wrote—"I have been trying for a year now to save him from an architect's office—he being clearly designed by Providence to be a wood-worker. His mother wrote as follows:—

'Did I tell you the result of —— visit to the Institute of Vocational Psychology? The report said that his general intelligence was higher than 90% of the public school boys interviewed, and they thought he would be unsatisfied doing a job entirely in craft work and strongly advised him to try for a degree in economics and later to do a Social Administrative job.'"

My friend calls this victimisation of the boy an "obscene racket." He was fascinated, he said, by the combination of fatuity on the part of the psychological pundits and the bottomless credulity on the part of the letter-writer. The episode is exactly like a scene out of Huxley's *Brave New World*.

W.M.B.   G

It is becoming mentally impossible for our civilisation to regard it as a satire.

The economic reasons for the almost eclipse of "craft-work", whether in wood or stone, are clear. But what was the æsthetic reason? Here, too, Halliday's pocket-book gave me the glimmerings of an answer. In the arts, it was the separation of the artist and the dealer from the craftsman; in stone-building, of the architect and the business man from the mason. In the pocket-book, the mason was still a designer, like Henry Yevele himself. But he was by then only the draughtsman of a finished work, not the "onlie begetter" of a new one. And when I left Stamford, I had seen what was Ireson's mission—to bring them together again.

II

His office was much more an expression of his inward self than the rest of the house. He had stripped away the Victorian fireplace to disclose an ornately carved baroque one of painted brown marble and honeycomb brick; he wished he could find out why nearly all of the old fireplaces, when in brick, were honeycombed. Round the walls were many beautiful prints of Stamford. They included that of Turner's water-colour, a copy of which he prevailed upon me to accept. It was taken from the Bull and Swan, where Turner used to stay, the only inn in Stamford Baron with a pargeted front to one of the gables. From this Inn you look down towards the Bridge over the Welland that divides Northamptonshire from Lincolnshire and the Tower of St. Martin's Church. But Turner faked his view by bringing in the ethereal broach-spire of St Mary's, over which and this tower he had poured streams of that unearthly radiance he was prone to over-dramatise. There was also a Morden Map of Stamford of 1753. It is of particular interest to Ireson because it shows the Welland joining the Nene at Crowland—the Nene being now 15 miles away. But Ireson is not only a local geographer—how rich and intimate is his geological and topographical knowledge I was yet to find out—he is also a sign-painter. On the walls among other drawings was a good head of Bernard Shaw. He also showed me a fine collection of mason's tools. Among them was a complete set of lettering chisels belonging to old men he had worked with, and a level, used by his grandfather before the days of the spirit-level. It was a triangle of wood from which a plumb-bob was hung for horizontal and vertical levels.

But as we passed from pictures of Stamford to specimens of the tools which had built its beauty, my eyes kept straying to a pair of carved stone heads on the wall. One was of a sour-faced man, the dolorous wrinklings and creasings of whose hard-bitten features caught the ripplings of his cap. The other was of a woman, serene and patient, with a coif round her head of the mediæval pattern. So completely mediæval they both were that I supposed them to be corbel-heads out of one of Stamford's six churches, so prolific in figure carvings like all the churches of the region. But they were not. They were the work of one Hibbins, a master-mason of Ketton, the village south of Stamford on the western arm of the Welland Valley. And Hibbins, the last of a line of village masons deep in time, died two months before I met Ireson at Stamford. He had no son to forge one more link in a chain which, as I discovered later, stretched back to the Middle Ages. Those heads were witness to a local continuity between the great broach-spires of the Nene and the Welland and their present era of iron and brick. What a revelation of timelessness! If external influences had left craftsmanship alone, it would have flourished to the end of the world.

During this evening and the next and on our journeys together, I heard something of the Ireson family which has striven with such vision and tenacity to keep the Age of Stone true to itself against the storms of our own. The Iresons have been master-masons for perhaps three centuries. The only one of them who left the Midlands was Nathaniel Ireson, who, in 1726, settled at Wincanton in Somerset. He left his home but not his profession. For at Wincanton he discovered a quarry remarkable even by the standards of the Midlands limestone belt. It contained easily worked freestone, limestone for walling, limestone for burning, sand that with the best lime made plaster and mortar, "overburden" clay that made a pleasing dull plum-red brick and pot clay. Ireson himself has never known such another combination. Through it Nathaniel

became a builder of credit and renown both in Somerset and Wiltshire. He made pots which are now collector's pieces, and bought Windmill Farm, on whose land the quarry stood. He became so prosperous as, in Ireson's words, "to give church towers and chancels away."

The present firm is composed of three Iresons—the father whom I met and his two sons. Ireson told me to look at his father's hands; the stumpy fingers are so spatulate and splayed out, the joints so thickened that he cannot close them. This has been the effect not only of hammer and chisel but of wicket-keeping for Stamford (he was also first bat) in second-class cricket. This twice-mayor of Stamford was also a great runner. When he was working on Oundle School, ten miles away, he used to think nothing of running to his work and back again. His spare, taut frame and fine features showed no sign of age. He is not the only craftsman I have met who makes me believe that the descendants of the pre-industrial craftsmen were beside the present workers a race of giants.

The men employed by the Ireson firm are not only bricklayers but masons, slaters and their apprentices from Collyweston and reed-thatchers from Salthouse, in Norfolk. They are all traditional craftsmen, with a very long lineage in the building trade and descended from craftsmen whose families had intermarried. No doubt this intermarriage was a form of self-protection as the urban workmen became more and more industrial-minded. But their numbers dwindle from old age and there are few or none to replace them. Ireson lost three of them during the War, one of them the best mason in carved stone surviving at Stamford. Ireson drew a sharp distinction between these traditional masons of Stamford and the modern bricklayers. In spite of being in the fashion (building in stone being regarded as outmoded), well paid and comfortable in their conditions of life, the bricklayers "seem unhappy, disgruntled fellows." They never developed, he said, the character, personality or skill of the masons. They lack the support of a family connection with the trade, and think of their work only in terms of the pay-packet. The more it becomes an automatic routine, the rougher and more careless its performance.

The interest of a man's work makes time irrelevant; lacking it, the bricklayer thinks of getting through the time rather than the work. He thus becomes the victim both of time and circumstance, while the craftsman's sense of vocation in his work develops qualities of "wisdom and disinterestedness, good nature and tranquillity." This exactly tallies with my own experience. He is "thinking about his work all the time" and so his craft is incorruptible. The bricklayer's isolation from anything outside his bricks contrasts with the mason's close relations with the quarryman on the one hand and the builder on the other. He feels part of a whole working community. Ireson does his utmost, as his letters indicate, to wean the young bricklayers away from bricks, in which the business of a modern builder compels him to work, to the traditional stone, where his heart and his inheritance and his chiefest skill lie. But even when he builds in brick, he has been partially successful in replacing the jaundiced Stamford brick (almost as nasty as pink Fletton) with the newly discovered Stamford grey, whose texture and shade are stone-like.

His master-idea is not to develop the master-style of Stamford, still less to imitate but to simplify it. That master-style is essentially Cotswold Gothic which outlived the Middle Ages up to and even beyond the Industrial Revolution which broke its back. For the good reason that it is the authentic vernacular of the oolite limestone ridge. It is independent of periods and fashions but not of place, and the modifications induced by different regions along the ridge.

The Victorians went wrong, according to Ireson, by reproducing the Gothic idiom without its peculiarly local spirit. There were still fine craftsmen, but they were separated from the architect in his office. The craftsman did his job with his customary skill and thoroughness, but he was expressing the wrong ideas. If you are part of the tradition yourself, the inevitable one of the region, you regenerate, not copy it. The great purpose of the Iresons has been to close the breech, as I have said, between the designer and the craftsman. Ireson himself is not only a mason and bricklayer but can do everything there is to be done on a house, from plumbing to electric fittings. He is the only builder in Stamford of such catholicity. The long roots of his family in the past of his own place equip him, as few men in England are equipped, for the great act of reconciliation. He only lacks the means to accomplish it, because the age is against him. It clings to an obsolete economic system and at the same time derides and discards the genuine, the English past, that built Stamford before this sham system was invented.

His views on the builder followed the same lines. The builder has become a business man more concerned with organising labour and his costings than with master-crafstmanship. Design has ceased to be his business. As one means of healing the split between architect, builder and craftsman, Ireson advocated a five-year apprenticeship as mason-bricklayer or joiner-carpenter for any young man desiring to become a builder or an architect. This should be supplemented by technical instruction and a study of carving and building geometry. Thus he would be continuously in touch with the actualities of building and the values of craftsmanship. Buildings could not be planned merely on paper; the draughtsman must be something of an artist as well as an engineer. He must become aware of the qualities and properties of his materials. Once this mastery is acquired, a few roughly pencilled sketches are all that is needed. The beauty was in the finished work. It escapes an elaborately drawn plan which takes no account of light and shade, of colour and texture, of proportions and perspective, and of the harmony with its surroundings of the finished building.

Of another purpose of Ireson's—to restore the old com-munion between village and town—examples occurred on our journeys. One of these took place in his home. Nevil Goodwin, one of his Collyweston slaters, came to see me straight from the roof he was repairing. In his dungarees with leather knee-pads and leather bag and brush, this long-faced man with his mobile expressive features and twisted smile looked to be in the middle forties. Actually he is sixty-four, and his father was still working on the roofs when he was eighty-seven. In his younger days, Nevil used to walk eleven miles to his roofing and eleven miles back again day after day. Ireson told me he is still like a cat on a roof, and always chooses the ladders with the thinnest rungs, worn to breaking-point.

Nevil proceeded without a trace of self-consciousness to give a dramatic exhibition of how the roof-slats are mined at Collyweston. To get at the "log" thirty feet down, the upper deposit of shale and sand has to be penetrated, the debris shored up and packed and the shale built up into piers. Then galleries are hewn with the pick just as in the Neolithic flint-mines of Grime's Graves. Along this "shim road" Nevil would crawl and pull himself to extract the log. This is hauled up by a winch and laid out to be frosted. Many a time had Nevil spent all night watering the slats so that his craft-mate, Jack Frost, should split the slats to the required slices. They are then stacked up in conical rings, shaped with the slat-pick and holed to be hung on the battens. When so, Nevil did his measurements entirely by eye. All the slaters at once distinguish between the Collyweston and the Easton slats where the seams are inferior, though the differences cannot be detected by the eye. Unlike the Cotswold slats, those of Collyweston are bedded in shale. They are imperishable and just as warm in colour, rich in texture, and prone to weathering as the Cotswold slats.

Nevil spoke and acted all these varied parts with gusto. He ended his performance with a recitative at a breathless pace of all the professional names of the different lengths of slats. He wrote these out for me, "as handed down from one generation to another." Some are North Midlands vernacular and have no parallels in the Cotswolds—Shorteens, Middleteens, Longteens, Outbows, Jobs and Mopes. Others are the same for both regions, and the third set shows variations in the same word—mumfits for the Cotswold movities, backs for becks and wippets for wibbuts. The diminishing sizes from the eaves upward are not only a structural virtue but create a rich perspective. The roof seems to rise into infinity.

Nevil is a gardener, too, and always brings Ireson and his wife a bunch of spring flowers, often lilies of the valley. I could not bear to think that such a man with such a father and of such a line of craftsmen should have no sons and sons' sons to be quarrying such slats from the pits and fitting them on roofs for all time. Especially as his apprentice gave up an unskilled job entirely on his own initiative to join him at twenty-four shillings a week less pay. Had Nevil sons, I asked Ireson? Two: one was a brewer's traveller; the other, now dead, had been a shop-assistant. They had gone up in the world,

III

Two hours of the next day, whose every precious drop was caught and distilled, were spent in the streets of Stamford. Ireson was the light-wave, I the receiving-station. I could not imagine anything less like the conducted tour. He had so great a love for the town that he spends part of every day looking at the old buildings and delighting in them. Being himself the youngest son of Stamford whose other building sons lie in the churchyards of its five churches, he sees things with filial eyes closed to all outside that great family of the ages. In the buildings he sees the quarries, the institutions, the ancient customs, the countryside and the people. In a house-front or elevation, in any jutty, frieze, buttress or coign of vantage, he sees the hands of his dead brethren who shaped them. In a mansarded roof he can see more than the influence of the Flemish woolmen; he notes differences of technique in the play of the chisel invisible to us. In one house he is aware of a particular scene in Northamptonshire, in another that to us looks exactly the same, of Rutland. In the blend over long periods of the Stamford style, he detects not only the kind of stone and the kind of man that made it, but even the kind of climate. His consciousness of an alien intrusion is sensitive as our coarser vision cannot be. He once wrote to me of the Stratford Memorial Theatre —"too much of ancient Egypt and not enough of Stratford, Warwickshire, England." The diversities of Stamford, Lincolnshire, England, are seen by him as more multiple than we can see, but disciplined to a local idiom that transcends its limitations in accepting them.

Stamford lies at the head of the Welland Valley where its arms converge upon the high ground which dips or "strikes" into the level Fens to the east, and continues north as the narrow ridge, almost a hog's back, of the Lincolnshire "Cliff." All round the town are deposits of lime, gravel and sand, of clay for bricks and for pots and of freestone. High barley land, pockets of wheat land, grazing water-meadows, wood and water were all accessible. In so kind a situation the town may be said to have built itself, and century after century lavished its creative spirit upon it. In fact, the Stamford quarries have been in use since 2000 B.C. A Neolithic skull was found in them by the local archæologist, a descendant of John Clare. The Dutch, too, were a fertilising power, and their mansarded roofs pierced with windows were subdued to the native style by their Collyweston slats. The dominance of Queen Anne and Georgian classicism, with its wealth of porches, doorways and window-frames, its abundance of keystones in high relief, was too mild a sway to oust the vernacular Gothic.

We began with Barn Hill, where Ireson lives. William Stukeley's house, with its portico of timber Doric piers, is on the crest. We passed Miss Trollope's house, which seemed an emblem of this retired little street, and came at once upon All Saints broach-spire, the flaming sword that guards Barn Hill. A little lower, a front-mask of sham half-timbering stands in the Butter Market. Ireson told me that the diagonals were the work of an architect, and clean contrary to the local manner of framing timber by uprights close together and horizontal beams only at the top and bottom. This was exactly how Ireson himself conveyed his information. The horizontal method of the guide-book, the plan of the town and the individual features of its architecture he interpreted in his own way. But the vertical method, foreign to the guide-book, was peculiarly his—the qualities of the stone, the differences between one stone and another, the incidents of the more recent building, the history of the interiors, the unending struggle with authority to maintain the traditional characters, the men who had built this particular house, the inhabitants of that one. Two hours more crowded with significant detail I do not remember; two hours that conferred upon uncommunicative grey walls the gift of life. On this essential Stamford he gave me the concealed right of way.

He knew the history of the very cobble-stones flooring one of the squares. When we passed St. Leonard's Priory, what he had noticed were depressions of the stew-ponds in the adjacent meadow. He made me see that poise of the monastic life which was its supreme justification. It was the balanced tension between the contemplation of the eternal, perfectly symbolised by the "stary-pointing" broach-spires, and the arduous earth-life of self-maintenance, sanctifying the "curse" of Adam. To work was to pray, but also to pray was to be still.

We passed what was once the theatre of Stamford, one of the six old local theatres left in England. Betterton, Kemble and others had acted in it on Race Day. Ireson's plan was to house the local dramatic society there and restore an even more intimate meaning to it than it had once had. He showed me the buildings he had done where the Ketton stone or the harder Clipsham was beginning to weather. He showed me a hideous house in the yellow Stamford brick, and I heard the history of how it came to be there and of the attrition of progress upon the old-established firms. A builder who desires to be "abreast of the times" leaves his native place, builds villas in London, returns with loaned capital, tempts the waverers among the older builders' men away from them by the lure of higher wages and exalts the idol of cheapness. If only, said Ireson, we were left alone, we builders of inheritance, Stamford would be in no peril of sacrificing her integrity.

These builders have saved Stamford from a worse fate even than that of the brick intruding upon the native stone and uniformity upon native variety. The most famous quarry in twentieth Century Stamford has been its own walls and buildings. Progress and Co., Ltd., have been the quarrymen. But the established local builders save and stack the old stone and roof-slats. Whenever the opportunity occurs, they use them over again both in restoring old buildings and erecting new ones. Thus a Queen Anne house, complete with gabled and mullioned bays and the date panel and demolished to make way for a printing-press, was rebuilt intact on a better site. Many of the stones of the dismantled buildings in Stamford are worked on the back with fragments of window tracery, mouldings and the like as evidence that they had been hewn out of buildings not for the first time. The contemporary Stamford builders have in building them up again acted by precedent.

What will always be bright in my memory was a corner of Stamford on the Rutland border. Here Rutland Terrace— a Regency row in stucco with high relief mouldings and every house slightly different from its neighbour, thin moulded piers, verandas in wrought iron, flowery front gardens and (before the War) a railing as comely as the iron of the balconies —faces the water-meadows of the Welland and the wooded ridge beyond them. The meadow land was once occupied by St. Austin's Priory. But all that is left is the richly ornamented Gothic Bedehouse, a little below and at right angles to the Terrace. Here were two styles of the utmost possible variation and yet good neighbours. Between them once stood St. Peter's Gate, and down to the Welland run the Stamford "Backs." The Castle was there, whose mounds are now levelled to a car-park. A bastion of the town's curtain-wall, part of the wall itself and a postern gate made one group; the water-mill, known as the King's Mill, and the warehouses made others. Once they were piled with wool which the barges coming up from Spalding and the Wash took in exchange for their merchandise. This assembly of ancient buildings is connected by alley-ways—Wool Row and King's Mill Alley—with the sheep market in the square above. Here still stands the mansarded Inn of the Golden Fleece.

But what I particularly noticed was a row of mansarded cottages at the foot of the slope. They were so placed that the architectural miscellany of the Backs grouped itself about them. On the first of them was written " FREEMEN'S COTTAGES." Ireson told me that these cottages had been occupied " tyme out of mind" by holders of free grazing rights on the Welland water-meadows. Now by some sleight of hand, or by the mere drift of tendency of which even he, on whose heart the chronicles of Stamford are graven, did not know the history, the grazing rights have gone, the cottages belong to the Town Council, and their occupants are tenants like any others.

In an age lost to realities, State or municipal ownership has come to be identified with "the people's" ownership. But there was once a time when "people" meant individuals in a community. What Ireson had told me was, in fact, modern history, just as the Backs are ancient history. The warehouses, the sheep market, the old walls and the King's Mill were founded upon a society of free men. The King's Mill here belonged to the King, the one person who could speak over the heads of prejudice, interests, privilege and nobility to a free people. Now the King's Mill is derelict and the cottagers have lost their economic freedom. The Backs are eloquent of an economy[1] whose loss has plunged the world into such desolation as our own period witnesses. Dimly odds and ends of people are beginning to discover that the recovery of that economy is (with the modern conveniencies thrown in) another word for self-preservation.

IV

Ireson also took me into the country. The broach-spire is just as conspicious there as in Oundle and Stamford, linking town and country together by the bond of the spirit. On the rare occasions when one or more of these spires is out of sight, something vital, even transfiguring, goes out of the landscape. It becomes no more than a landscape. The Perpendicular Towers of Somerset kindle the county in the same way. But they are much fewer. Here the broach-spires are like the studded nails in an old timber door. Ireson himself had inherited this integral relationship between town and country. Not only because his family originally came from the villages of Yarwell and Nassington, village masons, but because he is just as deeply versed in and familiar with the country scene as Stamford. There was not a striking house, a derelict mill, stone wall, farm building, church or village we passed of which he did not know the inner history. And because he could see under the green mantle of the earth where lay the material of his vocation, so he was aware of the rich farming land and of the poor, of the barley land and the wheat land. He translated the manuscript of the soil to me on our journeys as he did the printed word of the buildings.

We followed the western arm of the Welland Valley on our way to Liddington to see there the Palace of the Bishops of Lincoln. The grey stone turned from grey to brown as we went east along the Rutland flank of the Welland Valley. Farther on towards Oakham it changes again to a dull greeny-brown mottle. The explorer of this country can find out where he is by the colour of the stone as well as by the points of the compass. At Red Hill, where the Valley broadens towards

---

[1] *Of course* there were stresses and strains, ups and downs, in that economy. But that it was structurally sound is proved by the beauty and utility of its products.

Rockingham, the grey pile of whose Castle could be seen embowered among the trees of the Forest on the eastern ridge, marks of the desolation caused by the iron-working appeared. They mock the benedictive presence of the broach-spires. But here an attempt had been made to put back the soil. We were spared the lunar landscape of hills and gullies of slag farther south in the neighbourhood of Corby. But the aerodromes on the plateau had felled the trees and given it a stark look which these long uplands cannot afford. Down the slope Ireson showed me a derelict windmill and watermill and their ugly descendant at work, a roller mill, all visible within an acre of ground. The three buildings epitomised the rural tragedy.

Liddington itself is an ironstone village descending the slope as at Rockingham, whose greys are more pleasing than the oxydised tawny of the ironstone. None the less, Liddington had once been a handsome and spacious village in tune with the generous lines of the ridge, and roofed with Collyweston slats and a strong tradition of thatch. But now! The majority of the roofs were of French tiles, pantiles, blue slate, corrugated iron and asbestos. Fletton brick was an interloper among the few ironstone walls surviving. The village had been ruined in a couple of generations. Why, I asked Ireson. Because it is a village on a large neighbouring property. I found the same degeneration in other villages owned from the Great House. In other words, the revenues from the village went to the upkeep of the mansion instead of to itself. There was no local squire to give it his personal responsibility for it; there was only a great landlord, half-ruined by taxation like most great landlords, miles away. Not only crippled with Death Duties, but lacking that sense of local and functional stewardship embodied in Squire Dale of Trollope's *The Small House at Allingham*. It was an irony of Liddington that there is still a village mason's yard there. But the job of the mason, Bob Clark, a contemporary of Ireson's father, is now to put on the corrugated iron and asbestos.

The tawny pile of the Bishop's Palace, with its timber cloisters, its heavy buttresses supporting round chimney shafts and the magnificent hall with an intricate pomegranate frieze all round it and in the Bishop's sitting-room, was empty and falling to pieces like the village. It had a foundation going back to the eleventh century. One of the Bishops who had dwelt there was St. Hugh of Avalon, the "Hammer of Kings," in 1186, who neglected two of them to relieve the poor. As men hurry to build prefabricated boxes to house an inadequate number of the homeless, this noble building stands vacant. In the cloisters was a thatch pole, twenty feet long with its iron hook. It had once been manned to put out fires in the thatched roofs of the village.

Another journey was into the Fens by way of Barnack. Barnack's Saxon tower and fourteenth century broach-spire of the squat type was built of the Barnack stone, whose silvery tones and rough texture of egg-like or oolite granules are its especial beauty. Ireson, of course, knew all about its superiority to Ketton and Clipsham stone, and we ate his kind wife's farmhouse butter and oatcakes by the "'Ills and 'Oles," the humps and hollows of the exhausted deposits. The village is full of the decorative touches of sculpture by the great race of village masons who built the tower and broach-spire and the steeply pitched porch of the church.

One of the cottages with a plaque of 1684, a corbel head, dormered gables and dripstones over the windows, is where lives Watson, the woodturner of eighty-five and still working. Ireson often buys his work and we went in to see him. Without doubt, he is the most dexterous and highly skilled turner in wood I have ever met. In fact, he is one of the finest woodturners in England and the winner of many prizes. Yet, though he turns splendid candle-sticks, egg-cups and other small objects out of a great variety of woods, he fails with furniture. He is a perfect illustration of that cleavage between the craftsman and the designer made by the Industrial Revolution. It is Ireson's mission to close it. Shortly after I returned home, he wrote and told me he had been elected a member of the borough council. For the first time in living memory, father and son are members at the same time. The Ireson mission may one day become a policy.

Most of the villages on the borders of and in the Fens —Ufford, John Clare's Helpston, Glinton, Northborough and Maxey—are crumbling into the decay of Liddington. Not because they are Great House property here but simply because they are unlucky enough to lie within the Soke of Peterborough. The magnet of centralisation and vested interests is tearing them apart. Yet what villages they once were! Ufford and Helpston are rich in sumptuous barns, ranges of them, and many of them roofed now with corrugated iron. At Ufford, where the low eastern hills slide into the Fens, the quarries of small-coursed wallstone and roadstone are still owned by the Crowson family, village builders and masons for generations. Though not a freestone, Ufford stone is like the Barnack rag. Yet with the men and the stone and the vestiges of the old rural economy on the spot, Ufford itself roofs its nobler buildings with corrugated iron.

The exquisite manor farm of Glinton, with its ogee gables and ball finials at their ends, stands opposite the octagonal sky-scraper broach-spire of the Church. The Gothic-jewelled farm buildings of Northborough are a symbol of beauty, religion and husbandry in one. All this generosity in stone responded to the wealth of the black soil, less exhausted here to-day by continuous cropping without return than elsewhere in the Fens. It was significant that I saw here nothing but two-horse ploughs. There were no tractors. But if the prosperity was the gift of earth, the inspiration came from the heavens. Near Helpston, where sang the caged goldfinch of our poetic tradition, I could see four broach-spires at once, ghostly in the evening sun against a curtain of black cloud. It is impossible to understand the great Stone Age of the Northern Midlands except by man's knowledge of the communion between nature and supernature. He builded it because he was in a right relation with the earth and at the same time in a right relation with God.

But in my mind Ketton, on the western ridge of the Valley, was the flower of these country journeyings. Their various meanings and the relationship of these meanings to Stamford and Ireson converged there into a single point. We passed the cement-works, with hoardings as hideous as the buildings, and went first to the quarries. These are now owned by the Cement Company, which extracts lime and piles the debris into hillocks known as "powers." It only sells the Ketton building stone as a by-product. Ireson spoke well of this Company. But the replacement of individual ownership by the limited liability company, however well-disposed towards the tradition of quarrying building stone, has virtually meant the end of it. Even when Ketton building stone is bought, the traditional traffic between quarry and building site has ceased. By that system there was a continuous flow of inter-course from the quarryman through the mason and up to the sculptors and letterers. Quite apart from ownership and craftsmanship, the dovetailing of one job with another made for a stable community as a tie-beam makes for a stable roof. It was also a very useful system in times of slackened work or unemployment or when frost or rain held up the building. Blocks of stone would be quarried, dressed and stacked ready for the next order.

Ketton stone is one of the best oolites (the granular cells can be clearly seen in it) of the Stamford region. It weathers from pale yellow, pale brown or dutch pink in the quarry-beds to a delicate silver-grey with shadow reliefs under cornices, mouldings and sills. The darker Weldon and the tougher Clipsham, buffish with patches of blue, are the only other freestones that weather to this dove or silver grey. Though it now costs as much as Clipsham stone, Ketton is not so good because of the "flesh" which sometimes occurs at the ends of blocks of it and rots away. Ireson showed me several examples of this defect. But that it is worked at all in this age of brick usurping stone is something to be thankful for.

In the rather nondescript village, abounding in fine buildings and modern substitutes for them, Ireson pointed out to me a large cottage with oriel windows lavishly decorated with finials, quatrefoils, corbel heads and other ornaments, impartially Gothic and classical. It had belonged to the last of the Hibbinses, who died during the War. His were the two carved mediæval heads I had seen in Ireson's office.[1] The cottage had actually been sculptured by Hibbins' father and uncle, the village masons of Ketton. They had jointly owned their own quarry before the Cement Company took it over. The last of them, their son and nephew, had owned a mason's yard and his tools, and had worked on York Minster. Beyond the cottage the road drops down to the church and a packhorse bridge over the Chater, a tributary of the Welland.

[1] See Page 99.

It suddenly discloses a miracle of beauty. The churchyard, the Early English tower partly of Barnack and partly of Ketton stone, the Norman west front with its many orders of figured arches, the pierced belfry, the tapering broach-spire glorious in niched figures and canopied spire-lights, the bridge and the tree-bosomed river make a perfect unity. But to me the most remarkable part of this whole was the churchyard. It is lined just above the wall and on three sides with a continuous row of tombstones, more than seventy of them. All are loaded with ornament. The eighteenth century ones are of the utmost grace, the later ones overloaded and with some loss of grace, but still in the great tradition of monumental masonry. The very first of them figures the mason's tools— a pair of dividers, a square, a stone hammer, a crowbar, a trowel, compasses, a plumb-bob, a plumb-rule and line and a level just like the one Ireson showed me in his office.[1] And on several of the tombstones the name Hibbins was carved. I have little doubt that the whole set had been carved by the same family of village masons. And the same family, no doubt, had helped to build the church. In a long experience of country workmanship I have rarely, if ever, encountered so perfect an example of creative continuity.

It is through Ireson that this continuity between past and present, between village and town, and between the designer and the craftsman is precariously kept alive. Others aid in this great work, notably the firm of church architects I went to see in Stamford. But Ireson is the mainstay of this triple integration. At South Luffenham, between Stamford and Uppingham, I saw one of these village mason's men at work, and he still employs seven or eight men. The orders come through Ireson, who by personal contact delegates them to the surviving village masons. He himself is the last surviving axle of that great culture in stone which was planted on the stony ground of the limestone ridge and flowered into a demi-paradise.

On my way home I revisited its greatest miracle, the Eleanor Cross at Geddington, a miracle of sculpture, a miracle of beauty and a miracle of holiness. The way the richly decorated triangular shaft on its wide steps tapers above the three figures under their canopies to the cluster of crocketed

[1] See Page 99.

finials at the apex is in itself a miracle of structure. In building
this, Cross design and craftsmanship were at one. But there is
one more miracle to it: it was erected in a village; as Christ
was born in a village. This is Ireson's charge—to save a
culture like this from extinction. I left it to enter the age of
iron at Kettering and Wellingborough. Iron has entered the
soul of man to-day, and out of it has grown Belsen and
Buchenwald and the atomic bomb.

CHAPTER IV

THE PIGOTTS OF DODDERSHALL

"They dreamt not of a perishable home
Who thus could build."
WILLIAM WORDSWORTH.

"The resident native gentry attached to the soil, known to every
farmer and labourer from their childhood, frequently mixing with
them in those pursuits where all artificial distinctions are lost,
practising hospitality without ceremony, from habit and not in
calculation."

WILLIAM COBBETT

I

MANY JUDGMENTS have been levelled at modern industrial
civilisation. Not the least of them is its monotony. What
varieties of building survive in modern cities are none of
their making, and the more modern they are the less distin-
guishable they become. The suburb, the building estate, the
factory, the cinema, the government office, the department
store, the aerodrome, the railway and wireless stations, these
have no frontiers. It seems only by accident that their occupants
speak different languages. They are the repetitions of Cosmopolis. Manchester might as well be Montreal, Stalingrad
Sunderland. Identity is meaningless; there are only distances
to and from the same place. Different places are interested
in and so inclined to like one another. Those who live in
places separated by miles, not character, are inclined to shed
their human differences in the sense that they do the same
things in the same way. They are populations rather than
persons, and they do the same things because of themselves
they do nothing. They do what their industrial economy tells
them to do. What they are told to do has nothing to do with
what they would naturally chose to do, and in past ages could
do, and loved to do by virtue of being human beings. Doing
the same things day after day, they are bored—bored, as the

saying is, to death; and death plays a very large part in modern civilisation. It is mainly concerned with inorganic quantities. These are predictable because they always operate in the same way. So do the people who manipulate them. So hate abounds.

This boredom and this monotony are being steadily diffused into organic nature, the original home of interest and variety. So the incidentals of work—wages, costs, output, quantities— become, as in the town, paramount. Its essentials—what kind of work and how it is done—disappear. To measure human labour in terms of horse-power-mindedness and the bulldozer standard is merely to magnify monotony. A similar transformation affects the face of the country as it has done the various appearances of the old towns. If there is a wood, they are all the same trees; if a meadow, it is composed of a very few grasses instead of many, and many meadows are merged into one field. The cities not only spread their own sameness over the countryside and suck the rural diversity up into them, but what is still country becomes the same country. Hedges, those manifestations of difference, vanish. Lanes as tortuous as rivers are straightened out. Wild animal life becomes restricted to a few species like the few grasses in the fields. Utility supplants use; profit pleasure; expediency a way of life; efficiency, which is cost-cutting, craftsmanship. Such are the triumphs of dullness and sameness. Modern novelties like the bulldozer, the multiple plough and the combine harvester are like headlines that make the text describing a variety of doings superfluous.

II

Sometimes I go and see a small manor in my neighbourhood. It is extremely remote, though near the perimeter of the fifty-mile radius which is Metroland. It is not to be reached by a road at all, much less by a main one. A century ago, my hostess told me, even the difficult way I come did not exist. How did the furniture arrive over a period of six centuries? Presumably on farm-carts and wagons over the fields. To-day only gates between rutty half-derelict lanes give access to it. Even after it is approached, first by a poplar avenue, and then by one of hoary stag-headed elms, it is still invisible behind a dense grove of trees. Even when the water lilies of the moat shine out among these shades, it does not reveal itself. The moat surrounds a secret never to be discovered by the *Zeitgeist* of our age.

When the house does come into sight, it is as though it had risen from the earth, so suddenly is it manifest. So it did nearly a thousand years ago. It was then the house of a Saxon thegn, made out of earth but also water, the well of clear water still in use in the cellar. This was the original reason why its walls of wattle and daub rose in a waterless country far not only from a market-town but even a village. It was one of those rare manors that continued to be held by a Saxon after the Conquest, the holder being Alsi, daughter of Wlword, in 1086. It was first mentioned in an assize of 1205. It passed to the family which still holds it in 1495, the Pigotts, who came from Yorkshire and in the eighteenth century from Salop, two branches of the same family. The deeds grouped together in a small ante-room record transactions as far back as the early thirteenth century. Nothing remains of the Saxon manor except the well, and the first wall I saw, part of the wing of a minute courtyard at the back of the house, is of fifteenth century brick. Its parallel and opposite wall is of roughcast, declaring its attachment not so much to the past as to one of the idioms of its own countryside.

Much of the house, which is in two stories and the form of a half H, is also coated in roughcast. There are some stone quoins, and the roofs are both tiled in the local russet and slated. The main blocks belong to the sixteenth century and the south-west wing was built in 1689. The chimney-stacks belong to both these periods, the early sixteenth century cluster having a moulded brick cornice and moulded caps and bases to the shafts. Both have carvings in the brick of men's and women's heads, a wonder-beast and foliage. Carvings in stone of fleur-de-lis and a man's head east of the gabled porch of moulded wood with seventeenth century dentil ornament and voluted brackets, are a prevision of the extraordinary wealth of carving which distinguishes this house and its furnishings. Patchings of the nineteenth century are everywhere, and blue bricks of the late eighteenth century at one end of the south-west wing contribute to a composite house upon which century after century has lavished its workmanship. The interior has heavily moulded ceiling beams, friezes and moulded cornices round the walls, seventeenth century carvings round one of the fireplaces, splayed beams, an elaborately carved seventeenth century door and two seventeenth century staircases. The drawing-room has bolection-moulded panels, and doorways and fireplace are rich in seventeenth century moulded architraves. Fragments of fifteenth and sixteenth century carvings and traceries occur again and again. Yet the little manor is in no sense a show-place. It is simply a house that has been lived in for generation after generation by the same family. But that is the only sameness about it.

From the late mediæval period onwards, every age has stamped itself upon this house among the lonely fields, like a section of cliff representing a geological series. But this is only a partial and so misleading illustration. The presentation is simultaneous, not successive. Both architecturally and in the furniture the house fuses all the periods into one without any of them sacrificing their identities. It is not even an anthology within the covers of a single volume; it is a connected work compiled by different hands into an organic singleness. Presuming that Homer was a community of bards, living along the whole length of the Heroic Age, this house is like Homer. It thus differs organically from the Sussex mansion of Sir Adolphus Bland, described by Somerset Maugham in his short story, *The Alien Corn*:—

"It did not give you for a moment the impression of an English house. You had the feeling that every object had been bought with a careful eye to the general scheme. You missed the full Academy portraits that hung in the dining-room beside a Carlo Dolci . . . and the water-colours painted by a great aunt that cluttered up the drawing-room. There was no ugly Victorian sofa."

At the little manor there were no downright bad pieces. But there were some decidedly inferior to others: the quality was mixed as the periods were mixed up. It was the structural and decorative mix-up of the manor that warmed, charmed and humanised it.

To enumerate a few of these period pieces or styles arbitrarily separated from their total context would have been like picking out single scenes or figures in, say, a crowded canvas of Brueghels. I might have chosen as the loveliest thing in the earlier periods an Elizabethan dress of bodice and long skirt, embroidered after it had been made with a flower and its foliage in silk and gold and silver thread for every day of the year. This dress was like a song by William Byrd or a painting by Nicholas Hillyard. Beatrice in *Much Ado*, born under a "dancing star," might have worn it. It might have been taken as an idealised symbol of the whole Elizabethan Age, with its strife and sorrow hidden by that flowery mead. But to pick it out from the rest of the Tudor belongings of the house would have been invidious. It belonged, like everything else, not to an age but the house. So far from being a South Kensington piece snatched out of its context, it had been worn by the mother of the present owner in a fancy-dress ball at Malta, given by the Duke and Duchess of Edinburgh.

The house was so fertile in every age that, wandering through it, I could not think in terms of change or season, of spring and autumn, of effloresence and decay. British craftsmanship had changed its forms and idioms here between the reigns of Richard II (who with Anne of Bohemia is embossed on one wall) and George IV. But its qualities, its mastery, its inventiveness and delight in it had not changed at all. The house reconciled all the ages, just as the genius of Shakespeare reconciled the Middle Ages with the Renaissance. It extracted from each its virtue and enhanced that by placing it over against another. Here the ages of craftsmanship were neighbours in a community, no longer bound to time and so no longer parricides one upon another. And where all was a constellation of beauty, some stars, not so bright and fair as others, yet were parts of the unity. By itself, that cabinet in the drawing-room with Dutch inlay was perhaps too heavy and ornate, but among the rest it took its rightful place.

The richest single fitting was the late seventeenth century staircase. The great poppy-head finials of the newels, doubtless church-looted, were attached to panels with seventeenth century figures and the dado is of seventeenth century panelling. Along the well of the staircase was a full-length Zucchero portrait of an Elizabethan *chatelaine* of the house, dressed like the portraits of Elizabeth herself, but sufficiently different in feature to make it certain that she was once the queen of the manor, not of the nation. Close to her and in the sharpest contrast of habit and expression hangs a dour Cromwellian. The whole well is lined with portraits, offset by a couple of rich Wouvermann landscapes. Among the former is a portrait of the builder of the staircase, whose initials, C. P., bearer of the name which still occupies the house, are carved upon its wood. He was expelled from Parliament in 1606 for a racy speech against the "roguish Scots." A yet more intimate bond between the house and its furnishings is another portrait, that of Sir Edward Phipps, Queen Elizabeth's Master of the Rolls. He, as the Speaker, was responsible for the expulsion of Christopher Pigott from the House, which was followed by a brief imprisonment in the Tower. But this public breeze quickly died down, and a restored amity is made apparent by Phipps's portrait above Christopher Pigott's staircase. In 1603, a precise and elaborate genealogical table of the family was penned on white vellum, at least twelve feet in length, and sprinkled all over with crests, devices, ornamental lettering and figures of knights, judges and ecclesiastics. Unrolled, it took up nearly half the length of the drawing-room.

To me the inward meaning and interest both of the Pigott family and the manor on which it had lavished age after age of creative workmanship was the almost complete absence of public history from either. The house had never been besieged nor enlarged into a stately home. It had never been other than itself, the local residence of the smaller country gentry. Except for the squib about the Scots, the family had cut no historical capers. It had bided at home and minded its own local affairs. What they were is indicated by the very ordinary documents edited by Mr. Eland. They are records of local government work performed by the sixteenth and seventeenth century landowner. The more locally conspicuous of the Pigotts were sheriffs, deputy lieutenants, justices of the peace, commissioners, arbitrators and holders of various honorary

posts which entailed more labour than profit. They were
never Court drones nor national legislators nor fortune-makers
nor adventurers nor "Inclosiers" who rack-rented their tenants
or pulled up their smaller neighbours' boundary posts to pay
their debts. Their lives were more obligation than privilege;
they could have had little time for lounging, fighting or
speculating. Part of their duties consisted in acting as
"Regardors and Preservators" of the Crown Forest of Bernwood, and, after the old forest laws had fallen into disuse
and Bernwood had been officially disafforested in 1623, they
had rights and responsibilities as purlieu-men in a primeval
Arden of which only coppices and hedgerow oaks now remain.
They were never in the public eye like their cousins, the Verneys
of Claydon.

They were domestic as well as regional. How home-
keeping they were is revealed by the will of Thomas Pigott
to his son, Christopher. He bequeathed to him,

> "all the waynescott about the howse, glasse, Yron workes,
> tables, stooles, formes, tressells, chayres, cubbords, napkins,
> pictures, all furniture apperteyning to armes, bookes,
> the necessary implements of the baking howse, all the
> necessary implements of the dayre howse and washe
> howse, vessells for the use of the butterie and seller."

His self-supporting manor was a kingdom in itself. He
directed Christopher to

> "have the use and occupation of a carpett of needle-
> worke, a side-borde cloth or cubboard-cloth of needleworke
> likewyse, which were of my wyves owne working, and
> her needleworke quisshions now remayning in the howse
> of Dodershall, and my will is that the same shalbe used
> with the howse by the heires male of my bodie for the tyme
> being."

That is exactly how the house looks and feels—home-made
through ages of culture. The family not only owned it for
century after century and stored it with treasures. Its members
helped to make them themselves. A number of them had no

doubt been made by the estate carpenter. Family was fitted to house like hand to glove. They cultivated their given heritage for the love of home, and, as I sensed its tranquillity and peace, the very modesty of its richness, to the glory of God. No greater contrast could be imagined than with the mansion bought by a rich man and stored with Wallace Collection pieces.

In another of the rooms the very wallpaper was linen in a rich light brown stamped with intricate designs. The effect of this golden brown linen against an overmantel of heavily carved black oak was exquisitely repeated after I had left the house by a long foreground of recently cut meadowland washed in sun and backed by the flowing Chilterns ridge vapoured in falling black cloud. Wood-carving was everywhere, from sumptuous Jacobean chests and cabinets and a mighty dado of the late seventeenth century that ran right round one of the largest rooms to a noble Grinling Gibbons piece along a beam arching an alcove. Charles II appeared in person—his signature, that is to say, was affixed to a formal pardon for non-resistance to Cromwell.

Upstairs, there are two panelled doors of the seventeenth century and a fireplace of 1689 with a panelled overmantel and a very large architrave. One room has walls lined with bolection-moulded panels as in the drawing-room. Successive owners of the same family had been faithful to the organic character of the house age after age by never attempting to separate its furniture by period rooms and so to strike it dead and cold. This was graciously illustrated in what the family calls the William and Mary bedroom. The most conspicuous piece in it is a great Tudor bed with carved head and cornerposts of Welsh black oak, and it was Welsh because one of the family's long ancestral line had married a Welshwoman. In another of the bedrooms leading off the long Elizabethan gallery is a frieze of Tudor carving along the length of one wall with heraldic griffins of the eighteenth century on the architrave above the doorway.

From this gallery opened nurseries as well as bedrooms. It contained a pair of long windows with pointed arches of eighteenth century Gothic and a wooden children's gate at the end of the stairs of much the same period. Here had been

the nursery of the present mistress of the house. Running up
the stairs and clicking to the gate had been a precedent for a
couple of centuries after the long Renaissance gallery with
its bookcases, its carved wainscoting, its stucco ceiling and
its windows on both sides looking on formal gardens and
pleached alleys, had been converted. The fenestration of the
gallery included another window with iron bars which had
evidently been constructed before the era of window-glass in
secular houses. Thus the gallery alone had assembled a chain
of periods. Gently had age passed into age within this
dreaming house. As in a dream one had blended with another.
So linked, they half-destroyed the tyranny and inflexibility
of time.

I remember only fragments of the treasure of eighteenth
century craftsmanship gathered together in this undemonstrative, tree-hidden, water-environed, roadless little manor
among the empty fields. But in the room of light oak panelling
from which has been stripped eight coats of paint, I could
hardly forget a small needleworked Queen Anne armchair. It
stood in a corner behind a grand sofa standing on eight legs.
One of the most poetic chairs I had ever seen, it was very
simple, and was found to be stuffed with Queen Anne hay. It
was so unpretentious as to look demure. But just that turn
of the arms curving outwards at their ends and their linear
perfection with the back gave it a lyrical elegance.

It was in marked contrast with a judge's chair, a Chippendale, whose one arm ended in a lion's open mouth and the
other with it closed. By seating himself in that chair, solid as
the Constitution and broad as precedent, even Dr. Johnson
might have been said to have taken a certain liberty. It was,
as it should have been, magisterial. Near it was a superb
Chippendale globe, an *orbis terrarum* that expressed immensity
and totality neither by mere size nor rotundity but by sheer
generosity and fullness of workmanship. In my mind's eye
I think of it in conjunction with another piece that beside it
was like an interior candle-light to the moon. This was
perhaps a unique Queen Anne tri-cornered card-table covered
by the most delicate needlework of playing-cards and a floral
design. Classical marketry, furniture, rococo arabesques and
twisted oaken pillars, chinoiserie, a dumb waiter whose legs

touched 'the floor in buckled shoes, exuberant overmantels, a hand printing-press in carved oak—all represented that strange gallimaufry of foreign styles and fashions and *genres* which characterised the eighteenth century. Yet the native genius assimilated them as the house had assimilated every period of architecture and craftsmanship into the congruity of a continuous family home. Among the grandfather and grandmother clocks that were everywhere was one made by a local eighteenth century clock-maker. For the excellence of his workmanship and applied mathematics he might have been an apprentice of Thomas Tompion himself, buried in Westminster Abbey and the finest clock-maker in the world. This clock, made in the county town ten miles away, still further stressed the homeliness of all this lavish array of furnishings.

The only pen-portrait of one of the ladies of the house in this century appeared in the *Gentleman's Magazine*, and was reproduced in George Lipscomb's *History and Antiquities of the County of Buckingham* in 1838. Having "passed her hundredth year" and been thrice married, she died at the manor in 1781. She was celebrated for her wit, beauty and vivacity—"her cheerfulness and pleasantry throwing many eccentricities and failings into shade." She was "so much attached to the amusement of dancing, in which she greatly excelled, that she enjoyed that diversion, with unabated spirit, to a very late period, dressed in the liveliest colours, and moving ' on the light fantastic toe ' whilst many of her juniors were sinking into decrepitude." After she had passed ninety, she used to secure the best partners by presenting each one of them with a side of venison. This she thought of increasing to a whole buck when they showed signs of preferring younger partners, since, as she is said to have said, "I chose my first husband for love, my second for riches and the third for honours; and now I think of beginning again in the same order." She may have inspired some of her partners with terror and even horror; others may have looked upon her as a potential source of revenue over and above the venison; to others, again, she may have been a mere drollery. But in that long-lived house, she seems one of its tutelary spirits, carrying her indomitable years with an almost legendary charm and contributing to its ancient timbers that sense of timelessness which they evoke in me. Looking out of the window of the library, with its early editions of old herbals, other rare books and mediaeval estate map, I have the sensation of time stilled and come to rest. A large sun-dial of stone flush with the turf, a grass walk between high yew hedges leading to the moat, a cluster of ilex and mulberry trees to the right—they seem an immutable painting arresting the flux of nature.

Even the nineteenth century that wrecked the tradition of native architecture and craftsmanship had its place. A spinning-wheel, probably Welsh and of that century, added to the beauty of all the woodmanship of chairs, tables, cabinets and wall-carvings. The rare survivors of the Industrial Revolution were mostly congregated in the kitchen, one of the most vivid and personable rooms in the whole house. A magnificent dresser of seasoned elm was ranged along nearly the whole length of two sides of it, with open shelves above filled with Nanking and willow-pattern ware. Along the other two walls were ranges of lustre-ware and Wedgwood white basket china, together with a lively collection of early nineteenth century cartoons, many of them congenially occupied with Boney. Spits hung from the ceiling-beams. A small table in another room was made from the timbers of the *Téméraire*, of which a member of the family had been captain. It was the *Téméraire* that tried to pass the *Victory* as a consort to cover her at the opening of Trafalgar. Nelson called out from the flagship—"I'll thank you, Captain Harvey, to keep in your proper station."[1] These flashes from the greater world, hidden in the wood of the table like lightning in a cloud, gave the cartoons a brisk relevance to the house.

But every stick of furniture or fitting was relevant, even when it came from the workshops of Holland, Flanders or the valleys of the Black Mountains. Each one commemorated some incident, enterprise or home-thought of the family which had built the house and gone on building it for century after century. For instance, Brunel, of the Clifton Suspension Bridge and the Great Western Railway, had been a visitor there. He was aghast when one energetic member of the family, a woman, had pulled down the wall which supported

[1] *Years of Victory* by Arthur Bryant.

the seventeenth century staircase and left it suspended in mid-air. The pillars of twisted wood imitating the baroque ones in another room were erected to hold it up. The portrait of this lady is in the room with the linen wallpaper, She read French novels, but her daughter, a Victorian, far enough away from the Regency, read books of sermons.

In the centre of the kitchen, again, was a box-mangle, presented to the present owner's grandmother by the Duke of Buckingham. It had been made into a table for the kitchen, doubtless by some local woodmaster. Little histories like these humanised and integrated the bewildering variety and richness of furniture in the house, but I was particularly interested in this table for another reason. Its long beam connecting the two stout legs at either end in the manner of the refectory table had been the model for the supporting members of another table built by a living carpenter from the nearest village.

Thus the continuity of the manor had been brought up to date from the Plantagenets to the sixth of the Georges. The tradition of the great handicraftsmen and artificers had been preserved, however tenuously and in a minor key, against all the destructive and levelling forces that for a century and more have waged successful war upon British craftsmanship. Its union of use with beauty, function with fine art, had made our native craftsmanship a glory sustained through every economic change and social or political turbulence from the Conquest of Normandy to Manchester's victory over England. The idiom of each period had been like a new instrument swelling the symphony. It was a happy accident to discover that the family which had furnished its home with the effects of this union had fostered it in a manner yet more direct. In 1704, Thomas Pigott, a member of it, made a deed charge upon his estate of £4,000, £300 of which he bequeathed to the rector of the parish and three other trustees for the purchase of lands, the rents of which were assigned " to the placing and putting out and binding of poor children" within two parishes of the neighbour-hood " to be apprenticed." But the work of the contemporary village carpenter closes the last page of this volume of the household arts. This carpenter has no apprentices.

III

If this manor had been a mansion, it might have been regarded as a museum piece and its treasure a collection of antiquities. But it is small and had always been so. The love of home and beauty must have been the animating principle which had led one generation to leave it a little fairer and more gracious for the next. Its enrichment had been not expansive but intensive like the genius of Shakespeare. The generations had not "joined house to house and land to land," as a sixteenth century prayer had prayed that those "that possess the grounds and pastures of the earth" should not "after the manner of worldlings" set themselves to do. They had added piece to piece, adornment to adornment, within the circumference of the little moat. They had acted as the good husbandman does, or did, within the boundaries of his plot of land. Of this domestic piety the present mistress of the house may be called a lamp whose light has not been dimmed by the brightness of her legacy. Many words that at one time seemed the very structural timbers of the language have in ours either been vulgarised or fallen into disuse. Of the latter class the word breeding is a member. She wore it as an inward grace, with a gentleness and humility partly of her own self, but partly, I believe, crowned by her inheritance. Anything less like pride of blood could not have been. Yet this grace, this humility had in it a certain air, an elegance, that came from the blood no less than from the spirit. It possessed a fragrance like an old rose, an old rose that blooms as though it were young. So she bore her years as well as her heritage, years much the same as my own, and yet she moved to and fro, the perfect hostess, like a maid. I could not help imagining her as she must have been when I was a gawky undergraduate, in a broad-brimmed straw hat, with a posy of flowers at her belt.

The two Great Wars of our century have brought her a double tragedy, the worst that can befall the inheritor of an ancient line. The most recent of these also deprived her of household aid and made her caretaker and housemaid in one of effects that might have daunted a full staff of domestics.

Yet not a speck of dust nor cobweb nor tarnishing nor blemish of neglect was anywhere to be seen. She told me she used a paint-brush to keep the carved griffins' throats from becoming dens of spiders. She had taken down the fading linen wall-paper and washed it in lux. The polishing, the furbishing, the sweeping, the dusting, the mopping and the rubbing that house demanded could only be dimly imagined by the mere visitor. But its treasure had come from the heart and by the heart it was maintained.

In *Civilisation, Science and Religion*, Professor Ritchie writes of the Greek city-states—"The Greeks held that only in a small compact city can you have a real community, real societies, real living together. Large agglomerations of territory and large territories seemed to them just mechanical aggregates to be ruled by force and fear." Of this truth our own Shakespeare is the supreme vindication. The Hellenic idea of independent smallness as a cardinal virtue may be justly applied to the small manor. It was the big manor rather than the small which imposed itself upon the countryside and became a government building. In the Enclosures, the small manor suffered with the yeoman's farmstead and the peasant's cottage, and again Shakespeare is the example of how inter-dependent were peasant and yeoman and the smaller country gentry. The era of bigness developed from the mansion and the big estate to the big city and its big business. They in their turn begat the big fields of the factory-farm. By virtue of its littleness, the small manor was able not only to foster a continuity of craftsmanship but that sense of home which is a prerequisite of it. It remained in human and cultural contact with the local community. By staying small, it controlled that acquisitive sense which is the dynamo of expansion and bigness. It acquired but as a value rather than as a means to power. It acted as an integrating force and so expressed the quality and distinction of a neighbourhood, unlike the mansion which expressed itself at the expense of it.

It was mainly on these grounds that Cobbett, the crusader for the small man, praised the smaller landed gentry. They were the nerve-centres of the local organism, balancing leadership of it with responsibility for it. The records of local squires heading local contingents in the Peasants' Revolt are numerous. However imperfectly, the small manor embodied a way of life in tune with the self-government of the region. As William Sheldon, a cousin of the Pigotts and the squire of Barcheston, nursed the genius of Richard Hyckes, the tapestry-maker, in the sixteenth century,[1] so the family of the organic little manor of which I write had cherished and enshrined the craftsmanship of five centuries.

[1] See Page 20.

CHAPTER V

GOODCHILD OF NAPHILL

"As the homing bird released from its cage makes a few circles in the air and then, guided we know not how, hits the invisible path that leads infallibly to the place from which it came, so our minds, breaking the prisons of mechanism, find the direction proper to their nature and destiny, under a mysterious guidance akin to the homing instinct of the bird, and perhaps a sublimation of it."

L. P. JACKS.

I

NAPHILL stands high on the northern flanking wall of the Valley of the Wye in the western Chilterns. It must at one time have been a traditional village. Its mile-long street, with blind lanes branching laterally off it, was fitted loosely in between the wide common and the beech hangers curving steeply down to the village green of Disraeli's Bradenham, but long before him, Bradenham of the home-cured hams. In the climbing woods between clustered Bradenham and mile-strung Naphill, now occupied by an R.A.F. Station, the grunting of pigs rootling in the rich humus must often have consorted with the see-saw whirr of the pole-lathe and chisel of the chair-leg bodgers. Other woodmen enlivened these woodlands: besides its chair-making tradition Naphill once made use of much weatherboarding among its flint houses. But nearly every trace of the old village has disappeared. Even the site of the kiln that baked a sand-faced, plum-coloured, hand-made brick is unknown to the present villagers. It is easier to pull a rambling village to pieces than one like Bradenham. Naphill to-day is like an unattached suburb, with no more organic relation to the Chilterns than the R.A.F. Station itself. It belongs to nothing, not even, since its building materials have been imported, to itself. Its only resemblance to a country village is that it is still in the country and stops abruptly at the further end, not in memory of its past, but because a T-road happens to run across it on the crest of the slope.

This is where H. E. Goodchild the chair-maker lives in a seventeenth century flint cottage, with a seventeenth century barn attached to it, a minute trim lawn in front and an orchard in three acres of land behind. In the orchard he keeps his steaming tank while the barn-workshop serves as storage-room for his apples. Everything is linked up in Goodchild's home. He is a freeholder of the whole property, and he still makes chairs in the tradition of country Chippendale. Both in hand and mind he belongs to the culture of the cottage, the workshop and the orcharded bit of land, once the culture of the whole community. He is as remote from the rest of the village as in its present form it is from its own past. To proceed from one end of Naphill to the other is to step off the time dimension altogether. Once I am with Goodchild, the period in which we both live fades into thin air and leaves not a rack behind.

I have known him for many years and written about him. The yew-wood Windsor armchair he made for me and insisted on giving me is with me daily. But when I go to see him, I never fail to be startled to an almost physical giddiness by the abrupt transition from one world to another. At long and short intervals I have paid him visits throughout the recent tragic years. They have been years in which one peril or disaster is overcome only to give place to another. They have been and are years in which twentieth century civilisation appears more and more tenuous and ephemeral, ever deeper in gloom as the shades evoked by itself close over it. Each time I set eyes on Goodchild, his position as a chair-maker is more restricted and confined. There is to-day no hope at all of his recovering his former apprentices, and he has less and less time from making "utility" or "semi-utility" chairs to exert his genius on the chairs he loves to make. Though he could sell them readily enough if or when the controls are relaxed, the chairs that nobody in England can make like him are becoming more and more his recreation rather than his normal work. So tied is he by the controls that he is forced to give the greater part of his time to average chairs by the dozen. He goes on making the superlative ones he used to make but only by the compulsion of his inner voice. His reserves of wood for them are almost gone but he can get no permit for more. Yet in my later visits he grows more and more solid and real as the world I come from grows more and more unsubstantial.

There never was a man with a more profound sense of vocation than Goodchild. His integrity in and for his work has never yielded a hairbreadth, even through the very worst days of cut-price competition in the High Wycombe chair industry. It has always been a mystery to me how he came through them to win his mastership and ownership. He only did so by practising an asceticism hardly less rigorous than a fasting hermit's. He had worked eighteen hours a day for fifteen years, making 6d apiece for his "smoker" chairs and 8d for his Windsor chairs. The last time I saw him he was telling of how in his early days as a chair-maker he used to walk four miles every week-day from Naphill to High Wycombe and back again to earn, when the industry emerged from one of its periodic slumps, at the very most a pound a week. Sometimes his earnings were as low as sixpence a week, especially after the Boer War. The chair-making firms were often without orders and so had to turn off the men. For two years his wage see-sawed between a few pence and the peak of a pound a week. At the end of them hand-work was supplanted by the machine. Henceforward there was no chance for him to do any but the crudest work by hand, and for all the years he was working at Wycombe he made never a whole chair, but only the parts. Even these parts were not of the Bow Windsor type, in the making of which he has now no living rival. They were of the "kitchen" type, lathbacks, staybacks and stickbacks, not wheelbacks. Thus the step that he took to achieve independence in the making of chairs in his own supreme way was like moving at a stride from servitude to mastership and from commercialism to culture. The negative reason for such a mutation was the machine which drove him to escape from it because it denied him any chance of expressing the spirit within him. How different his history from that of the world without!

All the spiritual implications of vocational work are in him, while the world of industrialism outside his little fortress goes fatalistically on from one extreme of materialism to another. Yet in his presence I invariably feel confronted with the contrast between his stability and rock-firmness and the dream-like or phantasmal sense of the world to which he has never surrendered. A visit to him is for me like a sailor's homecoming to harbour after a perilous voyage out of sight of land and beset by treacherous and unstable seas. The more contemporary life occupies itself with security, the more insecure it becomes. The more it thinks in terms of comforts, of amenities, of material progress, of rationalising life and experience, the closer are the coils woven round it by the fantasy of money and debt.

The more worldly its desires, the more abstract is the science that ministers to them. "While a man by his own work often exerts only about one-eighth horse-power, by a medium-sized crawler tractor he controls between twenty and thirty horse-power : the costs per horse-power per hour are 10/- per human labour and 6d at the draw-bar of a tractor." Only in the world of fantasy can men and horses be changed into weights and measures. "Man, aided by chemistry and engineering, can beat Nature." Only in the world of fantasy is dead matter pitted against living substance. The greater, therefore, the success of science in banishing the intangibles, the X factor, from its calculations and operations, the more vainglorious are its ambitions and the more irrational and illusory the results. But in Goodchild's life and work the concrete and the natural are so unconsciously interlocked with the spiritual that conflict between them and the consequent revenge of the one upon the other do not and cannot occur. In so solid a world, however minute, the mind cannot but be at rest. The modern art critic speaks of "the natural evolution of art" into the nightmare forms of Picasso and his kind, as though art itself were dragged at the draw-bar of progress. But Goodchild sprang at a bound from the factory hand to the artist and from mass-production to the art-forms of the eighteenth century. "The hours of folly," wrote Blake, "are measured by the clock; but wisdom no clock can measure."

II

The rock-foundations of Goodchild's world are his anchorage in his own place. He belongs to it as a D'Arcy Spice apple belongs to Essex. He is, I am confident, a descendant of the Neolithic race which first colonised the Chilterns. His physical characteristics of shortness, litheness, small-boned suppleness and dark hair were theirs. Theirs, too, were his temperamental quickness of apprehension, mobile and sensitive features and consummate craftsmanship. When he twitted me for being responsible in his spending long hours in writing to people who wanted to become craftsmen in spite of the world saying no, the slanting light in his eyes and the expressive play of his features showed that he must, at any rate, have in him the blood of a people lacking the Saxon stolidity.

The wood for his chairs—beech, yew, cherry, pear, apple, elm, oak, chestnut and walnut—are all of his neighbourhood, and he lives where chair-makers and bodgers have always lived within human memory. He often gets his chair-legs from the woodmen who tread their pole-lathes in the beech-woods as did the turners of the Glastonbury Lake Village two thousand years ago. Though Goodchild now embodies alone the craft-traditions of Naphill, he maintains his contacts with the past as he does with the pole-lathe woodmen. For in his sitting-room it is impossible to tell the difference between the furniture he himself made some years ago and the furniture made by his family two hundred years ago. This rootedness, combined with his unique personal quality, is reflected in the chairs he makes, the "non-utility" ones. They never fail to strike a just balance between structure and ornament, between economy of material and freedom of flowing lines, between elegance and solidity. You see in them that union between the craftsman and the designer, the poet and the doer, who were cloven in half by the Industrial Revolution. Chairs so made cannot err, because the workmanship faithfully executes the rightness, both intuitive and traditional, of the design. Goodchild's chairs are made to be sat in, but also to be looked at; their grace and their comfort are married.

They are the heritage of a definite tradition derived from the eighteenth century. But so perfectly is the artist fused in them with the village workman that it seems an accident they should be of any particular century. They possess a kind of everlasting stability. Machines and machine-made products go out of use or fashion by their very nature. The craftsman-cum-artist put into theirs a touch of that timeless spirit that transcends periods. Posterity will see it as one of the oddities of history that our age has idolised what is transitory and ill-looking at the expense of the comely and the durable. Laminated and lifelessly mass-produced wood takes the place of wood that is animated at both ends, in the life of the tree and in the life the craftsman breathes into it. Thus wholeness is the key to the peace and security distilled from Goodchild's home. And wholeness is the harmonious interplay of relations between one thing and another which are distinct and appear to be apart. In this wholeness there is only a difference of degree between Goodchild and Hamlet.[1]

In past visits, Goodchild had told me exactly what it was that had revolutionised his life and in the end given him the power to achieve this wholeness. By chance he had come to see one of Chippendale's own designs with cabriole legs, and I repeat what he said to me—" When I saw how the old people made chairs, I knew I couldn't go on as I was doing." When I last saw him in the winter of 1945, he said to me—" I began to have a vision of working at home." So he bought parts of chairs out of his scanty earnings and worked on them in his spare time. Sent to Wycombe, they were stained to look like antiques. But by concentrating on the cabriole legs, he began to get orders by post to make chairs in the home of his fathers. This brought him back to the natural environment of the old chair-makers, the woodland. The wheelbacks are of seasoned wood taken from saplings of six to eight years' growth. His two years on a farm after leaving school prepared the way for this " return to nature." Then came the first Great War—" I, like others, had to go and see what we could do in the matter." He was sent East for two years and used " to sit under the mos-

[1] See Page 42.

quito net sketching chairs," with his mind ever on Chippendale. Invalided home, he at once started making his great and generous Windsors.

Thus, it is not taking liberties with language to call this first sight of a masterpiece a vision which was to create other masterpieces in its likeness. For thirty years a member of the village choir, he heard for the first time Handel's *Messiah*. He compared the effect of it to that of his first sight of a Chippendale drawing. Goodchild was, in fact, converted to making chairs as an autonomous craftsman as, to take the supreme example, the persecutor Saul was converted into the apostle Paul. The factory, from which he escaped to his own workshop in the home of his forefathers, persecuted good workmanship and the good life of creative ownership with it in its desperate scramble to cut prices down to that cheapness which is the sole "good" of our economic system. But in acting upon his vision, Goodchild won his match with the world by opposing workmanship to cheapness.

That vision of his came home to me on my most recent visit to him. I saw, standing in the narrow defile between the cliffs of bows, backs, splats, seats, stretchers, spindles, half-chairs and whole chairs stacked from floor to ceiling of his workshop, an armchair he had recently made. Unlike most of his chairs, which are bow-backed, it was a top-railed Windsor of half-scroll endings and with a richly ornamental banister splat resembling the top-railed chair which Oliver Goldsmith left to his friend, Dr. Hawes, in 1774. Both Goldsmith's chair and this one my eye picked out in the workshop were in their turn similar to the Chippendale design he had once showed me as the sign from the past which had saved him from the factory and guided him right out of our civilisation to the cottage of his chair-making fathers on the edge of Naphill Common. Though I have no room for it, I tried to persuade him to sell me this chair. I want it badly, as pilgrims in the Middle Ages would take any risk and spend their last groat to secure some precious relic. But my trouble is the other way round. Goodchild is reluctant to sell it me because he wants to give it me. I can only get it if I can somehow persuade him to charge me a proper price for it.

For the conversion to Chippendale changed his mind and

spirit no less than his work. From the moment that he liberated himself from the factory and by a self-discipline like that of the desert eremites made himself a master-man, he has opposed the principle of the mediæval just price to the expedience of the modern cut-price. During my long friendship with him, I have encountered example after example of his obstinate refusal to consider even a very moderate self-interest. He waved aside the offer of a dealer to pay him a price for making fifty chairs which would have enabled him to live in modest comfort for the rest of his life and without setting foot in his workshop again. Fifty chairs would have been nothing to a man who in his time has made thirty thousand. But no, something was involved that went beyond the dues of his profession. He was offered a large sum for a beautiful cherry-wood chair of the Gothic Windsor type. I should never have seen it and the tiny crack in it but that for that reason he had considered the price too high. The chair he made for me I had to take for nothing or do without it. He is as inflexible about charging his own prices for his own work as our economic system has been in buying cheap to sell dear. In all his transactions his way is precisely the opposite of the way that has built up the world of to-day.

Goodchild sells his chairs for what he considers they are worth, and no power on earth would induce him to make his price one penny more than his estimate of that worth. And it is as modest as are his letters to me when he writes the personal pronoun "i".

But what would bewilder the progressive mind or any mind that accepts the standards and valuations of our own age is the reason he gives for such apparent quixotism. It has in it nothing of a Puritanical or reformist zeal. When he refused the dealer's offer, he told him as he told me, "I only make chairs like that for pleasure." He refused to accept even the price of the wood for my own chair on the grounds that to do so would have clouded the memory of his pleasure in making it. The pleasure he receives from making a noble chair is in itself so noble that it must not be compromised nor tarnished by the intrusion of the trading or bargaining spirit. How astonishing that this aristocrat in creative pleasures had once been a factoryhand making shoddy! It had always been, as

I have said, a puzzle to me to understand how he overcame that market to become like his fathers before him a master of his house, his workshop and his land. For there seems something almost mystic about it, like the overcoming of death. I have come to see that it was his own inner light that raised him from that living tomb. That is not a quality to be explained. When Shakespeare left London for his country home, he said good-bye to his art. When Goodchild left the factory for his country home, he created his art. But however far removed in time as in power, they are alike in this. The country home was the foundation of the art of them both.

On my last visit to him he showed me four new armchairs he had made in the latter half of 1945. One was the Goldsmith-Chippendale; another was a very elaborate Gothic Windsor with a pointed back and tiny lancets and canopies carved into it. The third and fourth were like my own chair, but with splats as highly figured as a Decorated window. He had no idea what he was going to do with them. It had just been his mastership's pleasure to make them, and with no motive but that pleasure alone. They were the products of his leisure, his way of enjoying himself. The notion of offering this man weekly doses of cinema or other mass-entertainment in order to relieve the tedium of country life and raise the countryman to the high standards of the townsman was so fantastic that by it I was enabled to assess how completely he had walked out upon the age in which the jest of the gods had set him.

But perhaps their wisdom too. He is a living witness to a way of life grappled by hoops stronger than steel, not only to nature, but to one minute plot of green in our small island of shrinking country. Because not in spite of that, he became free to expand his spirit in creation. We sat round his stove in the dusk of a wintry day. The scent of his apples mixed up with his chairs diffused the warmth of summer's plenty. A pot of glue simmered on the stove like the hum of insects round forgotten flowers. It was for the ordinary wheelback Windsors he was making for a school. These are charming, an education for the boys who are to sit on them. But they could not satisfy him. He has in him the simmering urgent passion to make the utmost best that can be made out of wood, as the saints can never be wholly satisfied with this world, however radiant, however inexhaustible to human delight.

When he said to me that a century hence there would be nothing of our age posterity would find worth looking at, this break in the continuity of the Englishman's creative power to make England age by age more beautiful than her natural self is a personal affliction to him. But he cares nothing for antiquities. The past is to be honoured simply because it made good things. Goodchild is of the past because the present has lost the secret of making them. Hence the paradox in him, the gentlest of men, resisting with extraordinary fortitude and an iron resolution the pressure of the modern world. He is not a naturally melancholy man; he has had melancholy thrust upon him. For the moment he has beaten the world, and so going to see him is not so much travelling seventeen miles as one hundred and seventy years. But he realises how precarious his independent mastership is, though he could, if he were to relax his price-conscience, live comfortably on private orders to a ripe old age. There is in him a natural joyousness which often ripples across his habitual serenity. But for a reflecting man this is no time for gladness.

With quiet bitterness he told me that really good chairs could only be made now for export. It outraged him that the treasures English hands could make out of the natural riches of English country should be enjoyed by any but Englishmen: and as a sacrifice to the insensate commercial war of world-markets. Based, I added, on nothing but debt. The greatest compliment he ever paid me was that the chair he had made for me would find a good home. Starving our own country to enrich the cosmopolitan money-magnates was in his eye almost as shocking as bad workmanship—the deadliest of all sins.

I said to him, if our world went back to making good things for the good people of England, it would no longer be our world. It would be his. I know no better one. Piety is the right name for Goodchild's work, and his integrity is at one with the wholeness of his life and craft. There is in him a child-like tranquillity with an undercurrent of sadness the

sadder for his bursts of gaiety. He might well be proud that
he has won his own place and his own art against the world and
made of them what his Creator intended. But the only pride in
him is the pride he takes in the pleasure of making his chairs.
I find in this passion of his a reaching towards the illimitable
and the eternal, and of such as he is the kingdom of heaven on
earth. Francis Thompson once saw Jacob's Ladder at Charing
Cross. Through the vision of another I have had a glimpse of
it at Naphill.

CHAPTER VI

THE PERKINSES OF CHILTON

"Countries must be governed either by tradition or by force."
                                                          DISRAELI.

I

THE BEST EXAMPLE I know of what our world would call the picturesque or museum-piece craftsman are the Perkinses of Chilton. Many of our surviving craftsmen live in concealed pockets of our villages and country towns. The places where they live have grown away from them both in occupation and in habitation. So they are to be sought in corners and alleyways, bywaters off the main stream of business. The opposite is true of the Perkinses. Their home and workshop are the node of the hamlet of Chilton. Its lower part is tucked close up to the retaining wall of a broad ledge that overhangs the vast plain of the southern Midlands near the border between Buckinghamshire and Oxfordshire. The upper part climbs steeply towards the crest of the ridge whose crown is an exceptionally massive and commanding church. The Perkins buildings are scattered over a square platform about an acre in extent and exactly between the lower and upper portions of the hamlet.

Standing on the formal little bowling green, laid out to please Mrs. Perkins' taste for a fine turf, I look up at the knightly church in its armour of grey Portland stone; I look down a little row of half-timbered, red-bricked and russet-tiled cottages, and I look across at the huge red-brick pile of the manor, whose secular pride has too much grace to be ostentatious. The church looks north over the great plain, the manor looks south-east. The green and the garden, the home and the workshop of the Perkinses look west. Each point of the triangle has its own consequence. If the long sloping roof and low brick walls of the Perkins homestead could be put several times over into the church and the manor, it has a whole retinue of buildings that they lack. There must be at least a dozen of them. One has a tiny forge and anvil. Another is a wagon-house. A third is the sawing-shed, with a double hand-wheel in the centre. But it is nothing like the size of the towering hand-wheel for sawing out the hubs of carts and wagons in a corner of the fourth and principal building—the workshop. Most of the others are store-houses for timber and iron of all shapes and sizes, not merely disposed about one room after another but hanging from the walls both inside and out. Generations of tools find a home and an almshouse here.

To wander about this green plot, in and out among the toy houses containing their multitudinous forms of wood and iron, down the bowling green bordered by flowers and vegetables and timber frames for roses, among the stone troughs for rock-plants on the lawn in front of the green and by the open barn-like door of the workshop with its bench strewn with tools, its walls hung with them, its floor covered with the parts of carts and wagons, would fascinate any lover of old England. Visiting the homestead on a Sunday afternoon, he would see the Brothers Perkins and Mrs. Perkins, the wife of the eldest. He would learn that they are a family of wheel-wrights, and wheelwrighting is associated in our minds with the prints of George Morland, George Stubbs, Birket Foster, Peter de Wynt and Samuel Palmer. The brothers have been wheelwrights for fifty years; their father, their grandfather and their great-grandfather were wheelwrights. Their main business used to be the making of the Oxfordshire hoop-raved wagon, painted yellow, red and black. They have a photograph of the last one that left the workshop in 1939, the year that ended the last phase of the culture of manual art. This wagon is still in use and has never come back to the workshop for repairs. The carving and chamfering of these brilliant wagons gave them a highly decorative air. But by balancing and lightening the weight without impairing their strength, the wheelwright increased their durability. Ornament was for use and use for ornament. From the Vale I once saw one of the hoop-raved wagons of the Perkins Brothers passing with a full load down the crest of the ridge topped by the church.

It looked like a "stately ship of Tarsus" sliding down a long smooth green wave.

The enquirer who loved the old crafts would also discover that the brothers have never thought fit to discard any but a few of the tools with which their grandfather and even their great-grandfather constructed their wagons. One of these is the grandfather's driving hammer for securing the oak spokes of a wheel into the five years' seasoned hub. It looks more like an axe than a hammer, strikes with the flattened back and has a haft more than three feet long. It seems the kind of implement Thor would have carried and worthy to be placed beside the club of Hercules. The elder Perkins spoke of the "dowle" (dowel) or wooden pin attaching spoke to felloe in the same sense as FitzHerbert used in his *Boke of Husbandrie* of 1528. Shakespeare has "dowle" in *The Tempest*, one more instance of his lavish use of technical terms derived from rural industries. The very names of the timber for the carts and wagons bespeak not only the great woods of England but the poets who have called them Arden and Westermain— oak and ash and elm. These wheelwrights have no machinery at all for converting these hard woods—some I saw had been seasoned for a decade—into the uses of farm transport.

The Perkins Brothers are thus as traditional a pair of craftsmen plying as traditional a trade as can be found even in the remotest parts of our Islands. If the green plot with its workshop, store-sheds, wagon-shed, forge and homestead were to be scheduled as a folk-museum, it would give the new England a kind of costume picture of the old, such as it now only reads about in *Adam Bede* and *Amaryllis at the Fair*, *Over to Candleford* and *The Wheelwright's Shop*.

The site, too, has the significance of symbol. The edge of the grassy platform has a fringe of trees whose branches are a patterned casement to leagues of level land, mountains and lakes of sky. I have stood there on a winter's day when flimsy clouds drove past it like the smoke from a bonfire, and their loftier curtain was half-parted to disclose the frailest hopes of a blue matched in the scenes of the Italian Primitives. The cloud-procession, the far shores of palest blue, the green close projecting into space gave me the floating sense of being aboard a ship. And shipwrights are the Perkins Brothers who once made the painted galleons bearing Ceres from farm to farm. A more romantic site for the folk-museum could not be.

II

That is the picture. But it is only half of the reality. It is only the necessary background to that reality, and the background to craftsmanship is all that our generation can see. To the busy actual foreground it is completely oblivious. When I was last at the workshop, the Perkins Brothers were making felloes out of seasoned planks for the hubbed cartwheel that lay on the floor between them. The word hub nowadays is hardly more than a metaphor. The thing in itself, with its riveted iron cap, has to be seen between the spokes of a wheel in the making to realise its meaning. The years have given it the hardness of metal. But at the same time it is moulded, and each moulding takes a different chisel. The morticing and chiselling by hand of this shaped block of elm (oak would split) is a measure of the tough elementals with which the craftsman is always contending. He is, as it were, the artificer of foundations. All the glories of his handiwork, which in the past have filled the world of men with flowers, proceeded from this bedrock. We say that the craftsman works with nature. But he also works in the primal substances of nature. To place him in the past as a museum-piece is to uproot human life.

It gave me almost a shock to learn that this wheel was destined for a new dung-cart. The last dung-cart I had heard of in the neighbourhood was in the early years of the war, when one was put up to auction and failed to get a single bid. The wheel had come full circle when a traditional wheelwright was making a new one. Is the chemical age beginning to pass away in the dust-clouds of its own making? Opposite the workshop stood a newly painted factory wagon within the open door of its shed. The elder Perkins took me to see its new undercarriage he had fitted and the farmer's name he had painted on the foreboards. The difference between these and the rest of the wagon was like the difference between parchment and paper.

This shed was never empty. No sooner had one of the factory wagons been patched up to run better than when it was new than another broken-bodied specimen rumbled in. Year by year the mechanised farms kept calling for help from the most old-fashioned of craftsmen. Besides repairing the mass-produced wagons, the two Perkinses, whose own wagons were built to last a century, were busy all the hours of daylight in making farm-carts for farmers progressing further and further away from an old-fashioned husbandry. The new could not get on without the old, and the old was overworked in making the new. This strange intercourse between them, so ironical in the light of modern doctrine, was illustrated in the workshop itself. Behind the elder Perkins, who was spoke-shaving a felloe for the new dung-cart, stood a door encrusted with particles of red paint two inches thick. His wife gave me the right word for its rich and glowing appearance. It looked like coral. I looked down vistas of the past when one Perkins after another had wiped his brush against that door. Coral-like the paint had budded and branched in the quietness of slow time.

But the Perkinses are not only wheelwrights. Smithying having died out in one village after another, they are also blacksmiths. There being no carpenter round about them, the elder Perkins has become one. In his *spare time*, he told me, he is also a cabinet-maker. As though he has nine lives like a cat, he also makes Christmas toys for children. He showed me his gaily painted scooters and a sumptuous steam-engine with painted wooden wheels and body. The hub on the floor was a symbol of more than the craftsman working at the quick of nature. These brothers, who had been wheelwrighting for fifty years, were once more the hub of rural activity. In *Country Planning: A Study of Rural Problems*, Dr. C. S. Orwin wants to abolish small villages as well as small farms—"The village of a few hundred people cannot survive as a healthy organism . . . It cannot maintain any of the social services." For miles round the hamlet of Chilton the countryside was depending upon the Perkins Brothers. Their "social services" overflowed their own village like a flood.

Their plot with its array of buildings looks like the settlement of a small community of workers in wood and iron. They two, with the help of the elder's wife, a country-woman of Cobbett's metal, who grows vegetables and flowers and even in winter gets 120 eggs a week from her fowls, do the whole work of such a community. The family has no sons to aid it, no apprentices to follow it. It has sought for the latter in vain. Our age is pleased with the sentiment of the museum-piece craftsman. For him to carry the countryside on his broad back through all the ages, through every change and crisis, in tribulation as in plenty, this is quite beyond its horizon.

On the premises of the Perkin Brothers I could see a self-supporting England in miniature. The nucleus of it was in being there. In the company of such men at work, anybody could see that the notion of a people only able to live by international trade was delirium. Men like these could ride out the collapse of a whole world. It could well survive briars and couch-grass creeping over the paving-stones of the City. For this corner of reality at Chilton to become their playground would be a national calamity. The kindly, burly younger brother looks after half a century of work as though he were in his prime, and could shoulder our tottering civilisation through hurricanes of adversity. The elder is more reflective, the gentlest and quietest spoken of men, whose tranquillity, partly inborn and partly work-born, radiates a sense of security the reverse of the prospects of his trade. Yet how can the countryside do without the likes of him? He has a habit of smiling with a suddenness that transfigures his worn face back to his own heyday and the days when his trade was honoured for what it is—the pillar of an organic commonwealth. Whitehall thinks it runs the countryside. He and his kind do run it.

Remembering a wheelwright I know in Somerset who welcomes a machine he has for cutting felloes, I asked Perkins about it. He wanted it badly, together with a band saw and a circular saw, heresies to the craftsman under the glass case of modern sentiment. But his reason would have been a still more flagrant heresy to the mechanist. He did not merely want to cope with an overplus of work which left him only the leisure of fatigue. If he could have these three machines to do the donkey-work, he said, he would gain from them a "greater satisfaction" in his own more highly-skilled work. For, according to him, the real object of work was to derive a personal satisfaction from it. That was impossible unless it was done as well as it could be done and better. Having far too much work to do, he could not in the time do it well enough to feel the pride in it that is its reward. This was what he said to me. Pride has been rampant in our century, every pride but this, the noblest.

I asked him about his economic position. A man who works all day, has done so for fifty years and grows much of his own food, is little concerned with spending money. A man who finds satisfaction in his work is less concerned with what he gets out of it than others who find none. What did concern him was his tenancy to the big house. He had nothing but good words for the squire. But to be a squire's tenant nowadays is to be involved in his highly precarious fortunes. In our century the target of the town, the rural priority of the squires is nothing but a liability. This one, like others, was faced with having to sell his land. But over and above Perkins' natural anxiety in the fact of living and working upon his little portion of that land, he wanted to be its independent owner. Not only for the sake of the land itself, the beauty of whose site has been beyond measure enriched by the loving toils he has spent on it, but for the sake of being his own master. I can think of some who have earned such ownership as nobly as he, of none who merit it more so. To give it him would repay but a fraction of his services to England.

The age which discourages such ownership and has all but extinguished craftsmanship rewards such services to itself by regarding men like the Perkinses as picturesque figures and nothing more. Those services go beyond lifting it out of a tight corner and are greater than it knows. Almost every day I receive a letter which asks, "How can a real life be lived in modern society?" The answer is in the lives of men like the Perkinses. They do what they can to save that society from collapsing but are not of it. They belong to a society that has been, and will be, because it must be.

CHAPTER VII

ST. PETER OF ABBOTSBURY

Ah! I do think, as I do tread
Thease path, wi' elems overhead,
A-climen slowly up vrom Bridge,
By easy steps, to Broadwoak Ridge,
That all thease roads that we do bruise
Wi' hosses' shoes, or heavy lwoads;
An' hedges' bands, where trees in row
Do rise an' grow aroun' the lands,
Be works that we've a-vound a-wrought
By our vorefathers' ceare an' thought.

WILLIAM BARNES.

I

FOR A DECADE I had been absent from Dorset. Once I knew its contours, villages and towns as well as a flycatcher knows his transitory home in an English garden. But my memory was not so good as his, and the war had come between me and Dorset. Came "Contumelious, beastly, mad-brained war," and another wound with it. The old familiar face of her southern Downland, which, with the massif of the central chalk watershed, had been dearer to me than all other downlands, was renewed. But only through loss. New eyes sprang from dimmed memory like spring from winter. Yet it was no accident that found me taking my way westward in the line of the prehistoric coast road. It runs from Ballard Down, where the chalk reaches the eastern sea in Purbeck Isle, over Nine Barrow Down, down to the Arish Mell Gap, up again to the cliff of Flowers Barrow Camp, stormed by the sea, past the Mupe Rocks, on the crest of Bindon Hill to the Chaldon Downs, where Llewelyn Powys lived and wrote, rejoiced and suffered, over White Horse Hill, by the cap of heathland and its stiff plume, that Powys called "the lucky unicorn's horn of the county," the Hardy Monument on Blackdown frowning down upon Abbotsbury and high above the Bredys to the great hill-fortress of Eggardun. This last is the axle of three great land-masses—the large-limbed, chalk serenely confronting the tumbled lias and the narrow belt of oolite limestone cutting athwart them towards the north-east. I was fumbling my way back to the misted haunts of memory, the memory not only of my own past experience but of that earliest England that stamped the chalk with its peculiar culture and was drawn into its wide breast.

In its leisurely communion with the ranges, the great road is quite unlike the Roman one that passes to the south of Eggardun from Dorchester. It is so studded with tumuli along its entire length as far as the estuary of the Axe that they must outnumber those of Salisbury Plain, the key-country of the megalithic culture. What did the dead in the barrows come for? For flint, their industrial raw material. For pasturage and to grow upland barley, flax, hemp and perhaps other crops. To hunt the bustard and to catch fish, prawns and molluscs. For gold on Dartmoor and for pearls in the rivers of the west. But their primary purpose was to live in England.

I can guess no other reason for their intensive occupation of these southern Downs than because they liked them. Who could fail to love them? There is everything here the heart of man could wish; everything to satisfy all but his grosser ambitions and that demon of self-will that motived Shakespeare's Tragedies and has prostrated civilisation after civilisation like trees uprooted by a gale. "The climate's delicate, the air most sweet." The soil is kind, and in the sheltered places like Abbotsbury rivals in productiveness the more fertile lowlands of the Midi. Exotics flourish in Lord Ilchester's gardens; the Tertiary deposits of the chalk are apt for wheat; the best building stones in England, Portland and oolite limestones, are here for the taking. The geological war of the clashing strata offers to man abundance and variety on the one hand, an everlasting drama of sublime beauty on the other. Snugness is next door to grandeur, retirement at one with the adventure of sea and light.

I marvelled now, as I marvelled ten years ago, how England could have deserted her native land when Dorset is part of it, and when, as the War proved, her existence depends upon it.

The dead thought differently. On these southern Downs, seven types of culture from the Neolithic to the post-Reformation ages have found, as their relics testify, a fortunate home. All left Dorset more beautiful than they found her. Each one, that is to say, practised a way of life peculiar to itself, but always a way of life. Dorset absorbed them all into itself without effacing any of them, Bronze Age round and Neolithic long barrow, Celtic hill-town, Saxon village, mediæval tithe barn, Renaissance and Georgian manor. These monuments by their attunement to Dorset earth are a visual testimony to their builders' authentic ways of life.

Between Upwey and Abbotsbury the lower Downs fall in swelling breakers to the cloven edge of the sea. They are graciously withdrawn from the desperations of the outer world. The pinnacled and battlemented towers of Upwey, Portisham (Captain Hardy's "Possum"), Abbotsbury and the Bredys, some with bold stair-turrets in the Dorset idiom, are the cousins of the great Perpendicular towers of Somerset to the north. But a modest grace replaces their splendour. These grey villages of thatch and milky Portland stone are hidden from the open country of sheepwalks. Dry-stone walls hang with hart's-tongue ferns, coppices of ilex and gentle winding terraced roads speak shelter. There is no abrupt contrast between the shy villages and these secluded Downs of no great height. The lagoons of the East and West Fleet, whose placid waters are protected by the bright scimitar of the Chesil Beach, are their shore-line. The undulations of the Downs are toned down to the whole scene. The small manor houses of Whaddon and Rodden have a simplicity and linear purity that accord with the serenity of the subdued Downs on the one hand and of the lyric church-towers on the other. All the way to Abbotsbury the spirit is bathed in peace.

But beyond it, and all the way north-west through Little Bredy, Long Bredy, Litton Cheney, across the highway between Dorchester and Bridport to Askerswell and up to Eggardun, the scene changes. As different as the great pile of Kingston Russell House is to Whaddon and Rodden Houses, so are these majestic Downs to their lesser brethren strung along the coast to Upwey. The farmhouses are lonelier among these tremendous shoulders and sweeping dry combes than among the balmier miles behind me. Theirs is now the epic style, and no description of them is possible. But there are parallels on an even grander plane. One is the lofty chancel arch of Wimborne Minster, the other the interior of Romsey Abbey. The titanic columns and mighty arcades and soaring walls of this noblest of the Norman Abbeys paraphrase the sublimity of this Downland. But something is added: nature is infused with supernature, and the quintessential harmonies of her forms are transfigured.

The Celtic eyrie of Eggardun crowns the promontory of a range that here terminates the formal but aerial contours of the chalk and meets the tipsily gay shapes of the liassic heights of West Dorset and Devon. The ground drops so steeply to the east and north into a wooded bowl that the white clouds seem but another range of hills. Vastness, solitude and majesty are three in one. Time and space are contemplated as variations of the same mystery. Round Eggardun, whose triple ramparts furrow the hill-flanks in lines of archaic sculpture, there are Bronze Age barrows built as many years before the hill-citadel as from King Alfred to our living selves. Yet the ageless Downs make them seem contemporary.

It is in places like Eggardun that the rise and fall of civilisations are viewed with a certain equanimity. Eggardun does not encourage Utopian illusions. There must have been some flaw, some inward corruption that resolved them, one after the other, into silence and the earth. But one fundamental thing goes on in company with essential human nature—the arts of husbandry. All else perishes again and again. Toynbee in his monumental *Study of History* has inquired into the breakdown of twenty-one civilisations. I have noticed in reading him that, whatever the radical weakness, war or tyranny or centralisation or a vicious economic system or what not, it was its effect in dislocating the arts of husbandry that was the knell of every civilisation.

II

This set me thinking about a phenomenon of miles of these chalk Downs I had already but idly noted. They are terraced into perpendicular baulks and wide platforms in so many places that I lost count of them. There is a particularly fine set of these linces, or lynchets, or irrigated cultivation terraces, at Askerswell, below the wrinkled brow of Eggardun. And they are nearly always in the neighbourhood of the tumuli which grace these Downs more thickly than molehills in a neglected field. The theory of these "shepherd's steeps" that holds the field to-day is that they were formed by the eight-oxen plough of the Saxon open-field villagers. When the co-operative plough-teams of the village community reached the foot of a down, they continued to plough across the hill-slope, travelling only one way. The terraces, according to Henry Seebohm in *The English Village Community* (1883), took their present shape by the natural tendency of the soil to fall downhill. This assumption has been in our own time supported by O. G. S. Crawford, who has denounced all other views as the heresies of the amateur.

There are many objections to this orthodox dogma. Many of these southern lynchets are high up the steeper slopes, several hundred feet away from the valley bottoms tilled by the Saxon ploughs. Nor is there any topographical correlation between the downland terraces and the sites of Saxon settlements. The vertical sides of the platforms have only a slight batter, whereas the drift of the soil downhill must have formed them at an obtuse angle. Again, many of them in various counties were artificially faced with flint or sarsen stone. They occur, too, on rock-formations much less yielding than the chalk, and with only a few inches of top-soil. But even on the chalk, the depth of the terraces is sometimes twenty feet. Dr. C. S. Orwin has shown that the plough-teams would have had to plough ten feet in order to form the terraces. In less than ten feet a ploughman would strike the "clunch" or building stone of the chalk. Quite apart from the fact that only land-shortage, non-existent among the

Saxon settlers, would induce a ploughman to attempt the often steep slopes of the chalk, how could a wooden turn-wrest plough lay a furrow among such blocks?

But the terraces of Purbeck stone west of the southern Dorset chalk ranges give a mortal thrust to the Seebohm-Crawford theory. On the almost precipitous flanks of one of these sea-vexed promontories between Peveril Point and St. Aldhelm's Head, near Worth Matravers, has been hewn a wide and deep series of cultivation terraces out of the solid rock. It is inconceivable that even an iron plough could have made any impression upon a stone surface only a trifle less resistant than basalt or granite. The coulter and beam of a wooden plough could not have stood the strain for five yards.

Who, then, did build these wonderful terraces, build them by hand and not with the ox-team? Not the Celts, who, like the Saxons, had their own field-system, still visible in many regions of the chalk downland. Only the Bronze Age barrow-builders are left. And that the megalithic culture did subsist very largely on its irrigated terraces is world-proven. They were the agricultural pattern of the Incas of Peru who terraced the Andean slopes. They exist on Mount Lebanon, in the Cyclades, in Polynesia, in Africa and elsewhere in those regions where once dwelt peoples who had not yet entered the Iron Age.

III

So by devious but not casual downland pathways I arrive at Abbotsbury, the centre-piece of this itinerary of remembrance. At Abbotsbury, St. Catherine's Hill is terraced by a most beautiful stairway of lynchets encircling the entire hill from foot to crown. On it stands the heavily buttressed and vaulted Chapel that was a beacon to mediæval seamen. That it was built by the monks of St. Peter's Abbey for that purpose is all but the only thing known about the monastery. All that remain of its works are the Chapel, the Tithe Barn and the Parish Church of St. Nicholas, which contains a fine carving of an Abbot in the porch. All that remains of its history is that it was founded by Orc and Thola, his wife, in 1026, during the reign of Cnut. At the Reformation, when the village was still what it had always been, a fishing hamlet, it was "given" to Sir Giles Strangways. He and the villagers long after him used it as a quarry, while his own Abbey House was burned down by Sir Anthony Ashley Cooper in the Civil War. All that is left of the Abbey is, in fact, the now substantial village which literally grew out of its ruins. Many of the houses contain carved stones and arches removed from the Abbey. Such is the mean salvage from oblivion. Among the nearly eight hundred pages of Dom David Knowles's *The Monastic Order in England*, I could find nothing about it beyond the fact that it had always been small, like its Dorset fellows at Milton Abbas and Cerne Abbas. Not a single record of its Abbots survives. The only direct reference to it was that it was "poor and uninfluential." In other words, it remained provincial all its life. It minded its own affairs, without meddling in politics or doing big business in sheep or lands.

That was what interested me about it. St. Peter's Abbey was a monastery with no history, just as the peasantry and the yeomen and craftsmen and smaller squires who built up rural England had no history. None of them had any history because they lived by their own lands and workshops and little estates, secular and monastic. Whether as individuals or communities, all of them lived a way of life of their own, based on what nature had to offer them in their own particular places. These unhistoric monks of St. Peter's Abbey had lived for a millennium and a half upon the tension between universal heaven and that spot of Dorset earth I have loved for many years. I wanted to find out how they had done it. I could only do so by trying to read the manuscript of earth in the neighbourhood of the Abbey I was revisiting. It was the only text available.

That these monks of the Dorset coast were flockmasters and corn-growers is an obvious inference from the Tithe Barn. Yet it is not plain barn any more than St. Catherine's Chapel is a chapel and nothing more. As the Chapel looks with meaning over the sea, so the Barn looks to heaven. It is something more than a great storage chamber. The projecting porch resembles those of scores of other barns. But its ecclesiastical piers, arches and buttresses make it like the porch of a church. It is stone-walled and thatched like any other barn in this county of thatch and stone. But its walls have string-courses, its gable-ends finials. The western end has the usual slits. But the canopied niches and the battlemented supporting piers, like the battlemented towers of the South Dorset churches, turn it into a west front and the slits into lancets. What is it, a church or a barn? Both: a testimony in stone and straw to the communion between nature and supernature. This Tithe Barn is the monument of a sacramental husbandry. It is a parable in stone of a wholeness which is holiness. In creating it the monks were expressing the Doctrine of Creation.

Wherefrom did they get the wool and corn that filled it? Though few the sheep now, the seaward-rolling Downs of Abbotsbury are ideal sheepwalks. They are sheltered from the north by the parapets of Martin's Down, Whatcombe Down and Blackdown, softened from storms by the Chesil Beach and the calm waters of the Fleet. Between Toller Porcorum and the Roman Road to Dorchester a little to the south, I heard a sound I had not heard for many years. It was the sweet, thin, lucid, uplandish tintinnabulation of sheep-bells. But the monks of St. Peter's Abbey must have heard it every day.

Where did the corn come from? From the terraces of the Bronze Age heathens on St. Catherine's Hill. They are just as ideal for the purpose as the sheepwalks were for sheep. Contour ploughing and terracing are two of the more radical methods used by the Soil Conservation Bureau of the United States for stopping sheet erosion and building up fertility. But the prehistoric peoples of the world practised terrace cultivation without being conscious biologists or ecologists. The historic moderns, scared by the results of an acquisitive modernism, to save themselves have reverted to the methods of our first colonisers who have left no history behind them. St. Catherine is the Christian version of the Celtic Katterne. She herself was a kind of mother goddess descended from an archaic prototype who ruled the western Mediterranean from which the ancient mariners directly or indirectly came. They chose wisely. The slopes of the hill are almost immune from frost by their elevation and proximity to the sea. The rain but not the soil slid gently down its flanks and spread over the plat-

forms guarded by their sunny baulks. Perhaps, too, the monks
used the side of the hill facing the sea and the sun for a vine-
yard. If the monks acknowledged the derivation of the saint,
they would scarcely, good husbandmen as they were, ignore
the practical advantages offered by the pagan cultivators who
were the first farmers of Abbotsbury.

They lived the good life, those monks. Nor can it be con-
ceived that they lived by a fishing hamlet without catching
sea-fish in the Fleet less than a mile away. Depressions
immediately south of the Tithe Barn mark the site of their
stew-ponds for fresh-water fish. Waterfowl and waders have
always been abundant on the Fleet and in the marshy land
adjoining it. There is a local tradition that the Swannery
was founded by the monks. The swans feed on the Zostera
weed, but it was an ancient practice to fatten the cygnets on
barley. Yet I feel that monks who could spend art and a sacred
devotion upon their Tithe Barn must also have loved the wild
life that gladdened and graced their little estate by the sea. At
any rate, the Celtic monks and missionaries did. Without that
delight in the delights of nature the wholeness would have
been incomplete. And who could live in Abbotsbury without
the love of nature? Her colours and forms there might well
have been for the monkish husbandmen a foretaste of
Paradise.

There must have been, too, the workshops of masons,
carpenters, farriers, blacksmiths, wood and stone carvers,
glass-makers, saddlers, weavers, illuminators and others in and
about the hamlet and the monastic buildings. Five miles
away as the crow flies to the east lives a blind basket-maker in
the thatch and stone village of Osmington. From him I
bought a stout and serviceable bushel-basket. Fifty years ago
he had a gun accident which cost him both his eyes. He
immediately trained himself to be a basketer. All his withy-
rods come from Sedgemoor and are of two colours, which he
uses to an instinctively decorative effect. The white are
steamed, stripped with the "brake" and annointed with oil;
the brown steeped in water during the winter. John Tizzard
makes shopping, bicycle, scuttle, bushel and other baskets,
sitting with legs crossed on his lapboard in the workshop like
a Buddha. His sight is in his hands, which unerringly pick

out the right withies for each successive stage in the weaving. Invariably selecting the right colours, they are hands that see. He twists and wattles the rods without a trace of fumbling or hesitation, staring ahead with eyes that see not. By his courage, pertinacity and self-taught indomitable skill, there is no longer need for him to see. His baskets are as perfectly finished as though he had never failed to see.

The earliest of the barrow-builders in Tizzard's county were basket-makers. Assuredly they were present when St. Peter's Abbey was a hive of local industry. All through the ages they have had the consolation of their craft for this world's ills. At Abbotsbury they must have had something further. It was the consciousness of living in a community of their fellows and that the work of their hands was blessed.

No self-supporting monastry was without a mill to grind its corn. The one at Abbotsbury lay just below the stew-ponds to the east of St. Catherine's Hill between the Swannery and the Tithe Barn. Though the mill of Bindon Abbey survives, all traces of St. Peter's Mill on an affluent of the West Fleet has vanished. The nearest one that still grinds, not corn for men but grist for cattle, is three miles to the east at Upwey. The divine is interwoven with the natural there as at Abbotsbury, for the Holy or Wishing Well is fed by the same springs as feed the stream that feeds the mill. Upwey is hopelessly suburbanised. But the mill lies close up to the Downs. The stream flows past the battlemented church at their foot and reaches the overshot wheel about a hundred yards down, canopied by a bank of lofty trees. It is as noble a building as its site is exquisite. It stands three stories high, and has a crown wheel for each of them. On the water-wheel the cogs are of oak, while those engaging the spur, crown and other wheels are of metal.

The miller delighted to show me all the niceties of Upwey Mill and exactly how the mill-stones were dressed by the mill-bill which he gave me. The actual grinding is done in the slopes of the furrows near the skirt. The bedstone had only two brasses for taking the strain of the runner-stone spindle, one of oak and the other of copper. The runner-stone itself was entirely without balancer boxes. Yet the miller told me that the whole mechanism of this antiquated type was so delicately balanced that a woman could turn it. He demonstrated to me the uses of the mill-staff for testing the balance of the stones and of the "damsel" which regulated the feed from the hopper. Thus I was seeing at first hand what Rogers, the millstone-dresser of Chapter IX, had so often described to me by letter. Every stone-grinding mill has an indescribable smell compounded of dust, grain, meal, flour, damp timber, old timber, sacking, sawdust, rope, water-weed and spray. It is a smell like no other in the world. By its means I was able to sense the mill of St. Peter's Abbey at work. It would have differed in no essentials from the living one at Upwey.

IV

All this country, in a triangle from Eggardun to Cerne Abbas and Weymouth, has, since I last saw it, changed very little to the outward eye. Internally the decay goes deep. But so gently and undemonstratively has the old rural economy crumbled that only an attentive eye discovers it in the thistled fields, the many ruinous buildings, the unkempt thatch, the rarity of sheep, the coarsening of the turf and the exceeding loneliness of the country off the high roads. The reasons are many, but they are radii from one primary source. The self-supporting economy of which I have taken St. Peter's Abbey as an illustration has ceased to be. West of Weymouth the signs of that dissolution are negative, east of it positive in numerous disfigurements. For it is only by a self-sufficient economy that this countryside, any countryside, can live. It may and should exchange the overplus of its produce and products with what is not Dorset. But to do more than that is for it to bleed slowly or swiftly to death.

To-day, the last place where Dorset fish and Dorset corn and Dorset milk and Dorset lambs are to be enjoyed is in the region where they were caught and produced. More often than not they leave Dorset altogether. A Dorset man was prosecuted in 1945 for selling a catch of mackerel locally because the transport system had broken down. Carriage to-day comes before the production of what is carried. So mackerel cannot be eaten fresh when to be fresh is to be edible. Many of the

smaller villages are falling into utter decay. The county
Education Committee would have completed the process had
it been successful in its proposal to close down two-thirds of
the existing village primary schools. But on the motion of
Mr. Rolf Gardiner, this decision was reversed by the narrow
vote of thirty-five to thirty-one. This is the solitary victory
of Dorset for Dorset in our generation. The centralisation of
the senior schools (age groups 11-15) is already accomplished.
Thus the children follow the food.

Both have followed the local craftsmen and the land-
workers. So the buildings fall down because there is no labour
to keep them up. There would be no money to pay for them
even if they were present. Money, piping its devil's tune, has led
the procession of those who have been compelled to desert
their native place or lured away by the fictitious appeal of
higher wages in a factory. In Winterbourne St. Martin, I saw
a whole street of cottages roofed with corrugated iron. On
the western cliff above Weymouth, to be seen from a dozen
points of vantage, now stands a row of prefabricated hutches
with a few inches between each metal box. They have been
built at the very point where four primary building stones
geologically meet—Portland, oolite limestone, cornbrash and
chalk clunch, with clay-pits for brick within easy reach. When
reason protests, the answer is always that it is cheaper in money
—that false measure—thus to deface England than to accept for
nothing but the trouble of extracting it what nature offers at
our very feet.

The prevalence of this delusion has been universal. But at
the end of October, 1945, Mr. Christopher Hussey wrote two
articles in *Country Life* about the houses Mr. John Campbell
designed and built on Chapel Point by Mevagissey, remote
from all the world. The photographs of these houses showed
their clean sweeping lines, warm and spacious roofs and their
simple but effective and harmonious lines. Some whimsy
touches there were, probably due to the welling of exuberant
relief in the designer progressing backwards and joining hands
once more with the immemorial order of English building.
For they are entirely traditional in form and character, without
being in the least slavish like Victorian Gothic. They were
constructed by Mr. Campbell with the aid of a master-mason

and a master-carpenter in exactly the same way as the mediæval
builders erected parish churches. Except for a very limited
use of concrete, they came straight out of the earth on the spot,
the local Devonian stone and the local grey-green Delabole
roof-slats. They grew up like flowers out of their native rock.
But the fact most confounding to the combines in building
materials was that they were built at a cost so exceeding
low that no mass-produced house imported into Cornwall
could compete with them. There is nothing but fatalism and
the combines to prevent all the country builders setting to
work with the double purpose of relieving the housing shortage
and restoring to England the loveliness she has been losing
like Villon's beautiful armouress.

Though straw is now burned on thousands of acres in the
neighbouring county of Wiltshire, and Dorset is one of the
principal thatching counties in England, there is scarcely
a thatcher left to a score of villages, and he has no apprentices.
Yet at Iwerne Minster, Colonel Ismay's experiment made the
village not only self-supporting in local food and building
materials but so rich in crops and stock that it was enabled to
set up a creamery and bacon-factory for exporting its surpluses.

This ebb of Dorset's life has been accelerated by the military
occupation of the last few years. The littoral all the way from
Lulworth to Purbeck, unexampled for the variety and complexity of its strata, unparalleled for its perspective of bay and
promontory, cove, cave, pinnacles and ledges, cliff, arch and
snout of rock, has continued a military reservation long after
the end of the War. Much of it is to be permanent, so far as
any military works can be said to be permanent in the age of
the atomic bomb. The modern mind has become as slow to
peace as Providence is to anger. It goes on fortifying itself
against the irresistible whether by the moral surrenders of
a false appeasement or the physical armament of a false
security. The land within this military zone has gone back
to waste. Foxes and rabbits multiply, and erosion, aided by
tanks and military works, spreads on the high places. Parts
of Egdon Heath now look more desolate than Thomas Hardy
made them.

The lofty Downs between the stone circle at Poxwell and
the main road between Dorchester and Weymouth are crossed

by the Ridgeway whose course I have traced. It is festooned with groups of barrows. Half-way across and on the crest of White Horse Hill, Came Wood and a cluster of these barrows look down on Chalbury Camp's green dome and Weymouth Bay beyond it. On the further edge of Came Wood the deep-furrowed cirque of Maiden Castle comes into view below the northern scarp. Still further to the north across the soft chequered Vale the mid-Dorset chalk midrib divides it from Blackmore Vale between the Stour and Beaminster. The Bronze Age, Celtic, Roman and Saxon cultures are all to be seen from this height at a single glance, resting in the friend-ship of a common oblivion upon their common but here princely earth. Here, too, lies the Dorset of William Barnes and Thomas Hardy, who have written the last chapters of the rural culture of four thousand years. Both Barnes's Came Rectory and Hardy's Max Gate can be picked out by the experienced eye. The place has a tranquil agelessness that has often drawn me to it.

Since the War the road has been widened. The bulldozer has been busy, uprooting trees and hedges. Came Wood, though not severely felled, has been stripped naked of under-wood. It is no longer a retreat for birds and men against sun and wind and rain and the very vastness of the scene. It is no longer the immemorial woodman's workshop. The mounds of the dead that gaze into distance, the green ramparted citadels, the thatch half-hidden among the valley trees, the hulk of Portland floating between clouds like icebergs and a mother-of-pearl sea, were as I had always seen them. But the height from which I saw them was no longer the same.

Something alien had broken in, not obliterating the place where I stood but in a subtle way changing its spirit. Perhaps the meaning of this change may be conveyed by the difference between William Barnes and Thomas Hardy as interpreters of the spirit of Dorset. Both were Dorset countrymen who de-lighted to clothe Dorset humanity in immortal dress. Barnes did so more completely, if in smaller compass, than Hardy. But Hardy introduced an alien element, and it is a fact that he is not revered in Dorset as Barnes still is.[1] There is a radical paradox

[1] Shepherd Fry on Mr. Rolf Gardiner's beautiful and devotedly husbanded farm at Springhead, near Shaftesbury, loves to recite his poems.

W.M.B.   L

in his work: his intuitive rural perceptions clashed with his intellectual philosophy. This was a fatalism controlling those perceptions and crystallised in such terms as the "Immanent Will," "Necessitation," and even "It." Such conflict between the ruralist and the thinker never occurred in Shakespeare. But Hardy's pessimistic determinism, like the optimistic Marxian "Historical Necessity" and the theory of automatic progress, is as foreign to the rural as to the Christian conceptions of life. It was, in fact, imported from an inorganic urban civilisation and grafted on to Hardy's native ruralism. They were incompatibles, as the forced marriage between the urban and the rural always is and always must be.

CHAPTER VIII

FLAX FARMERS OF THE WEST

If you in Do'set be a-roamen,
   An' ha' besiness at a farm,
Then woont ye zee your eale a-foamen!
   Or your cider down to warm?
Woont ye have brown bread a-put ye,
   An' some vinny cheese a-cut ye?
      Butter—rolls o't!
      Cream—why bowls o't!
Woont ye have, in short, your vill,
A-gied wi' a right good will?
                              WILLIAM BARNES.

I

IN THE St. Luke's summer of 1945, I found myself for the third
year in succession judging flax-ricks. This year it was in a
competition between the West Country farmers, who for
the needs of war, and now of what is called peace, have been
growing this most ancient of English crops. The country
and the circumstances were quite different from those described
in *The Wisdom of the Fields*. But my fellow-judge, J. E. Hosking,
was the same. In controlling several flax-mills, his aim has
been a much wider and more subtle one than the production
of flax for the market. That necessary work has only been a
foundation. His greater purpose is to recreate a rural culture
sprung from a mutuality between agriculture and industry as
close as that between hand and brain.

The flax industry itself has been in the hands, both in war
and peace, of a bureaucratic machine whose concern is not
with values but their reverse—mass-production, financial
cheapness, statistics and quick returns. This machine is itself
subject to an economics which acts only in terms of arith-
metical profits and the foreign trade that has offered the most
lucrative fields for exploitation. As for the countryside where
the flax is grown, its culture has ebbed to vanishing point. To

restore the continuity, to reforge the lost links between the fields and the mill, to make the fields once more productive of human character and skill as well as of healthy crops, to turn the mills into the workshops of a genuine community, such has been and is Hosking's endeavour. He is very far from having realised it: the whole age is against him. But he persists, and in many ways he has already accomplished wonders. One out of many of these enterprises has been to make the flax-growers among the farmers compete for the best three ricks. My round with him in 1945 was among the farmers of West Somerset and West Dorset.

It is a measure of this remarkable man's partial success against the oppressive machinery of modern governments that he has recently been having a hand in two more flax-mills besides the three he originally founded. Both are in the West, and one of them is at Lopen, between Ilminster and Ilchester, off the Fosse Way. It lies in a small valley surrounded by small meadows watered by a small stream. But the stream is large enough to be trapped for the retting-tanks before escaping on its own natural way.

Since Hosking arrived on the scene, the mill has been slowly waking to life from the relaxing grasp of the absentee land-lordism of the State. In front of the hideous urban buildings erected by the State and obscuring the gracious lines of the old mill, flower and vegetable gardens have appeared. They are fertilised by the "shive" or skin of the flax-straw. Hosking's manager is now installed. One of his many discoveries, he is a quiet and knowledgeable man who comes of a family of small craftsmen-owners at Market Lavington who suffered the same fate as the Durbeyfields. The workers are being weaned from their absorption in the pay-sheet to considering the quality of their work, which alone can ensure the quality of the flax-fibre. That quality is beginning to put an end to the wastage of purely quantitative standards. The organic discipline of work is beginning to displace the purely arbitrary discipline of a remote administration. Hosking has ideas of how to use the old rope-walk of Lopen, a hundred yards long. Mr. Callow was not mechanically minded enough to attract the notice of the State before Hosking made him one of his fieldsmen at Lopen. Being a countryman by birth and instinct,

he was, as one naturally concerned with quality, slow on the
uptake of quantity. Now he has scope and has blossomed.
Lopen is like a man rescued from drowning and recovering its
breath.

Mr. Callow accompanied Hosking and me in our rick-
visitings over most of West Somerset. He is not only a
countryman; his own fortunes have been analogous with
those of his particular countryside. Even to-day there are
sufficient flax-names, flax-pools and flax-buildings remaining
to indicate that West Somerset was once a prosperous flax-
country. There were once spinners' mills that made the sails
of Nelson's *Victory* at Merriott and at Crewkerne, where
Wordsworth walked in every morning from Racedown under
Lewesdon to fetch his letters; I saw a fine yellow-stone flax-
mill and a row of spinners' cottages of the same Ham or
Upper Lias stone. Castle Cary also had its flax-mill and on
the ridge between the Parrett and the Isle the flax-land is
nonpareil. Since the Upper Lias is as kind an earth as the
deeper soiled oolite limestone for flax-growing, it is evident
that West Somerset was in the past a regional centre for the
integrated growing and spinning of flax.

Mr. Callow, too, was once an integrated man. Like Cobbett,
he began his field-life as a bird-scarer but soon left it for flax.
Flax died and, before Hosking stepped into Somerset, was
artificially revived for the War by Government. Mr.
Callow got into the Lopen factory but only in a humble
position. Since Hosking promoted him, he has been recovering
his flax-instincts. But I noticed how they had to be dug into
through an intervening stratum induced by mechanisation
of the plant. His normal attitude had a semi-fatalism grafted
on it entirely opposed to his organic sense. He had not
surrendered to the machine but had acquired an inferiority
complex towards it. He had no doubt at all which made the
best linen—the hand-pulled or the machine-pulled flax. The
machine can only "handle" a standardised article which, of
course, nothing grown by nature is, flax least of all. But
Mr. Callow was at first evasive in answering me, not out of a
divided mind but simply because any stranger who was not
machine-minded was something new on him. He has to
recover under Hosking his confidence in the truth. So the

Lopen Mill has now to unlearn the false standards before it can achieve the values and produce the quality of Hosking's own Devizes Flax-Mill. Hand-pulling and hand-processing of flax are like hand-milking. Hand-skill in both is incomparably superior to automatism. But when that skill is lost, the machine will do the better job.

What is true of the Lopen Mill and of Mr. Callow proved equally true of the countryside we travelled and of the ricks we inspected for the competition. It is also true of the local building. The red marls, the Upper Lias of western Somerset and the oolite of eastern Somerset all supply building stone fit for palaces. A few village masons, so Mr. Callow told me, still exist. But they all are forced, as in Northamptonshire and Lincolnshire,[1] to become bricklayers. It is "cheaper" to import brick, just as it is cheaper to import butter from New Zealand, bacon from Denmark and flax from the Baltic than to produce them next to our own doorsteps. And the "interests," of course, are strong in brick. In the quarries that remain open, the building stone is used for road-stone, which is like using butter for grease. Only at Ham Hill, which produced the golden stone of Sherborne Abbey, does the remnant of the masonic tradition survive.

We crossed the Blackdowns which drive a marly wedge between the Upper Greensand and the Upper Lias of the extreme west of the county. It is a poor farming country of bracken, bramble and "fuzz," starved pastures, decayed coppices and beech hedges along the roads. That is to say, it is a hill-sheep country. But, as hill-sheep are now "uneconomic," we saw no sheep. So, in an age which puts last things first and makes money more important than what it can buy, the Blackdowns are tumbling down into the waste from which the hill-sheep redeemed it. But we did see a herd of Ayrshires which, for all that the breed is highly strung, can stand the cold of the heights. But no North Devons, the hardy native beef-breed of the West. They also are becoming "uneconomic," because they are not milk-machines. How maladroit an industrial-financial civilisation is with a countryside! When the magnates and monopolists have no use for it, it goes into the workhouse. When war comes or starvation threatens, it

[1] See Page 96.

has to be fetched out again and forced into a suit of economic clothes that neither fit nor could ever fit it.

It is fine to get the first view of the other side and to see the elegant ridge of the Quantocks on the left and the sea-like Bridgewater flats to the right. Other countries change in miles and leagues; ours changes in furlongs. No wonder it breaks one's heart to see how that sweet diversity is being ironed out. Beyond Wellington we were in quite a different country. Stone walls succeeded beech hedges, lanes thirty feet high in sandstone cliffs the windy upland roads. Reddish stone from the Stogumber quarries replaced the yellow or grey stone we had left behind. Rich pastures with a bloom on them (though not fully grazed) followed upon the penurious ones, cider orchards upon gloomy spruce, snug little farms upon lonely drifts of bracken.

Mr. Callow told me that there were big farms too. What did he mean by big? Three hundred and fifty to five hundred acres. In Wiltshire to-day they would be considered Tom Thumb farms. Some of the farms still had their mixens. Their farmers had not yet been taught, as Hosking said, that this was all wrong, nor been thrown out if they disagreed. We saw carts carrying dung and here and there folded sheep and cattle-yards to keep the artificial manure bill down. We walked in orchards so thick with windfalls of Tom Putt apples that the foot stumbled. Their scent intoxicated the air. Mistletoe grew on the trees; Dorset Horns and North Devons kindled the eye. We were far from the Artificial Insemination Centre at Ilminster where there is everything of the bull except the bull. At the village of Halse between Milverton and the Quantocks, we saw a dog ambling down the road between the cob cottages with their black stone plinths. I had the illusion that all was well with these villages and farms. Children and dogs would play in the road for the next thousand years as they had done in the last.

But it is not well with them. If the observer has had enough experience to know that the mixed farm is the only good farm, the kind of farm which is still wrapped up in what the Press, clinging to the privileges of plutocracy, calls " the old illusion of self-sufficiency,"[1] it is far from well

[1] October 13th, 1945.

with the small farms of West Somerset. Nor is it at all necessary
to walk over them to perceive the evidences of decay. They
appear in the milk-stand by the side of the road. This is what
Hosking calls the symbol of a "creeping paralysis" breaking
up the economy of good farming. Everything is ultimately
sacrificed to this cash-crop—first the sheep, then the beef-cattle,
then the fodder-crops and finally the fertility. Yearly the farm
is drained of its calcium and phosphates which find their way
to the sea; the farmer gets into the hands of the chemical
merchant and he himself becomes a mere "teat-puller." He
begins exporting his farm and to that there is only one end.
This is what is happening in the lowlands of West Somerset,
and it is one phase of financial dictatorship. The mixed farm is
being driven back to the hills. How long will they remain
its refuge and strength? The Quantocks are still none too
easy of access. We kept losing our way among the winding
corridors of their high-banked lanes, wise provisions of our
forefathers against the downhill soil-drift of slopes like steep-
pitched roofs. Here this firm husbandry still holds, but
precariously.

The abandonment of good husbandry by these Vale farmers
is welcomed to-day as a measure of progress. I happen to
possess a first-hand record of what one of them was like some
eighty years ago. It was written for me by the son—himself
now eighty years of age—of Professor James Buckman, who
discovered the Roman Villa at Cirencester and founded there
the museum of which he was the first curator. In 1862, he threw
up his Chair of Botany and Geology to become a farmer,
renting a farm of four hundred and fifty acres at Bradford
Abbas between Yetminster and Sherborne, some five miles
east of the Ilminster country Hosking and I were travelling.
The soil, a sandy loam, quick-drying and easy to work, is very
similar to that of the farmers we saw. The farm's most
important crop were the sheep, five hundred of them, flocks
of Dorset Horns and Hampshire Downs. The cattle for
fattening were Herefords and Black Scotch; the dairy cows
a couple of Jerseys to provide milk and butter both for the
household and the market. A whole herd of pigs was kept and
the rest of the livestock on the farm were poultry, half a dozen
Shire horses, a carriage and a riding-horse. The farm pupils

sometimes kept hunters. So, as the Professor's son told me, "there was no lack of manure to keep the land in good heart."

The farm was mainly arable. But it maintained twenty acres of water-meadow, twelve acres of permanent pasture and two acres of cider apples. Sufficient cider was made to last the community through haysel and harvest. All hay and straw were consumed on the farm. Up to 1873, all the corn was cut by hand except the barley, for which a hay-mower was used. It was never tied but "pooked" (put up into cocks) and treated like a hay crop. "Except in the black earth district of Cambridgeshire, I have," Buckman writes, "seldom seen crops of wheat to equal my recollection of some of ours. I can remember my father showing me some ears of corn measuring little short of six inches and pointing out the unusual number of seeds per bract." After a mild winter when the corn was too forward or "frum," the sheep were run over it in the spring, "after which it would stool (tiller) out and five or six stems would appear where one was before." It was sown by special drills that spaced the seed widely apart in contradistinction from the modern practice which sows far too thickly. The purely cash crops were such as are never grown to-day. Among them were nightshade for the chemists, Savory and Moore, and Stremonium (Datura), a handsome plant with long trumpet-shaped blossoms and broad leaves on a thick stem, processed into cigars, tobacco or snuff and also used as a specific for asthma. It had the effect of enlarging the eye pupils of those who handled it, one pleasing to the women as enhancing their beauty.

A dozen men were permanently employed on the farm, including a pair of carters and shepherds. "In the good old days I have seen twenty men reaping corn and as many women binding after them. Wages, it is true, were miserably low, but our head carter, getting only sixteen shillings a week with extras at hay and harvest, brought up twelve children and put them all out well into the world. What with his free cottage, his garden, his pig and a rod of tater ground on the farm and Vinney cheese at fivepence a pound, he spent little on food. I doubt if the modern labourer is any better off or more content on his three or four pounds a week." I may add that carters used to get up at four a.m. and spend two hours without pay in polishing their horse-brasses. Though the modern land-worker is richer in his money-wage, he is poorer in everything else. Machines were readily used on the Buckman farm—an American reaper in the seventies, an early binder, a threshing machine, an elevator in 1884 and occasionally a steam plough for a deep tilth. But they were strictly subordinated to the human values and economy of the farm. They did not cause unemployment nor depress the manual craftsmanship of the farm.

Was this farm at all exceptional? During 1945 there appeared in *Blackwood's Magazine* some instructive figures given by Mr. W. G. N. Dobie upon the comparative yields per acre in Scotland in the early nineteenth century and the present. The average crop of oats to-day is forty-three bushels per acre; Sir John Sinclair (the first President of the Board of Agriculture) gave the nineteenth century figures "in good seasons and fertile districts" as fifty-nine to seventy-two. Barley is now forty bushels per acre; then, according to Sinclair, it was forty-seven to fifty-three. A good crop of potatoes then and now was and is seven and a half tons per acre, but fewer tubers were sown in each acre more than a century ago. The decline in the turnip yield has been much steeper. In our time seventeen and three-quarter tons is the average; in 1809, forty-eight tons per acre were considered "a good crop." How were such figures that so deflate the fashionable statistical arrogance of to-day achieved? First, by adequate labour—one Lothian farm of six hundred and seventy acres was worked by ninety-one labourers and another of seven hundred and two acres had a hundred and sixty-three. No labour was considered too laborious if it contributed to the fertility and improvement of the soil. The tenants erected dry-stone dykes at their own expense and summer fallowing involved six or seven ploughings together with repeated rolling, harrowing and hand-weeding. Secondly, the most liberal applications of dung came from the "mixed middens." But compost as well as dung was freely used, and beside the residues on the farms was made up of seaweed and town manure, peat and wood-ashes, slaughter-house refuse and crushed bones. In 1801, in fact, Lord Meadowbank developed the Indore Process under another name.

A third reason for this very marked superiority over our own farming was that the farmers themselves knew a great deal about soil, minerals, crops, leys and rotations. Fourthly, the actual workers on the farms were much better fed, worked much harder and were incomparably more highly skilled. The wages were low but a high purchasing power more than compensated for shortness of cash. Moreover, each labourer had a house and garden of his own, a cow for which he received rations, liberty to keep pigs and poultry and an allowance of oatmeal. Mr. Dobie's record obviously makes mincemeat of the preposterous claims for modern farming made by the scientific "experts," who have relieved the contemporary farmer of that knowledge about his own farm which his forefathers possessed.

Professor Buckman died in 1885 and his son carried on the farm for nearly a year. But he was forced to abandon it by a succession of wet summers and the expansion of the highly profitable market in cheap food imports. The father's independent action in resigning his professorship to become a working farmer was reversed in his son, who left the farm to become a portrait and miniature painter. But he has always looked back on his farming youth "as the happiest time of my life."

No criticism of the modern dairy farms to the west of Bradford Abbas could be as scathing as this record. The more modern they become and discard their traditional husbandry, the more deeply they penetrate into the *cul-de-sac* which caused Mr. Buckman to leave his father's farm. Modern progress is largely based upon the cardinal error of those cheap food imports which ruined the Professor's handiwork and brought to nothing the act of self-sacrifice which turned him into a farmer. Nevertheless, if we escape its most recent manifestations—the atomic bomb and a world food shortage—we shall return to farming on the now obsolete model of Professor Buckman. The professors, the economists, Whitehall and I. C. I. may "tire the sun with talking." But grim necessity will talk rather more to the point.

On the whole, the flax-ricks were disappointing. They were well-intentioned but we did not see one which deserved Hosking's term of "classical." The year had been against the stack-builders; it is easier to build a stack with short than with long flax, which is inclined to be bow-shaped and so difficult to pack. The year 1945 was a long-flax year. But hardly any of the ricks were sprung, and straw well over the eaves to prevent drip is essential with straight stems. We seldom saw a generous use of straw over the eaves and proper footings to the bottoms. Only one rick was faggoted. The idiom here is parallel lines of straw bonds from eaves to the "wad" or stiff mane of the roof-ridge, the roof being sometimes supported by poles at the eaves or along the line of the gable-ends. But the thatchers had been working like men feeling their way back to a lost land without the compasses of memory. They were careless copyists, not heirs, of the tradition. And the ricks were often built much too high and wide, exposing them to the full force of wind and rain. This is all very well with a corn-rick. But a flax-rick must protect the roots and the straw which encases the fibre, not the seed. These towering edifices were too bold with the weather. No flax-rick should offer a broadside to wind and rain. None the less, they were experimental attempts to swing into the rhythm of a past craftsmanship. They were in the same transitional stage as the Lopen Mill.

II

The other flax-mill is at Netherbury, a mile or so south-west of Beaminster. There the chalk watershed of Dorset comes to a full stop and the Upper Lias forms ridges and cones of an entirely different landscape. Netherbury itself, among its concourse of joyous little hills, is one of the most enchanting villages in England. If the reed-thatched and Purbeck slat-roofs of its warm yellow-stone cottages and mullioned farm-houses had not been nearly all replaced by Welsh blue slate, it would almost be the equal of Castle Combe in the south-western Cotswolds. Castle Combe excels both in the architectural graces and in situation; green and gardened Netherbury now chiefly in the last. The stone walls and winding lanes are set along parallel terraces down the flank of a shapely valley, watered by the bowery Brit. Three sister hills overpeer the village on one side, Great Parnham House on the other. The church, as in so many of the secret villages of the Lias—and Netherbury is bosomed deep in cider orchards and lofty trees and hedges—stands high upon a mound. It is visible where the village of which it once was the beacon is screened by canopies of foliage. The cottages and farms of Netherbury are like the fruit of a leaning apple tree.

The mill[1] lies on the Brit at the bottom of this pocket in the hills. It is ideally situated for flax both in water-power and by its easy communication with the spinners and weavers of Bridport. But in its insolent red brick and corrugated iron it is so ugly that it looks like a practical joke in a raffle-sack. The old water-mill at the back, comfortable in line and mellow in the texture of its stone, is hidden by this offensive stranger, belching out smoke from its chimney-stack like bad language. Hosking has his work cut out here, for the mill is still under Government control and he himself has only a superficial authority in it. Nevertheless, the manager and fieldsman are his own men and the flower-borders are again being cultivated under the forbidding walls of the mill. The beats or stooks of flax stood on one slope and the retted flax was drying out on the other. At least, the first page of a new-old manuscript of England's organic life was being re-written. In the manager's office, a stethoscope was hanging on the door, used here for starting some electrical appliance. Hosking asked if it was for the heart. You may not, he added, be able to hear the heart-beats yet. But if Slape Mill does not peter out altogether in the future[2] and Hosking ever becomes its physician, the heart-beats will no longer resemble the ticking of a red-tape machine.

The Ministry takes little interest in the flax-rick competition. But it gives Hosking his head over it. Accordingly, six of us, ourselves the judges, the manager, the fieldsman and a guide set forth. The guide was a silent Dorset man of the old dark race which built the first walled town of Maiden Castle more than a thousand years before the Iron Age Celts enlarged it. We should have been lost without him. It was here that

---

[1] Rebuilt and restored to flax-processing in 1939 by Mr. Rolf Gardiner of Springhead before becoming a State-factory in 1942.
[2] In 1946, it was arbitrarily closed down by the Board of Trade.

Charles II lost himself after Worcester. The country of West Dorset between the Bridport-Lyme Regis highway and the sea—our main objective—is still one of lanes and green tunnels twisting up and down the liassic mounts and downs. The farms are still isolated from more accessible communications. Sometimes the only way to reach them is by cart-tracks and green halter-paths. There could not have been a more perfect way of feeling the heart-beats of the deeper Dorset, faintly pulsating under the rush and roar of modernism. A country-side can be seen from within only when a definite purpose takes the traveller into it, other than sight-seeing. The sight-seer looks at, not through, the country.

But in the morning our journeys lay more or less between Bridport and Melbury Osmond. It, too, is a patch of country of very few highways and those secondary; it is a maze of circuitous lanes. Into the middle of it the narrow strip of oolite limestone forces its way up from Burton Bradstock between the lias on the west and the chalk on the east. Wherever such collisions occur, and they are frequent in Dorset, the tempo of the landscape quickens and it is full of confusing splendours and variations. Both the lias and the less brashy oolite are first-rate for flax-growing, the crop grown on the latter being of a saffron tinge, indicating a high quality fibre. But though the full-bodied curves of the chalk may at times appear indistinguishable from those of the oolite, Upper Lias never deceives the eye.

We were inspecting a rick at Melplash Farm which is girdled by a small amphitheatre of these playful liassic mounts, and I was able to take full measure of their singular beauty. Every liassic hill is individually distinct from its neighbour, though certain types recur like the cone with a plume of pines and the flat-topped like a gate-legged table. The odd live-liness of their varied slopes lends an air of careless happiness to their countryside and makes real the Biblical "laughing hills." Round Melplash Farm there was a whole festival of them, some carrying groves or woods in a thoroughly rakish fashion.

Their invitation to the good life made the sights of this farm the more melancholy. The long farmhouse was rich in dignity and two cedars spread fingers of autumn shadows over its grey walls and thatched roof. All else was in ruins. Isolated

lengths of crumbled wall stood deep in nettles or were overgrown with briars and ground elder. The once solid bartons
were either agape or sheeted with corrugated iron. The low
Dorset gates lacked bars, ivy wound its coils round the trees,
the yards were ankle-deep in litter and hummocks of grass
were the graves of activity. Here progress was a synonym of
decay, and in the village the school was on the point of closing.
The dangerous and feverish outer world had sucked up the
life of Melplash Farm and would soon leave it nothing but
the epitaph of the picturesque. Yet with sheep and pigs this
warm-hearted countryside could be reclaimed—the Dorset
Horns for the vales, the Dorset Downs for the uplands.

In the old coaching inn of the George at Ilminster is a
superb grandfather clock made by "R. Summerhayes of
Ilminster." Above the dial is the carving of a clipper in full
sail at the entrance to harbour. At the striking of the hours,
doubtless the ship moved towards its anchorage. When the
local clockmaker disappeared from the local town, the logical
end of the process is for Devons, Downs and Horns to vanish
from the local farms. A spiritual no less than a material
fertility vanishes with them. As Shakespeare well understood:—

> "And as our vineyards, fallows, meads and hedges,
> Defective in their natures, grow to wildness,
> Even so our houses, and ourselves and children,
> Have lost, or do not learn for want of time,
> The sciences[1] that should become our country."

In vernacular stacking, the West Dorset rick still differs
from that of West Somerset and the Quantocks. The thatch
of the flax-ricks we saw generally lacked both gables and
parallel bonding. The straw bond, perhaps still twisted by the
wimble, is mostly confined to supporting the "ridge-wad."
The spars are arranged diagonally in courses, though seldom
properly staggered to prevent the rain from forming runnels.
At Mangerton Mills under Eype Church, whose lofted tower
looks down between twin-pointed nipples of the lias, we viewed
a rick with terraced or ripple thatching from ridge to eaves.
The sense of beauty, once an intuitive heritage, had been

[1] *viz;* country crafts.

recovered. But, here as elsewhere it failed in fusion with practical service. The essence of the old country life was this fusion and so its complete justification to an age that in sacrificing the one has lost the other.

III

The old rope-town of Bridport, slung like a hammock between the green hills of the east and the green hills of the west, is the boundary line between my earlier and later associations with Dorset. All to the west is country I have lived in as a young man, but had not revisited for more than thirty years. To break our mission at the Greyhound there, before prospecting further west for ricks, was therefore the threshold of an adventure for me. And Walter Trump's Greyhound, with its shelves of Victorian books in the dining-room and cartoons of Victorian celebrities along the staircase, has still a fragrance of the past. Opposite is the relic of a still richer one. "Beach and Co.—Pharmacists," with its bow-windowed front, panes of panelled glass and beautiful little eighteenth century Gothic oriels on the first floor, reveals not only the graciousness but the integration of that past. It is flanked by the shop-fronts of Timothy White, the World Stores and the International Stores, expressing not only the gracelessness but the disintegration of the present. Though this decadence had begun long before my young days in westernmost Dorset, it was during the thirty years of my absence from it that those shop-fronts had appeared, so incongruous with Beach the Pharmicists.

With the keener pleasure against these reflections I heard from the manager of the Slape Mill at the Greyhound about Mr. Legg and his son of Shipton Gorge, whose flax-rick we were to examine. They are, said the manager, what the towns-man would call "country clodhoppers"—slow in speech, slow in gait and slow in manner. They are proper mixed farmers, keeping sheep, fowls, goats and a few cows on a fifty-acre farm and this year had grown two acres of flax. They never made any trouble about the grading. Though they had no help but that of their two selves, they had offered to pull their own crop. When their neighbours were short-handed, they worked for them even better than for themselves. This was good. But it was even better to hear that these were the characteristics of all the small mixed family farmers in the region between Bridport and Lyme Regis.

What is more, it is the smaller farmer who grows the best crops of flax. This is also true of the crops commissioned by the Lopen and Devizes Mills. Yet the average size of the family farm in the far west of Dorset is only between thirty and thirty-five acres. I asked the manager why this superior flax came from the family farmer. Because, he said, of the personal care and interest he devoted to it. True, he had an inducement, because flax is a cash-crop to put against the rent in place of the old wool crop. And the fibre of flax, unlike milk and wheat, takes nothing out of the soil as an export. But, since what I had heard from the manager tallied with what I had observed for myself in 1944 among the small farmers of the Quantocks, it was evident that these qualities are common to many small mixed farmers wherever they farm. They are stamped upon their husbandry. Always provided that they are not tempted or coerced to become degenerate "teat-pullers." The manager's warmth was the more illuminating from the fact that he has emerged almost scatheless from his service in a State mill, to being as he is one of Hosking's men. But he kept on using the word "factory" to describe it, to be gently corrected by Hosking's "mill."

We stopped first of all at Mr. Legg's round rick. It was to the normal rick what the Dexter is to the Shorthorn—a toy. Two ears cocked up at each end of the roof-ridge gave it an almost comical air. But it was very well packed, of a good colour, with the eaves well covered and footed with bracken. Sturdily and serviceably it confronted some of the grandest and noblest, wildest and loneliest country in the south. We had gone east a mile or two and then turned south towards the sea just short of Askerswell and the Bredys, themselves set in a landscape for kings and saints. Mr. Legg's pigmy stack had a prospect of an even greater majesty and purity. But it is a country not of kings or saints or heroes or poets but of the small farmer. I am content it should be so. These wonderful hills and ranges confer upon his littleness a dignity that is his by right of his observance of fundamental laws and principles. By right, too, of his crucial service to every nation in all ages, whether he be fostered by it or, as in modern civilisation, despised and dispossessed. It is charming to know that the Dorset W. A. E. C., unlike its fellows in most other counties, is a help to the small farmer in time of trouble.

Although we stopped at a dozen more farms between and north of a line between Burton Bradstock and Chideock, the epic quality of the country never faltered to a lower key. Its expression changed but not the magnificence of its features. We travelled along green roads, up and down deep cuttings in the russet rock, down Pineapple Lane where the hazel boughs meet overhead. Wherever we stayed to judge a rick, it belonged to a small or smallish farmer whose cluster of farm buildings was staged in a Miltonic setting of Downs, varied with the fantastic contours of liassic hills. Rarely was there another building in sight. Only one of these farms—Doghouse Farm— had as many as a hundred acres. It lay under the corrugated brow of tawny Golden Cap whose profile, bronzed in the low autumn sun, stared, Nature's Ozymandias, into the mirror of the sea. There were four well-thatched corn-ricks here as well as a flax-rick, stoutly armed against the winds to come. It is to be noted that a good rick is never dwarfed by its natural surroundings, however grand. Nor is man ever a puny being against the immensity of the universe, so long as he is in an organic and so a right relation to it. It is only modern man, with his grandiose pretensions and expulsion of God from his idea of the universe, who seems insect-like and poised on the edge of the abyss. Shakespearean man was never so. Was Lear, white-headed, broken, cast out, puny against the elemental storm? Or was his Fool?

Nor were we ever without company other than our own. Though we did not often see the farmer, there were always the animals. At Lower Ash Farm under Boat Hill near Bridport, —though even a small town might have been a thousand miles away—we had geese, poultry, horses, bees and well-knit Devons, all congregated on a tiny knoll. Yet I have travelled over the mechanised farms of Wiltshire and seen never an animal for mile after mile. The more solitary the farms, the more complete they were and usually the better the buildings, sometimes finely reed-thatched and always solidly constructed of stone. Very few were without orchards, and it is on these remote farms that the strongest cider in Dorset is made. Nor is a sweeter and more melting blackberry to be found than along the high hedgerows of these family farms hidden among the hills. The tilthy red soil like a cushion to the foot imparts a bloom to the beasts and a savour to the fruits, abetted by the wine-like air.

A farmer we did meet was Mr. Chubb of Lower Ford Farm. His farm stood on a green platform high among the hills. It is occupied by the farmstead and its outbuildings, a magnolia tree with one gigantic October flower, the paddock with two Shire horses and the flax-rick built by the father and thatched by the son. The orchard of Bramleys and cider apples would have pleased Mr. Raymond Bush.[1] It shelved steeply down at the edge of the platform, was planted in rows and so frost-free. The cider we drank from it pleased me. It was the best unsweetened cider I remember to have tasted, and lit up the whole body. It had been made in a traditional timber cider-press and there were fifteen hogsheads of it in the farmhouse. But so hard did this family work that there was rarely much surplus to sell. That there was so much at the time of our visit was due partly to the fact that it had been recently made and partly to the fact that 1945 was a sunless summer. There was not so much sweat to put back.

Mr. Chubb, short, thickset, power-limbed, white-haired and with brown eyes like a sheep-dog's came to us almost at a trot out of his field of kale. Before we arrived, he had been pulling his kale by hand so as to leave the land rootless and at once cultivable by the harrow. This is the kind of farmer Mr. Chubb is. It is one of the oddities of history that such devoted husbandry as Mr. Chubb's should in the eyes of our own age actually be prejudicial to him and his like. His status would be raised beyond measure if all he did was to sit on a tractor by day and in a cinema at night. In himself an example, he was even more interesting about his father. This man had been not only a grower of flax on his own land but processed it with his own hands before selling it to Scuttle's, the Bridport spinners who survive to this day. He deseeded and dew-retted

[1] *Frost and the Fruitgrower.*

it on his own fields, well aware that flax, being retted on the grass, has a stimulating effect on it. He "swingled" it, just as William Barnes's labourers used to thresh the corn with the "drashel" or flail, the striking staff of which was called the "swingle-tree." "Swingling" performs in one the dual processes of breaking and scutching the flax in the mill, and the old Flemish term for a flax-mill, so Hosking told me, was a swingling-mill. Chubb the father also cocked his flax into "barts" (in Ireland "sheighs") in the very paddock where we stood talking to his son.

All that Flaxman means to the nation to-day is a telephone number. But there was a time when it indicated a countryman intimate with the earth, with the subtle characters and pro-perties of the natural plant and with all the delicate processes that converted it into dressed yarn. Mr. Chubb, following our talk with his shrewd but gentle dog-like hazel eyes, was maintaining the tradition by still growing flax and by having built a fine workmanlike rick of it. It was among the winning few.

IV

Lower Ford Farm stood under Lewesdon, one of the giants, like Pilsdon, Waddon, Windwhistle, Lambert's Castle, Coney's Castle and Golden Cap, among the great hills of West Dorset. By taking a few steps, I could see the nick against the sky in the long calm oval (a lion couchant) of Pilsden Pen, the cap of greensand to the west of Lewesdon. These great natural sculptures, Jacob Pilsdon and Esau Lewesdon, were the outposts to others of the little farms tucked under their great shoulders —Huxter's of Broadoak, Harris's of Monkwood and Bowditch's of Bowood, for instance. Pilsdon and Lewesdon are not merely conspicious; they are a necessary discipline to a liassic land-scape. For all their loveliness, its inconsequent forms lack the order and serenity of the chalk and limestone ranges.

What was a revelation to me on a day perfect as a flower was the discipline, not apprehended for thirty years before its advent, these twin stars had exerted on me. Now as in that distant past I was profoundly conscious of them. I was always looking for them from farm to farm, and for the tiny high-hedged fields, intensely green, of the Vale of Marshwood to which they are the gate-piers. In this land of family farmers, cupped by the chalk, the lias and the greensand heights, I had lived without at all realising their unconscious influence. But now I did know. It was they which had been the decisive pull preventing me from being absorbed in an urban intellectualism from which, after leaving West Dorset, I barely escaped. Just before joining Hosking in the West for the flax competition, I had been reading *The Unquiet Grave* of Palinurus, regarded in London as a minor classic. But its minor literary qualities, derived from the minor figures of modern French literature, are the instrument for expressing a self-conscious miasma of the soul, a final negation of life, a sense of doom from which there is no escape and no salvation and for which there is no remedy. But these are terms too high for the puny nihilism of this book. The thunders of the old rationalists end in pop-gun shots at Christianity behind a hedge of self-absorption. *Tout est Dégout et Misère* is the text of Palinurus. And this doom, this sterility are the logical end not only of a purely urban intellectualism but of the whole civilisation to which it is irretrievably committed. There but for the grace of God, there but for Pilsdon and Lewesdon . . .

What was wonderful for me on that day of enchantment was to see this memorial countryside virtually unchanged since I had last seen it. What an experience if we could see Weymouth Bay as Constable painted it in his picture in the National Gallery! Change, of course, there had been. But it was not written like Belshazzar's fate across the face of the land. But how immense and calamitous had been the change that has overtaken not only the rural scene elsewhere but the form and pressure of the whole age! Since my foot had last trodden the Vale of Marshwood, the world had progressed from the pre-automobile to the post-atomic era. Rudely awakened from their dreams would our Victorian forefathers be if they became aware of descendants, some of whom think and even speak of the total dissolution of society and whose despair even reaches the last question of all. Will the whole world be calcined to ashes? Not by an act of God but by the crime of man. Such men have begun to think in the mood of *King*

Lear and in terms of the early Christians and the Seventh Day Adventists, but without supernatural hopes and without any faith at all. These thoughts visited me in contemplating Pilsdon and Lewesdon. But now I understood that here in this blessed land of England, among the changeless hills and downs, in the secret vales, in the farmers who cultivated them, in the craftsmen who transformed their riches and in all men who loved them, lay the real wealth of the nation. A wealth not subject to the economics of strife, glut, artificial want and ruin, a wealth nursing human welfare and a wealth that could make men rich not in power but in the incorruptibles.

It was the rick of the last and thirteenth farm that won the first prize. Ninety acre Redlands is perched above Broadwindsor, west of Beaminster by Conegar Hill. William Barnes wrote of Beaminster—

"Sweet Be'minster that bist abound
    Wi' green an' woody hills all round."

This is true of most of the villages and small towns dibbled in among the ranges—Shipton Gorge, Symondsbury, Bradpole and Broadwindsor, where Charles II took refuge after Worcester. Most of the thatch in Broadwindsor has given way to blue slate. But the special ripple style of the thatching survives here and there above the tranquil stone of the buildings. There is a quality of refuge about Broadwindsor that even imported blue slate cannot estrange from the hills.

The rick stood boldly out on the uplands, and Mr. Marsh who with his brother owns Redlands, was ploughing the field where he himself had built and thatched it. He was ploughing in a singular manner, as though his tractor were a pair of horses. He was, that is to say, looking at the plough and the furrow all the way, not straight ahead like most tractor drivers. When we went up to congratulate him on coming out top, he complained with smiles of the bad finish a tractor always made. In driving a machine he had not ceased to be a craftsman. His rick showed the metal of his craftsmanship, the only example we had found of Hosking's "classical" style. The bottom was generously faggoted, the stem well sprung, the spars were staggered throughout, the trim straw came well over the eaves, and the "ridge-wad" was as clean and orderly as deft fingers could make it. The straw-bonds, striped with diagonal spars at eaves and ridge, were masterly. The rick had only one fault: the flax itself was a little rough, having been machine-pulled by outside labour instead of hand-pulled. All the same, it was as good a sight as Conegar Hill itself. And it put the seal on a day of ten brimming hours in this high wild garden of the West. Beethoven's Pastoral Symphony calls it back to me.

How far the revival of flax-growing and Hosking's example in the West can heal the wounds of factory farming and centralisation depends on too many incalculable factors to be reckoned. In three years' time from now (1945) the whole industry may be scrapped. The magnitude of such a disaster can only be appreciated by coming into close personal contact with a rural industry based on the land. If cheap Baltic flax, produced by slave-labour, floods the market in the near future, our flax-mills will close down. Some thousands of men and women will be doing nothing and earning nothing. Hundreds of farmers will be deprived of a useful cash-crop whose export does no harm to the land. Hosking's experiments in training craftsmen in the fields and the mills will be blacked out. And the promise of a regenerated England working and living upon the wealth of her own land will wither with them. We shall sink under a load of debt as heavy as our shame.

CHAPTER IX

ROGERS OF FROME AND STOUR

O Jay betide the dear wold mill,
  My naighbour playmeates' happy hwome,
Wi' rollen wheel, an' leapen foam
  Below the overhangen hill,
      Where, wide an' slow,
      The stream did flow,
An' flags did grow, an' lightly vlee
Below the grey-leav'd withy tree,
While clack, clack, clack, vrom hour to hour,
Wi' whirlen stwone, an' streamen flour
Did goo the mill by cloty Stour.

                          WILLIAM BARNES.

I

THERE IS only one resemblance between the letters of the
master-builder already described in Chapter III and the letters
of the master-millwright in this one. Both are masters and
delight in expressing the passion of their work. But from
that common base their respective fountains diverge. I found
it almost impossible, for instance, to classify, arrange and
co-ordinate the subjects of Frank Rogers's letters. Dr. Edmund
Esdaïle, a distinguished schoolmaster, gave me an interesting
definition of craftsmanship. He called it "manual literacy."
For Frank Rogers his manual literacy is all-in-all. His absorption in his work, the fusion of his very heart and soul with it,
make his recollections of it a by-product from it. He would
very much prefer to be doing his job with me watching him
than talking to me about it, and he would very much prefer
to be talking than writing to me about it. And he is so
immersed in it, or rather his memories of it, that they come
flowing on to the paper like one of his own mill-streams over
a weir, smooth and unruffled, with no hold-ups of punctuation
to obstruct its even course. He inserts a comma or a full stop
when he happens to think of it. That is so seldom that he

never dreams of bothering with a capital letter for the opening of the new sentence. His phonetic manner of spelling accomplishes such opulent, oriental-looking words as "rithum."

Rogers remembers neither me nor himself; he remembers only his work. I wanted him, for instance, to tell me more about himself in relation to his work. But he brushed this aside as irrelevance; he was only incidental to his work. So too occur, like blue succory in a wheat-field, odd bursts of poetic digressions. They are scattered over a text severely concerned with precise information. They concern not only his own craft of millstone-dressing but every other connected with those 27,000 country mills now vanished, derelict or museum-pieces. After I had had half a dozen letters from him, I let him have his own way, belatedly seeing that it was the best way for him to regard himself as an aside, the way of a speaker off-stage. Rare as are these casual revelations of himself, they are at times poignant and heart-moving in a sense almost impossible to describe. They are brief lightnings, yet flashes that illuminate more than himself. They show me the inward view of the master-craftsman's way of life like a sailing ship beating up against roaring seas.

His own neat and sometimes elegant diagrams, all drawn from memory, are a great help in elucidating his text. Without their aid, his profound knowledge not only of millwrighting and stone-dressing but of engineering, all self-taught, would be overwhelming. For Frank Rogers is so consummate a manual craftsman that his technicalities are often baffling.

The very rare pieces of autobiography slip out here and there from his objective memoranda, like those trickles of water he describes that find their way into the buckets of an overshot water-wheel and set it revolving when it should be at rest. His father, who lived till he was over ninety, was a cabinet-maker. As a young man, he used to help a relation of his gearing wheels and the like at a small windmill at Hemstridge in Somerset. Later he took over this mill altogether. He reconditioned it, put in new gearing throughout, together with a new overshot water-wheel, and some years later adopted the novelty of steam power. After thirty-two years as a country miller, he failed in a lawsuit against the Rural District Council which took his water for domestic supply. He lost his mill and became a jobbing carpenter and builder, but still held his own as a craftsman. He kept in touch with his lost vocation of owner-craftsman by being called in for millstone work by the millers or gentlemen farmers of the neighbourhood. Except for stray allusions passing across the page like a dimly seen master-trout across a deep pool, this was all I could gather of Rogers the father. There are only two references, one in the middle of a sentence, to the grandfather who was also a miller. He used to sing a "ditty" about the sound of the piece of mill-mechanism called "the damsel," a couplet of which ran:—

> "Yet fancy still echoes the merry clic-clack,
> When neither the mill nor its labour was slack."

The self-references are hardly less scanty. As a boy, Frank Rogers worked as a dresser at Bindon Mill, adjoining Bindon Abbey near Tess Durbeyfield's Wool in Dorset. After he had served his four years' apprenticeship here, the water-power from the Frome of this ancient mill, founded by the monks, was replaced by a roller plant for grinding wheat-meal and, of course, extracting—for greater profit—the wheat-germ. The two pairs of water-powered "Derbyshire Peak" millstones were retained only for "serving the provinder department," that is to say, grinding grist for cattle. For cattle and not men to reap the benefit of the whole grain, became the only method of saving the country water-mill and the windmill with it from falling to pieces. Rogers moved on to West Mill, Stalbridge. Mr. Moore (the miller) asked him if he could "pack the neck." Rogers said yes. "Well," said the miller, "your father could turn out a good sack of meal and the job is yours." "Speaking for myself," said Rogers, "I carried out my trust efficiently for about six years. Father was delighted I had adopted his love of the occupation and often gave me useful tips."

Here Rogers not only "packed the neck" but became conversant with every phase and branch of making and mending in milling. He often mentions West Mill with affection, especially before Mr. Moore, "well-known throughout the west country as an honourable tradesman," like the

owner of Bindon Mill, "had to concentrate on provinder or
pass out." Here too, "the trusty Burrs" (French Burr Stone,
of Norman granite, the best of all millstones) were replaced
by Derbyshire Peaks. This mill had "a splendid undershot
water-wheel by Hindley of Bourton, Dorset, dated 1893, and
is still doing a service (grinding grist) in these days of war and
ploughing up. The mill is situate rather off the beaten track
in the Blackmore Vale." The former miller, Mr. Scammell,
combined baking with milling. "The old machinery, which
had seen good service, being well in its prime in Lord Nelson's
time and the Hearts of Oak era, is gone." If the hackneyed
associations of "Hearts of Oak" be dropped from the mind,
this phrase of his, leaping out of the business-like text, reminds
the reader of Shakespeare's evocation of the remote past in
"When Noah was a sailor." It was while Rogers was at West
Mill that he used to dress the stones of King's Mill, two miles
up the Stour, "in the parish of Marnhull, Hardy's ' Marlot,'
he does not mention this mill." No, but Rogers, in the charac-
teristically off-hand manner of this bare reference, reveals
how well he knows his great fellow countryman. West Mill
went derelict, and when Rogers revisited "this delectable
spot" while on a week's holiday in later years, his old boss
(Mr. Moore) exclaimed, "What part do you come from now?"
It made him think he must be "an exile."

This is exactly what Rogers is, an exile, "eating," as
Richard II said, "the bitter bread of banishment." To be an
exile from the work and its setting in the Dorset countryside
(he now lives in the mining district of County Durham) and
from the manners and customs of the old life and pre-eminently
from its craftsmanship, from all to which his hands and his
heart belong, this is his tragedy. "I am fifty-five," he writes,
"and simply long to do more millstone dressing." He was
bewildered at the art dying out on such a scale almost within
his own lifetime. But die it did and left him an exile. His own
real life became a ruin like the life of the country mill. Rogers
is the survivor of what is virtually an extinct culture. What
haunting home-sickness there is in these halting words!—"I
have always gone into every item thoroughly. My reward
would be the thought of a job well done, and no employer
ever interfered." The millers were surprised at the smooth

and hitchless working of their mills. One of them at Berwick St. John, in Wiltshire—where Rogers had dressed the wheat-stones at his small mill—said he had never seen such meal as Rogers ground. Then in his customary fashion my correspondent breaks off from the interruption of personal reminiscence to plunge once more into the technics of millwrighting, once his "labour of love."

He is silent as to why and when he migrated up north and how he came to take up his present job. If he is conscious of its supreme irony, according to his impersonal habit he gives me no clue. With the resignation common to nearly all craftsmen, he accepts the *débacle* of craftsmanship. Only in one solitary passage and, as is common with him, in the middle of a sentence, he writes " . . . at my present employment, which I may say is punishment working as general hand . . . " In the last of his letters he told me what that punishment was. As usual, he speaks in that parenthetical way which is second nature to him on the seldom occasions when he is talking of himself. He became an unskilled routine worker in the roller mill at Bishop Auckland. The captain had been degraded to the ranks of the modern machine-minding proletariat. But not from age nor dereliction of duty nor the winter of his skill but because the revolutionary step from craftsmanship to automatism has been taken by the era in which he lives. Yet there has been a drop of compensation for its bitterness. For this roller mill to which progress has forced him to come down "is the only surviving private firm of flour-millers in this county that has not been swallowed up by the combine." "I do not intend," he says, "staying at this job, there is no soul in it." But where to-day is the opening for such a man to exercise his multiplicity of skills?

So, what was once this man's daily work and his delight became the hobby of his occasional brief holidays. Whenever he could get away from the mechanised roller mill, that, like all roller mills, takes the life out of the grain, as its machines take the life out of a man's work, he went back to the old organic life. He played at what was once his livelihood. I have already mentioned his holiday visit to his old work-home of West Mill. At another time, he spent his week's holiday with a farmer and his family where a small country mill joined the farm. The farmer told Rogers that he had been crowded out by other farmers wishing to get their grain milled (for grist). The millstones were in a bad state, but the farmer had no idea how to set about stone-dressing. Rogers told him he could help. "His pleasure knew no bounds, and to-day the old mill is going once more." These breaks from the routine jobs at the roller mill became the highlights of his life.

Another opportunity, not of working but watching, came when Rogers was serving in the Middle East during the first Great War. He was out with the Dorsets from 1914 to 1919 and used to watch "two women grinding at the mill." This was a handmill still in use. "One woman sat turning and facing an opposite still sitting, a younger person fed the grain by hand." The sound reminded him of the water-mills at home, and so off duty he went peering about and listening for it. Sometimes he got a glimpse through a half-open door, but was careful to observe the strict Mohammedan rule "not to force my presence where it wasn't wanted." He spent some weeks on Imbros and Lemnos and often visited the windmills on the Islands. "I was also invited inside a primitive water-mill at Gerisha, near Jaffa." One other chance he had seized of what nowadays would be called escapism. He wrote voluminously to me about his old craft, "a welcome break" from work which had ceased to be one. And he was delighted to learn that I was taking care of a thrift and mill-bill with which he had once dressed so many stones.

II

Rogers is almost as reticent about his workmates as he is about himself. Only in one letter do I get more than a glimpse of them, and only one of these is more than a profile. This was Billy the "workmate-craftsman," who worked at "Factory Mill, situate astride the two parishes of Fifehead Magdaline and Marnhull." Billy, who, he said, was old enough to be his grandfather, was "of a jolly disposition, never seemed ruffled come what may and with a rosy complexion. His frame was the only index to years of toil, with a gait of walking with one shoulder higher than the other, medium height, a good memory for events that had taken place during an active life in the occupation of milling. Any one looking at the splendid country type of face in that lovable character would observe tattoo-like pock-marks of blue, indicating fragments of steel. The application of the mill-bill had not only splayed the backs of his fingers but the fragments had penetrated the sides of his nose." In the old days this was "the hall-mark of a millstone dresser."

There is no consecutive account of the aged Billy because my correspondent gets lost in his lovingly elaborated description of the water-powered machinery of Factory Mill. It was sharply printed on his memory because he had paid a visit to it with his father after he had become a bankrupt from the lawsuit. The mill had been closed for many years and his father was eager to set it going again under his son's name. But while father and son were mooting this happy project, two men arrived to pull the old mill down—"I can still picture with pain seeing them engaged with cross-cut saw eating through those venerable wood shafts as big round as a man's body. This was my first introduction to scrapping of which I have seen plenty. To my boyish mind at the time it appeared nothing less than sacrilege."

At last Billy reappears but only in relation to the miller and "a certain William Parsons" who knew how to dress stones. This miller "often wore a top hat which resembled a concertina by coming into contact with the beams that carried the floors. Billy would add you weren't dressed in them days without a box hat." Parsons was "a gentleman on tramp" who called for work at the mill. These "knights of the road" often journeyed from one district to another, the millers handing over the stone-dressing to them. They would stay for a time but "the wander-lust had got into their bones" and off they went. Billy took one glance at Parsons whom he had never seen before, and, intuitively divining him to be the "splendid craftsman" he proved to be, persuaded the miller to engage him. "Although a new water-wheel had been installed, the timber beams carrying the millstones were in a very dilapidated condition—a big job—but this man mastered this and many other things . . . often working all day and night to get a job finished. Wood, iron or stone, it would be all the same to this clever craftsman." Once, when a carter accidentally snapped a shaft of his wagon, Parsons saved him from getting into trouble by working well into the night preparing a new ash replica.

Parsons and Billy seem to have kept the whole small and active rural community, revolving like a wheel round the hub of the mill, in running order. They took a pride in maintaining the old mill up to the old traditions for which she was built. Rogers never knew Parsons but "the work of an artist (leaves) a legacy of enduring properties. What more could a man require than that his memory be perpetuated through the medium of our native English oak?" There, as Charles Lamb said, is poetry enough for anything. In another book, I gave an account of Pike of Tinhead, a wheelwright, who died many years ago. But the memory of his wagons was also perpetuated in the thoughts of unlettered men who had never known him in the flesh. A mythology gathers about these great and unknown names. Through them the dignity of craftsmanship lingers on into an age to which it has become a mere antiquity.

The versatility of the old wheelwrights made them particularly serviceable to the millers of the stone-grinding water-mills. I know of a Buckinghamshire one who built van, wagon or trap from the log to the finished article. He cut the planks from the tree in the sawpit, made the wheels, turning the hub on his wheel-lathe, and did his own tyreing. He painted and lined the vehicles, writing the name on the board in gold-leaf. At the age of seventy, he used single-handed to turn a wagon upside down for repair, a task impossible to the young workers of to-day who, with their slogan of do as little as possible for as much as possible, would not do it even if they could. Wheelwrights like this one were constantly summoned by the millers to repair or renew the cog-wheels or timber-work of the mills.

After some years, Parsons left—"the wander lust claimed her own, he gave notice and never came that way again." But Billy stayed on, almost as old and tough as oak. He was never late, though he lived nearly three miles away in his thatched cottage at Marnhull. First, he hung up his rush-basket. Then he milked the cows. At eight a.m. he appeared bearing "two pots of hot tea" for the men's breakfast. Then began the earnest work of the day. It was not so exacting as to oust time for conversation and village news, "the old mill adding her contribution of chatter and orderly rithum." The mill and the community—a seamless circle, a society of organic wholeness, a complete culture in little. No wonder that, when the country mill was sabotaged by the combine, the whole organism fell to pieces.

In heavy rains the Stour flooded and the mill-work was held up, there being little fall in the stream to allow the "tail" water to get away. When the tail or back water rose to the level of the "head" water which supplied the driving power to the undershot water-wheel, "the order of things" was "baffled" and the mill became "tail bound." The power was dispersed over the fields instead of projecting itself against the water-wheel. The "tail race" reminded Rogers of a ship's wake set up by the propeller, a spectacle "of a power and a beauty that belongs to the countryside." The overshot water-wheel was less at the mercy of flood-water because it depended on the fall and so weight of the water filling the buckets from above—not the drive from below in the undershot wheel. Rogers's father, who had an overshot wheel at his mill, had several control points on different floors to raise or lower the mill-gate. These were lacking at Factory Mill. But in both mills the surplus water was controlled and released by the hatches ("clewers" in the north) or flood-gates.

When these emergencies occurred Billy was in his element. "I still remember as I write, Billy after heavy rain would throw up the casement window on the top floor (of the mill) to scan the snakish contour of the Stour. He called out with concern, ' that water be fernal high.'" According to Rogers this was the nearest he got to swearing. To Billy it was a "language unknown." When flood threatened, he would speed up the work of the mill. He operated the sack-hoist to remove the sacks from the basement, manipulated the hatches and mill-gate[1] and made everything ship-shape or rather mill-shape, bustling about as though forty years had dropped off his great age. He had been known to grind three hundred sacks of barley with hardly a pause, working day

---

[1] See later. Page 204.

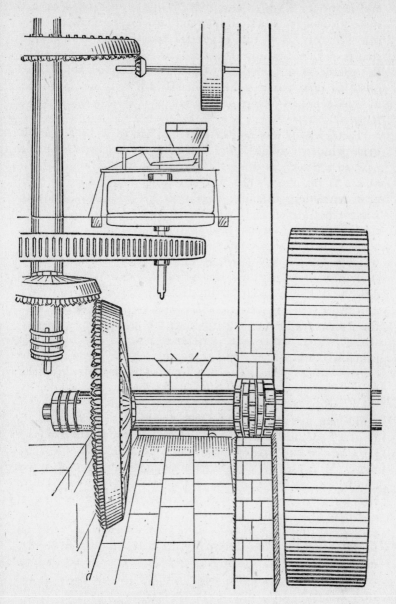

CROWN-WHEEL, SPUR-WHEEL AND PIT-WHEEL.

and night for a week. Our modern aim is to save work, not merely drudge work, but good work, individual work, difficult work, work that engages a man's whole being, work that is its own reward, work that creates, work that ennobles the character, any kind of work. Thus the recital of deeds like this one, accomplished not only by Billy but countless unknown heroes of our countryside as it once was, appears a fable.

Factory Mill was not, of course, what all mills but a few grist-grinders have become, a factory. It happened to stand next to a flax-factory which had been a manor house and is now a farm. Rogers had a vivid recollection of Factory Mill, now with thousands like it defunct. It had two undershot water-wheels, each a self-contained unit of timber construction throughout, the water-wheel shafts "veritable hearts of oak, adzed to many square angles to carry two wheels each, the water-wheel and pit-wheel, transmitting power to a vertical shaft also of timber and the heart of a tree." Rogers then describes the mechanism of this mill as it appears in diagram I. As can be seen, the vertical shaft carried three geared wheels, the lowest engaging the pit-wheel, the middle one the spur-wheel which drove the millstone pinions (more lightly pencilled), and the top one on the next floor of the mill the crown-wheel. This engaged a number of horizontal shafts by bevel gear (one of these is given) for driving the sack-hoists, the flour-dressers, the wheat-cleaners and others.

Rogers goes on to mention " the gudeon," which he describes in detail in another letter. He means, no doubt, the gudgeon pin, the pivot or axle at the end of a beam on which a wheel works. Two can be seen in the drawing beyond the pit-wheel and below the lowest of the vertical wheels, secured by three iron bands. The timber shafts thus banded were the product of "that great timber age" when "there were no foundries," except the founding of bells for parish churches by itinerant founders. Rogers must have relied here on local memory, not formal history. Castings of gear bodies, firebacks, cannon and other objects go well back into the Middle Ages, as the iron industry of the Sussex Weald clearly reveals.

He then refers to the illustrations of a wooden crown-wheel and a spur-wheel with wooden cogs in Walter Rose's *The Village*

Carpenter. In time these shafts and spur-wheels, which some-times were from eight to ten feet in diameter and contained as many as three hundred cogs each, were replaced by metal wheels. Some wheels were cast whole, others in two parts "called a split-wheel and bolted up to permit of easier erecting." But many mills retained the vertical shafts of timber, and this required that the bush of the new wheel should be a hexagon or

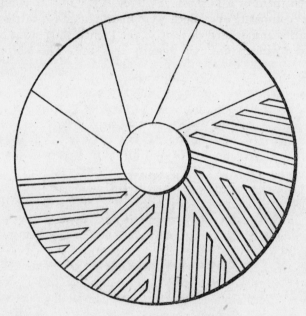

GREY PEAK RUNNER STONE.

octagon. The wooden arms or spokes of the old wheel passed into mortice holes in the shaft, squared out with the adze "centuries ago." In order to "wedge and key" the new wheels into position, these arms had to be sawn off at the required lengths to make the wheel run true, and the old millwrights were experts in such adjustment. Rogers even told me he had "often noticed a slight wobble in the shaft, although the wheel itself was running perfectly true." What a tribute to the ingenuity of the old craftsmen!

III

The mill rather than the mill worker is Rogers's paramount interest. First must come his own particular craft of hand-dressing the millstones. The diagrams II and III show the "furrows," led by the master-furrow, the longest, and "lands" between them of a Derbyshire "Grey Peak" millstone and an emery[1] composite one. Both were mainly used for cattle-grist and barley and dressed clock-wise, the French Burr stone being dressed "widdershins" or against the sun. The stationary

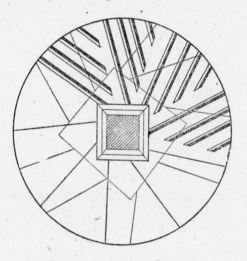

EMERY COMPOSITE STONE.

bedstone (diagram IV) rested on a timber frame called the "hursting," while the felloes of wood holding it were known as "skirting boards." The harp-shaped divisions were the same in both runner and bedstone. But, of course, the two sets of furrows in each of them worked across one another when the runner was engaged.

The French Burr, the master-stone of all, was made of "selected blocks of granite built up, neatly jointed and bonded," with three or four "balancer boxes", each holding several

[1] An emery stone can be more deeply furrowed, but darkens the meal.

pounds of lead. These balancer boxes, situated in the back of the runner, were weighted with lead "to get a good balance." Rogers remembered a boy once answering what they were for. "Where the boss keeps his savings."

Peak and Burr stones were usually four feet in diameter and "the dressing was determined by the drive of the mill," clock-wise or anti-clockwise. Rogers compared the "formation of the furrows" to "the setting of the type for a simple printing-press." The master-furrow played an important part both in the output of meal per hour and in the draught and distribution

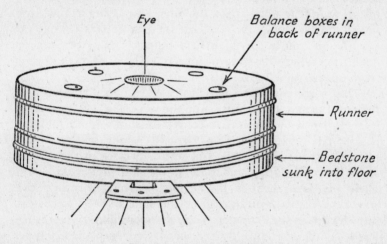

RUNNER AND BEDSTONE.

of the wheat during the grinding. The Burrs, if they were well looked after, required little attention from the dresser, unless the feed from the hopper was allowed to fail. An alarm bell used to be connected to each set of stones at work as a warning that the feed to them was running low.

For lifting the runner or top stone, weighing eighteen hundredweight, to be dressed, some mills were equipped with "gibbet and thread with screw crossbar and two arms shaped like calipers," with two pins for fitting into holes in the millstone edge. The runner was lifted bodily, swung round and turned face upwards clear of its partner, the bedstone. Other mills raised the runner by "blocks and falls" or chain blocks. But sometimes the runner was just "manhandled" out of its bedding. A broad chisel was inserted between runner and bedstone and a pair of wooden wedges with a long ash lever called a handspike fitted to their ends. A wooden platform fixed to the floor took the edge and weight of the runner when it was raised diagonally half-way. Rogers himself used often to accomplish this feat unaided. Two men were usually called in to grasp the ends of a rope passed through the central "eye" or hole in the runner. At the back of the stone a third man, the heaviest of the trio, used the lever or handspike, also secured to the eye. "At the word ready he lays on his weight to good effect, the other two lifting at the same time." "With comparative ease," the runner was thus lifted upright and pushed over upon a couple of bags of bran or chaff " to cushion the sudden impact." The dresser could thus work on the stone well off the floor.

This work was done with the steel mill-bill, drawn and tempered by the local smith, and the wooden shank turned on a lathe driven by the mill. To get the right stance, Rogers used to rest his left elbow on a small cushion of bran, half-reclined on his thigh. He first tested the face of the runner with the mill-staff, some four and a half feet in size and made of three sections of mahogany glued together and riveted to form a straight edge on the underside. It was of the same length as the diameter of the millstone and to the miller was what the straight edge is to the mason. Its plane had to be true. To prevent it after use being out of the true, it was tested by the "staff-prover." This was a straight edge of steel, kept in a case of its own and from time to time wiped over with oily sacking to prevent rust. Some mills used a joiner's plane for testing the mill-staff. But this was bad for the plane on account of the particles of stone that lodged themselves in the mill-staff. Rogers himself used pieces of glass to pare off the uneven surface of the mill-staff wood. He then painted a red or black pigment on the staff and lightly swept the slightly concave, exposed grinding face of the stone with it, so marking where the surface was worn.

First, the "lands" between the furrows, which have a glaze on them, were chiselled with sixteen clean cuts per inch. This "cracking" or "scratching" provided a sharp surface for grinding. Then the furrows, down which the pulverised wheat-grains pass to the edge or skirt of the millstone, were cleaned up and their feather edges freshened up with a broader chisel striking a harder blow. These furrows on both the runner and the stationary bedstone "produce the scissor action" in motion as "the furrows kiss in opposition." Good dressing was impossible without the co-operation of the black-smith. These "admirable craftsmen" were familiar with tempering every kind of chisel for Peak, composite or granite Burr stones, and for the granite they "must temper hard." Rogers used to aid the smith in tempering the blades and grind-ing their edges on a wet grindstone to a "diamond point." Otherwise they would "fly" or "batter."

Further tests, expounded in a wealth of data, were applied when the runner was replaced in order to detect whether its stone face was out of parallel with the bedstone. Many millers used to grind a sack or two of choice barley through the stones to carry away any grit left from the dressing. "A newly dressed stone was always a joy to me," and after the dressing they would grind well over a thousand sacks before they required re-dressing. The "high pitched hum" of the grinding-stones, more noticeable with belt transmission than when gear-driven, was "not unlike the singing of a kettle."

The dresser also had to "pack the neck." The neck was the all-important bearing or collar in the centre of the bedstone on which the runner rested by means of a spindle between the runner's eye and the bedstone's neck. If the brasses of the neck (three in number and "contacting the neck to bear the thrust and wear in driving the runner") went slack or the dust got into them, if the spindle and "jack-stick" that fits on the the neck were unproven, the millstone was likely to be thrown off its balance. The cog-wheels of the horizontal and vertical wheels (see diagram I) were engaged at a slow and regulated pace. By means of the water-wheel, a quill swept in full circle over the grinding surface of the bedstone, showing at once whether the spindle was out of plumb by failing to sweep all parts of the surface. Instead of brasses, blocks of lignum, oak, ash, beech, box, hornbeam or apple tree were often used. "Wood is splendid, something alive, eliminating wear it retains the lubricant and is not so apt to fret and heat."

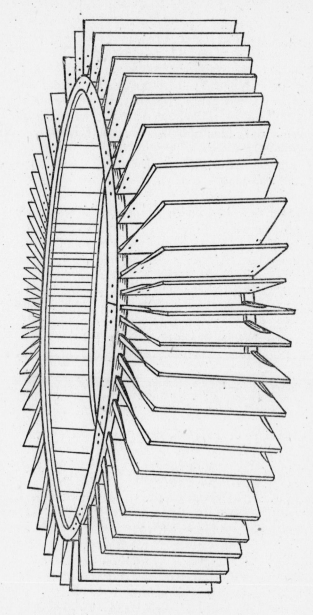

UNDERSHOT WATER-WHEEL (Primitive Type).

The purpose of the neck was to take the thrust of the drive either by belt transmission or gearing. Lubrication, therefore, was essential. In the old days, tallow candles mixed with cotton-waste or sack-string teased into tow were the lubricant, with mutton or other animal fat as a substitute. "The delicious smell of sweet tallow," wafted abroad when the flying belt or massive geared wheels had warmed up the neck, used to attract the "mill pets," and cat and rats forgot their ancestral enmity to enjoy its savour.

Clamped to the eye of the runner-stone is a "stirrup," a steel spindle whose three fingers engaged a hinged shoe. This was part of the millstone harness for feeding the corn, or rather by which the stones themselves did the feeding by conveying a "reciprocating movement" to the shoe. This fitting was called a "damsel." When hand-forged by the local smith, it added a "merry ring" of its own to the singing of the stones. At Gant's Mill, Bruton, there were three of these damsels to three pairs of stones, Burrs and Peaks. "Outside the mill, abounding with bird life, I picked out a very strange incident. As a boy I had often noticed the starling imitating the clink, clink of the mason's trowel, and also in the vicinity of the blacksmith's shop listened to his version of the ring of the anvil. However, this bird happened to be a chaffinch actually recording the song of the damsel. The sound or beat is not unlike a pony that has broken into a canter on the hard surface of the road." Doubtless William Barnes had the same note in his ears when he wrote:—

"While clack, clack, clack vrom hour to hour,
Wi' whirlen stowne an' streamen flour
Did goo the mill by cloty Stour."

Thus the music set up by the engineering subtleties of balance and stress, friction and transmission in the mill, were related in the mind and memory of this Dorset countryman with the organic voices of nature.[1]

[1] A dispossessed miller I know, Horton of the Chinnor Windmill, who has a fund of nautical terms for the sails of his mill, described the song of his damsel as "Take it Bob, take it Bob, better than tea." He now carts bricks in a lorry.

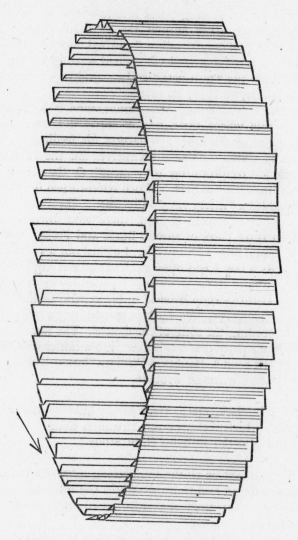

UNDERSHOT WATER-WHEEL (Improved Type).

IV

Rogers is right in claiming that the old millwrights were the true pioneers of engineering. The remarkable thing is that he himself, a village craftsman concerned with stones not engines, should have at his fingers' ends and after long years of absence the ingenious mechanism of the old water-mills. Every country craftsman of the old school was, of course, intimate with his own job. But he also had a more than nodding acquaintance with every other rural industry nearly or remotely related to it in the interwoven fabric of the local community. I often had to wrestle with Rogers' meaning. He grasped the subtleties of that mechanism, as distinguished from the vast intricacy of modern machinery, too well for me always to follow them through the curious windings, the over-eager rush of particularities and the disdain of connecting links, transitions and punctuation which mark his epistolary style.

Leaving stone-dressing, he takes up the problems of the water-wheel and gives a lengthy description of the figures in diagram I. He analyses the niceties of the "brick barrel arch" through which the oaken shaft passed from the water-wheel to the pit-wheel, of the "gudeon" (gudgeon) at the bonded ends both of the vertical and horizontal shafts, of the "foot-step" bearing on its tripod in the masonry, taking the weight of the vertical shaft with its three cogged wheels and of the "bridge-tree" to which the "footstep" was bolted. To the fittings and contrivances given in diagram I he adds variations in different mills he had known, with exact illustrations of how they were operated. The richness of his actual knowledge is astounding, the spurts of poetic feeling that emanate from it full of unexpected charm. But the communication of that knowledge is often bewildering.

The undershot water-wheel appears to be the more ancient of the two types, with their intermediate forms like the breast-shot and the mid-shot. In diagrams V and VI, Rogers presents a more primitive one and an improved one which he calls "a power unit that came near to perfection." "It speaks volumes as to the perfection our ancestors attained before the end of the great timber age." The wooden rims of the first type were built up by felloes (the wheelwright's word, felloes, suggests that the earlier water-wheel may have been an adaptation, with the addition of the paddles or "floats", of the wagon wheel) to which the oak arms (not shown) were tenoned and morticed. The arms themselves were bolted to socketed metal collars to prevent any weakness in the joints when the wet wheel was at rest, and the floats were secured by wooden

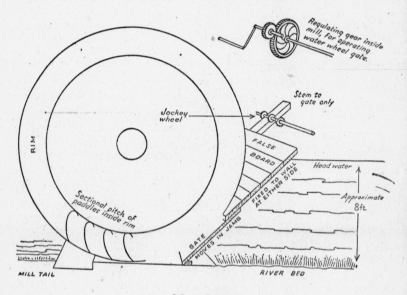

MILL-GATE.

struts with oak pegs at each end of them. The floats themselves were sawn out of elm boards. Rogers recalled a " water barn" at Burton, near Bindon Mill, where he had worked, in which an early type of threshing machine was driven by an undershot wheel.

The improved version of undershot wheel (diagram VI) inclined the floats at a tangent to ease the strain when they struck the water. When the rivers silted up and became weed-clogged and overgrown with riparian bushes and trees during the long agricultural depression, the right-angled floats were

impeded and lost power. The tangential readjustment enabled
them to slip out of the tail water with less labouring. A further
improvement came from adding a half-back to the floats
which, on impact with the volume of rushing water, saved
power by getting a better grip of it.

Nearly all the water-wheels were once equipped with a
vertical hatch or gate to control the water-power. According
to Rogers, the invention of the inclined gate was due to the
eighteenth century firm of water-milling engineers, Maggs
and Hindley, of Bourton Foundry, Dorset, who adapted it for
" their splendid water-wheels of iron." A sketch of this gate
ᵢₛ given in diagram VII. It omits the spokes and cross-stay,
that strengthened the wheel "as an added protection against
side-thrust," on the same principle as the driving wheels of the
steam traction engine. The "false board" in the diagram was,
of course, fixed, while the lower jamb was movable and
could slide open inside the base of the fixed board some six
or seven inches. The timber was in some mills replaced by
steel girders and gates, easier to move. The gate was operated
by the miller within the mill by means of larger and smaller
cogged hand-wheels. One of these is given in the sketch with a
crank, a shaft and a pair of engaged cogg-wheels. The pinion
was engaged to the "rack-wheel," whose spindle and rollers
were for preventing "the gate stem from springing out of
gear when the handle is turned inside the mill." Rogers'
father, as I have mentioned, used several of these controls on
different floors of his mill for the mill-gate to his overshot
wheel.

The height of the water was regulated by the weir, the
surplus running over its sill. It was also a means of diverting
a stream to the mill which had to stand by the road. In rainy
weather, the flood-hatches were lifted when the water level
rose. When Billy noticed how "fernal high" the water was
rising at Factory Mill, it was these flood-hatches he had to
attend to, together with sliding up the mill-gate to maintain
the speed of the water-wheel. But when the head water
continued to rise, the mill had to close down and the flood-
hatches to be drawn to their fullest extent to let the flood pass.

In another letter, Rogers compares the undershot with
the overshot water-wheel, a sketch of which is given in

diagram VIII. Its advantage over the undershot wheel seems to me to be conclusive. For this simple reason that, depending on the weight of the water from above to fill the buckets instead of the drive of the water from below to propel the floats of the undershot wheel, it was more independent of a good head of water. In fact, the overshot wheel, as Rogers himself says, needed to utilise only a quarter of the water demanded of the undershot wheel. He maintains

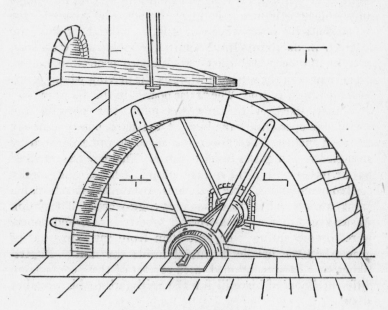

OVERSHOT WATER-WHEEL.

that it was just as efficient as the modern water-turbine, whose only superiority in performance is that it cuts out the maintenance of heavy gears. The buckets were supplied by means of a wooden trough at the wheel-top. After three or four buckets were filled, "you sense a prodigious amount of power as the wheel begins to run and the buckets start discharging," turning upside down at the opposite side and spilling the water before they reached the base of the wheel.

There were, however, three disadvantages to the overshot wheel, two authentic, the other completely irrational. Though it required less volume of water, it depended upon a greater fall than the undershot. A characteristic of the overshot wheel, again, was "a tendency to a sudden burst of speed with any slight decrease of the load." The miller had at once to adjust the mill-gate to correct this irregularity. The third disability is a comic example of human credulity handicapping this glorious human contrivance for utilising natural power. When the water had been shut off at the close of the day's work, a trickle from a slight leak would sometimes fill a few of the buckets and away went the wheel, setting the millstones in revolution. Rogers' ingenious father used to counter this tricksiness of his overshot wheel by cutting a slot across the trough that fed the buckets and fitting a narrow lid to it. Opened at the day's end, it let the trickle run harmlessly down the back of the wheel. But elsewhere, this mysterious self-momentum in the night gave the mills with overshot wheels "a very bad reputation." "Belated passers-by or a loitering courting couple would hear the mill start up in darkness and decide that it was haunted." Billy with a dry smile used to say, "it must have been the old chap."

In the numerous mills that Shakespeare knew on the banks of Avon and its side-streams, the overshot wheel was built entirely of timber. In the metal wheels it appeared in the wood-linings in the shafts to carry the geared wheels and in the oaken axle with a gudgeon. Rogers was enthusiastic about the "breast-shot wheel" he sketched from the Evercreech Mill in Somerset. Here the buckets ran flush with a curved chute of stone at the circumference of the wheel. This stone breast-work encircling the side of the wheel was hewn out of the natural rock of Evercreech. This economised the water-power by preventing any of it escaping. Conserving the water usually spilt by the buckets on the down grade, enabled the mill to be run even when water was very low. At the mill of Croft Spa, the wheel was mid-shot instead of over-shot, the water entering the buckets at the height of the axle.

From this fascinating world of man's apt control of natural forces[1] in co-operation with not "conquest" of nature, Rogers

---

[1] The windmill is a striking example. The sails were adjusted to the wind by slats operated like those of Venetian blinds. By this device, a stalked post-mill could harness all but the roughest of gales.

passes on to some general reflections upon the main purpose
of the water-mill—to make bread whole and out of corn fresh
from the home-fields. "You are," he says, "one of the few
who realise all that is wrong in the mass production by a
combine of an essential of life." Though "this combine has
starved and bought out thousands of individual millers, the
question still remains, what but the rural mill can handle the
local-grown cereals with such efficiency?" The modern roller
plant has nothing whatever to do with either local or national
needs. Its steel rollers and steel conveyors and elevators make
a "two-mile course of process" simply to extract the wheat-
germ and its vitamins B1, B2 and E, together with a reduction
almost to vanishing point of the natural calcium, phosphorus
and iron in the berry.

Our native wheat, Rogers goes on, "is always derided by
the machine-minded, mass-producing so-called millers." To
grind it on millstones would be "to revert back once more to
Mother Earth." By this method misuse is impossible. No
machine yet invented "can match a pair of French Burr millstones for output per hour." The roller plant by a series of
specialised machines reduces the wheat and then the coarse
semolina to starch, besides separating the germ by "plan-sifters,
centrifugal flour dressers, etc. English wheat cannot stand
up to such treatment and still retain baking qualities." It
is despised simply because the roller mill depends upon foreign
hard wheats. If a vote had been taken among the old stone-
millers as to which was the better, English or foreign wheats,
it would have been unanimous against the foreign wheat.

Rogers had noticed a newspaper paragraph about a man
who had died while his teeth were being extracted. Had I
observed the accounts in the press of human skeletons being
found in excavations for laying water-mains and the like?
The jaws were always filled with perfect sets of teeth. Why?
Because the owners ate bread that had not been stripped "of
all the essential bone-forming properties." It came from
wheat that grew in the very fields beneath which they were
buried and was milled on millstones whose murmurs they
had heard when alive. This stone-dresser from boyhood, who
had picked up all the engineering principles of the defunct
country mills only to become "a sort of general labourer to

the industrial machine" in a roller mill, testifies with authority
on the differences between them.

The roller mill has been one of the most approved testi-
monials of progress. The truth is that it was invented for
the sole purpose of being geared to a thoroughly vicious
system of acquisitive economics. Result—the loss of the bread
that was life, of a rural community that was stable and fruitful
and of a craftsmanship that enriched the character of the
mill-worker. To Frank Rogers, an exile from it for many
years, the mill by the stream became so intimately the bread
of life that after all those years he can resurrect every detail
of the old mill-culture and in a language to which he is a
stranger convey it to me.

There is a sequel to this story. Rogers is now happily
back in a water-mill which grinds whole-wheat flour from the
local corn. There are fewer than half a dozen of these left
in England. One is the Dean's Water-Mill at Lindfield in
Sussex. I happened to know the owner and Rogers is now at
work there. The wheel has come full circle. " We, the mill
and I, soon became acquainted." No words could better
describe the personal relation between a craftsman and his
workshop. The water-wheel at Lindfield is mid-shot, and the
water enters the buckets at the level of the axle by means of a
fall of four feet, a dam to lower it a further three feet and a
brick breastwork below the mill-gate to enclose the drive-water.
Before long Rogers was writing to tell me all about it, and
the wheatstones he had been dressing in his " capicity as
miller." By what seemed a miracle the past had become the
present.

V

In more than one sense the water-mill is a parable of
country England. Once more than 20,000 of them were throb-
bing and pulsating on all the streams, tributaries and rivers
of England. Within the lifetime of the older among living
Englishmen nine out of ten of these solid and keep-like
structures have vanished or are derelict hulks or have been so

transformed as to be unrecognisable as mills or carry on a
maimed and precarious life as crushers of cattle-fodder.
Constable's "Dedham Mill," though painted in the last century,
belongs as much to a past age as an interior by Hogarth. Thus
has the landscape of England changed and wide areas of it have
been obliterated or degraded so that the older among living
Englishmen can no longer recognise them. In thousands of
parishes the corn passed from the fields through the millstones
to the communal bakehouse or the cottage oven, all next door
to one another. So, when the water-mills went derelict, the
parish community was dislocated and the economy of centuries
disrupted. It was as though the linch-pin had been removed
from the wheel of rural self-maintenance. So, when the
water-mills went derelict, the various trades connected with it,
wheelwrighting, carpentering, smithying, sack-making, millstone-dressing, millwrighting, turnery and other skilled
occupations were either crippled or knocked out. The paralysis
of the country mill was like the fall of the mainmast on a ship
which drags down with it a network of stays, cordage and sails.

As the water-mills fell to pieces, the whole system of
regulating the flow of the water-ways on which they stood,
of controlling the water-power and of keeping the banks
clear of weeds and the bed from silting up fell into disuse. The
inland waters with their harness removed ceased to be clean,
fresh and orderly. Again, in none of its manifold uses did
English timber show to greater pride and advantage than in
the water-mills. Some of them were built of weather-boarding,
especially in the eastern counties. But those built of stone
contained on their wooden floors a mass of intricate timbering
of whose multitude of uses Rogers gives some indication. Some
of the great shafts were very ancient: a quantity of the
timbering at Beaulieu Mill in the New Forest, for instance,
is mediæval, and, being still in use, as serviceable as ever. The
nearest analogy to the timber adjustments of the water-mill
are the strains and balances of the cathedral. The same problems
of stress and counter-stress, of poise and counter-poise were
studied and triumphantly solved by the millers of the one and
the builders of the other.

Thus the price paid for cheap white bread, deprived of its
nutrients, has been a heavy one. It goes beyond the poverty

imposed upon what Shakespeare called "our sustaining corn."
For it includes the losses in a multiplicity of rural employments, in local self-help, in the mutual interaction between
field and home in a variety of skills, in the preservation of
the water-ways and in the careful utilisation of our native
hardwoods. Nor can it be maintained that the water-mills
were cumbrous and primitive contrivances legitimately ousted
by a more advanced and economical efficiency. It is doubtful
whether a more delicately balanced and supremely workmanlike instrument for human service has ever been invented. The
functional fitness of part to part, the distribution of power,
the pressure and the motion, all had to be harmoniously
correlated so that the flour might be pulverised to every particle.
The power itself was bestowed by nature gratis and the costs
of transport were infinitesimal. When the staff of life was
broken and given a lick of white paint, it was heavily subsi-
dised; the whole-wheat or wheat-and-rye loaf cost only a little
more than the price of growing and grinding the grain. The
people have eaten white bread for three generations, not by
their own free choice but because no other was on the market,
not because it was cheap but a source of high profits to a
combine.

If enlightenment were ever to reach the high places of
authority, the water-mill would be at once reconditioned and
re-opened. The only honest argument against it is the lack of
skilled craftsmen to operate and keep it in repair. Twice in
the forties of this century successive Governments have been
forced against their will to restore to bread a portion of its
nutritional qualities. Such is the unacknowledged confession
that the water-mill which preserves all those qualities and plays
no tricks with the grain at all is the goal to be aimed at. But
it needs a wiser civilisation than ours, a civilisation that puts
value first and profits second, to come to this logical conclusion.
All that can be done to-day is to dissipate mental confusion
and illusion. The water-mill is not, that is to say, an obsolete
institution which the march of progress has by the nature
of things left behind. If or rather when the food shortage
becomes in the future even more serious than it is already, it
is the means to halving the number of loaves that need to be
consumed and more than doubling the nourishing power of

the bread that is eaten to-day. If the whole-grain loaf became the standard one, we should only need one-eighth of our arable to provide every person in England with four lbs. of bread a week. Through the water-mill, the bridge between field and home, England can take root again in her own earth; through the water-mill, the bread that was once a symbol of communion between the divine and the human will be a mockery no more.

CHAPTER X

(1) *John Parker of Tickenhill*
(2) *John Birch of Bewdley*

"In the modern period the aim has been a worldly one, perhaps most simply described as the single word 'prosperity.' The result of giving priority to that aim is that we seek beyond everything else a kind of mechanical perfection, the chief object of which is a reduction of the immediate financial cost of production. We call it 'efficiency.' Efficiency may be a good servant but it is a terrible master. It is a purely economic conception and as such has become our master. So it comes about that we feel compelled to go on producing more and more cheaply, for whoever is most efficient can undersell him who is less so. We are forced to go on striving to reduce costs, and to do so, so to speak, at all costs, even at the cost of the quality of the product, the independence of the producer, and the fertility of the soil which makes production possible . . . We must acquire a new sense of purpose . . . It is safe to say that one of the signs of its appearance will be a revolt from the mechanistic view of the world and from the related conception of man and his fellow creatures being primarily cogs in an economic machine."

LORD NORTHBOURNE.

I

John Parker of Tickenhill

THE WORKSHOP and plot of ground of John Birch, the besom-maker, stand on the side of the road which was the main street of mediæval Bewdley. It runs steeply down to the "new" or Georgian town parallel and at right angles to the Severn. From the high stack of birch-bundles beside the workshop the eye ranges the horizon of the Clents and stops at Wychbury Camp, which in its turn looks across the Worcestershire plain to the Bewdley heights. They are flanked by the Wyre Forest, the source of the birch-bundles. The foreground is Bewdley itself. Its warm brick-reds and cream or buff plaster make as perfect a composition of unpremeditated planning as Leland saw on the further "ripe" of Severn: the town

> "sett on the side of a hill, so comely that a man cannot wish to see a towne better . . . att the rising of the sunne the whole towne glittereth, being all of newe building as it were of gold."

Here was, as Camden said a little later of English building, "the great bravery of building which marvellously beautified the realm." The plaster facings that once glittered have now been subdued to the tones of time and the softenings of nature but only by a maturer turn of beauty's countenance. Bewdley as Bewdley was and is has but changed from one comeliness to another. As such the time-weathered borough seems "half as old as time." But the craftsmanship that made it should not be subject to time at all.

Leland saw Bewdley from exactly the opposite direction that I saw it, both from Tickenhill Palace, where Prince Arthur was betrothed to Catherine of Aragon, and from the little plot where stood the birch-bundles and the workshop. I looked down on the town from a height; he looked up at the town from the Severn level. The effect is the same from above as from below, although the observers view entirely different townscapes from their relative angles of vision. The effect is the same whether you look up from Telford's seemly parapeted waterside and bridge to the town and the wooded heights that cradle it, or from the heights at the edge of the town to the bridge, the river that reflects the waterside houses and the village of Wribbenhall beyond them. The same because of the perfect unity of the total scene from any quarter. It is a complex unity, each related section of it telling a different story and conveying a different meaning. The town wedged in between the once great Forest and the still great River expressed home and travel in one. The flow of the town down to or up from the river was taken up by the river itself, whose boats plied up and down between Bewdley and the port of Bristol and its wide world of merchandise. The woody heights above the tilted town, with their oaks clasping the clay, were the making of it and determined where it should lie —near them for its brick and timber, near the river to take the surplus of its industries derived from those heights. The eye could see every portion of this composite whole. But it saw the differences of town, height and river as a pictorial whole, as they once were an interdependent one by human industry. Beauty and utility had been one, though now only the beauty is left, and craftsmanship is beauty and utility in one.

Beyond the water-front is a very different scene, a shack-town like a vast dumping-ground of refuse. Here people live or camp who have no other homes; here is disorder to deny Bewdley's order. No witness of the extinction of craftsmanship in our own age could speak more loudly than this wilderness. The same lack of any real purpose or meaning appears in the factories along the banks of the Severn between Bewdley and the Black Country, duplications of existing ones in the latter before the war. Now they say there is not enough work for them to reach their pre-war production, which was half that of the war. Yet the cry is for still more factories by Severn side, and in the irrelevance of the Tewkesbury Trading Estate the ambition is gratified. What for? Simply to go on producing for production's sake, in the void, on the Beveridge principle of digging holes and filling them up again. So in a fever of pointless activity the age drifts on towards the end of its *cul-de-sac*.

All the market-towns that survive in England were the direct and explicit creation of their local craftsmen. They worked to no architectural plan-sheet nor scaled drawings but according to an inborn pattern and rhythm of faculty they shared with nature but adapted to human needs. Of no pre-industrial township is this truer than of Bewdley, once a hive of crafts. Many of the names of these old tradesmen have come down to us—builders of the "trowes" that traded with the port of Bristol, coracle-makers, cordwainers, whit-tawers, rope-makers, tanners, chandlers, horn-workers, cap-makers and others. The continuity between past and present was "felt along the heart" as I looked down on the riverine town from Birch's workshop. The Wyre Forest has been the fountain of being for them both—birch and scrub oak have been Birch's "plant" for over half a century. The tanneries

(Bewdley once had fourteen), the boats, the forges and the pewter foundry with its charcoal fuel, the potteries, the timber-framing of the houses, the very names of streets and inns like Bark Street and the Wood Colliers Arms, owed themselves to the trees, the bark and the clay-pits of the Forest. The brick-works, dismantled between the two Great Wars, continued to make the mellow-warm roseate bricks that were the stuff of eighteenth century Bewdley. Snuff, made in the town up to forty years ago, was ground in a mill that made use of the local water-power. From Birch I bought a handle-less oak scuttle[1] which is a miniature in shape of the obsolete Bewdley coracles and was made in precisely the same way of woven oak-laths. But the rim[2] is hazel instead of oak simply because, as Birch bitterly complained, the tree-felling since the War has desolated large areas of the Forest. Thus town and workshop, twenty generations of vanished craftsmen and the living John Birch are seen to be in a biological relationship with their natural and local environment. As Severn and Wyre were to Bewdley, so in Shakespeare's time Arden and Avon were to Stratford. This alone explains why so many local crafts were mentioned by Shakespeare. He, too, was in a biological relationship with his home and country town.·

Above both town and workshop stands the old Palace of Tickenhill, founded by the Mortimers, under the hairy crown of the Wyre Forest, the eye as it were of the whole Severn scene. So it looks and so it was, for Tickenhill was the local government not only of Bewdley but the Welsh Marches. Leland gives a right picture of it—" A fayre Mannour, stonding in a goodly Parke well wooded, on the very knappe of an hill that the Towne stondith on." It is now owned by Mr. J. F. S. Parker, a business man from Birmingham. He is an enthusiast for the old life of Bewdley and his wife its local historian. Nearly the whole of the upper floor of this noble and rambling manor houses an unprecedented collection of bygones. Parts of the outbuildings have been fitted up in complete replicas of a wheelwright's and a tinsmith's shops, with further rooms containing quantities of what from a fire-engine to a roller mangle contemporary Bewdley has discarded.

[1] Swill, skip or shale-bucket in Cumberland.   [2] Bool in Cumberland.

The vast folk-museum of the top floor would take a month of examining before the wealth and multitude of its exhibits could be duly appreciated. It was the oddest and most bewildering heap of treasures I had ever seen. Far more abundant than the very fine collection of Warwickshire husbandry and craftsmanship in the outbuildings and barns of Mary Arden's yeoman farmstead at Wilmcote, it is nothing like so well arranged. It is an immense gallimaufry of indiscriminate rarities, and so did not bring Tickenhill to life as Mary Arden's farm is brought and Shakespeare's country ancestry with it. Mr. Parker showed me with special pride a convenience for drinking-parties, a pair of eighteenth century pewter chamber-pots, that were hidden, as the two-bottle bloods emptied their glasses, behind the curtains in an anteroom. The first type-writer of 1873, the first biscuit tin, the first bag of golf clubs, the first penny-farthing bicycle, all were there, together with every kind and manner of agricultural and craft implement, from the horn-maker's wherewithal to the pewterer's lathe. Here was the attic-grave of old Bewdley's manifold industry; here the cemetery of Worcestershire husbandry.

This burning apostle of over seventy has formed a protective Civic Society for the neighbourhood. In the great hall, so spacious that the musical box he was showing me could not have been heard at the other end of it, he expounded to me his dream of drawing a charmed circle round Bewdley. Birmingham and all its age and works would be excluded from it and the old town re-enriched with all of its former crafts and "misteries," with craftsmen and their apprentices to ply them. As a luxury group of trades? Yes, what of it?—there would always be buyers for good workmanship. And was the agriculture of the region to be restored with them to its former husbandry, since most of these trades rested upon it? This had not occurred to him but in no wise daunted him.

I looked at him, at that time a stranger to me, with mixed admiration, wonder and perplexity. Was he in a sense the conscience of his age, the better minority of it, but, because he was still of his age, the director of a Birmingham iron-works, sharing in the essentially unrealistic character of his age? Or did he represent the divided mind of his age, its "schizophrenia", with one voice uttering the shibboleths of industrialism but

with the still small voice repudiating it? Was he a great
pioneer who had reached the other side of industrialism and
was bent upon using his wealth to build up an "island of
example" of a better society? Or was this visionary scheme of
his a kind of insurance policy against the acquisitive society
from which he came? Did he want to make Bewdley a larger
edition of his folk-museum upstairs or to save it from the
imminent wreck of modern civilisation? Or, moved by
insight rather than sentiment, was he seeking to set in motion
a genuine experiment with the certainty of that collapse in
his mind? And how and where would he find his men to
become the new-old craftsmen of Bewdley? There was pathos
in him as well as resolution and largeness of conception. But
to these questions I found no answer.

Yet, when I came to know him better, I thought less and
less of him as the last of the English eccentrics, of that enliven-
ing breed that runs like a scarlet thread through the fabric
of English history from Tom Coryate of Odcombe, Andrew
Boorde of Cuckfield and Taylor the Water-Poet to Charles
Waterton and Beckford of Fonthill. I thought more and more
of him as the man of practical vision, tending a small flame
that threw fantastic shadows over the forms of our twentieth
century illusions but splitting the darkness in which we live.
These tenebrous forms are the fantasy; his design for Bewdley
is the plainest common sense which the monstrosity of modern
thought distorts from its proper likeness.

Prolific as he is in ideas, this man does not sit brooding over
them in the great hall of Tickenhill. One of them is to form
a Guild of Handicrafts whose business will be to recondition
the derelict water-mill and to revive the defunct horn industry
to make a homely start on horn cups, combs, buttons and the
like from the data he has gathered through his collection. If
such a Guild could set the stone-grinding mill in action once
more and act as an intermediary between whole-milled flour
and the local bakery, such service would be practical enough
among citizens who, like their fellows in all towns, eat bread
deprived of nutritional defence against the epidemics of the
European chaos. He is a power, too, on the local Council.
By his circulation of the articles on Bewdley that appeared
in 1945 issues of *Country Life*, he has bestirred the Council

to sanction buildings only in conformity with the traditional type. He has persuaded it of the need for proper roof tiling and to resist the shack suburb which has spawned on Severn side. Even the Council houses it intends to build would be an improvement on this degredation. The competition, "Bewdley as I would like it," promoted by his Civic Society, awakened dormant feeling in the neighbourhood against the lack of design, variety and sense of site in the Council house.

John Parker has many other projects for Bewdley in mind or in action. He is the first to acknowledge them to be nothing more than the scratching of a soil that needs double-digging to get the sourness and inertia out of it. But he has three promising allies on his side for the deeper operations. One is his indomitable self and the sacrifices he is prepared to make for a regional and so regenerated England. The second is the general feeling of the townsfolk, who, unlike those of Tewkesbury who have sold their birthright for an industrial mess, have a healthy suspicion of the Black Country mentality at their doors. The third is the largest issue of all. A self-supporting regional England is the sole salvation of our days. This truism is, of course, anathema to the powers.

Thus John Parker is trying to give an answer to the supreme question—what is the good life? John Birch in his workshop between Tickenhill Manor and Bewdley Town never bothers about his answer. A timeless tradition has given it him.

II

John Birch of Bewdley

Bearded John Birch is eighty-nine and looks like a mid-Victorian engraving of a shepherd in the family Bible. In his cottage he showed me a photograph of himself and his wife bundling birch-twigs: she died just before the fiftieth anniversary of their wedding. Two flitches of bacon hung beside it. The pig was on the same premises as the homestead, the copper boiler or "bosch" for steaming the oak-laths, the birch stack, the garden and the whitewashed brick "hovel," with its three stools on which his son and his two workers were pealing the oak-laths for binding the besoms. The antiquity of the two old men on their stools beside his son, portraits that Rembrandt would have delighted to paint, seemed a symbol of a craft whose roots are in prehistory. The integration was complete: agriculture was correlated with industry, home with business, the raw material with the finished products (Birch also makes whisks of green stripped birch-twigs for taking the fluff out of the Kidderminster carpets), family inheritance with employment: all were interwoven parts of a single whole. The total scene was an object-lesson in "ecological" unity.

Old man Birch himself, moving from cottage to workshop and illustrating the varied processes of his trade, now the woodman, now the manager, then the worker, was the node and so the master of the whole structure. He was a living witness to "the independence of the producer." His ownership of that tiny but crowded plot of ground was his guarantee of an economic freedom that released him from the bondage of human life to the "economic motive." His tranquillity embodied the dignity of the human person and rested confidently upon the continuity of a tradition embedded both in the soil and in the deeps of time. To call the two old men his employees conveys a wrong impression; they shared in the family relationship of this home-trade and as such were remote from the "operatives" or labour-units of a machine economy. Like Birch and his son, they were familiars of every note in the scale of production from the felling of the oak saplings in the Forest to the final binding of the besoms. The contentment stamped on their motions and features was due, not to the opiate of custom and conservatism but to the absence of those psychological strains set up by the sub-divisions of mechanical labour. It was obvious that this family business was an organism in itself, rooted in the organic life of nature and transforming the wood from one shape and utility to another without breaking away from nature.

Work executed as a complete chord and not, as in a modern factory, as a single note repeated again and again, is a very important element of craftsmanship. It means much more than security from monotonous toil because the series of orderly variations in a craft, from the origin in the natural material to the end-product used by human society, establishes a rhythm. Such rhythm is the key to a way of life, and a way of life answers the question that man has always asked—How is life to be lived?

This phrase-making, as distinguished from the reiteration in factory-work of one word in the phrase, was not confined to woodmanship but was once a characteristic of craftsmanship in general. An artillery Colonel sent me the following account of a weaver named Ross, still at work at Rogart, Sutherland. The whole of the processing from the raw wool to the finished tweed is performed by himself, his wife and a water-wheel, and so he has lived and worked for twenty-two years. There is nobody, of course, to catch up his honest trade when he is gone.

His patterns and blends of colour are all of the very best, and he has consistently refused to instal a power-driven loom for his own hand-loom on the ground that "you cannot get the quality with power-driven machinery." When the Colonel asked him about the future, he replied, "I wish I might be sure of another twenty years' weaving." "He complained that all the young men had few thoughts except to get a job on the hill or on the river. I pointed out that stalking, keepering and gillieing were skilled and lovely country jobs. He replied, 'Yes, they are, but such work creates nothing beautiful.'" He told the Colonel that he enjoyed every minute of his work; no matter how laborious it was, he "whistled with his shuttles." When the Colonel wrote to me, Ross had recently woven twenty-three yards of tweed in a single day. It was by no means an eight-hour day. The immensely complicated, contentious and virtually insoluble problems of modern labour do not exist for such men as Ross. They have only one problem: can they keep themselves and their crafts alive? To all but a fraction the answer of their age is no. It likes economic but not craft masters.

Like Ross the three men working on their stools in Birch's workshop were masters. Their knowledge of the properties and humours of timber conferred upon them one kind of mastery; their control of the design and technique of manipulating wood to serve a specific purpose gave them another kind and their interest and absorption and pleasure in their work yet a third. In translating an oaken rod, fresh steamed from the copper that smelled like toffee, into thin pliable strips like leather, they only used a pair of tools, a cleaving knife for nicking the top of the rod and a paring knife for removing splinters, knots and bosses from the sappy surface of the split lath. All the rest of the work was done not so much by the hand as the fingers.

The best instance of craftsmanship without tools of any kind I know comes from Stourbridge, where the Stour joins the Severn a few miles up the river from Bewdley. Here an old man named Squire makes the clay pots for the glass furnaces. These are domed and topped, measuring four feet in diameter and three and a half feet high. Squire shapes these pots by exactly the same technique as was used by the wheel-less potters of prehistory. They are built up layer by layer as in dry-stone walling, but smoothed off to a perfect finish. They are not fired at all but simply dried off, and yet are so resistant that a heavy man can stand on the roof of one of them without even cracking it. Another extraordinary thing about Squire the Potter is that he has an apprentice, his own son who works with him. He is the fifth generation in the direct succession since 1780. Our reaction to a tool-less craftsman like Squire and almost tool-less craftsmen like Birch's three workers is that their work is primitive and so rudimentary. We forget that they use a finer tool than man has ever invented or can invent—the human hand.

This finger-work in Birch's workshop looked easy, as craftsmanship always does look until you take a hand in what appears a mere dexterity. Actually it is much more. Such ease proceeds from command over the nature of living growth. Years of apprenticeship and practice cannot altogether accomplish it without an intuitive grasp of how nature works, born both of inheritance from father to son and a kind of internal rhythm in the worker himself. When these conditions exist, a "mechanistic view of the world" is a contradiction in terms. And it is clear that the variety in unity of Birch's home-workshop is a miniature of the more elaborate variety in unity of the town of Bewdley. We can have no doubt of the beauty of Bewdley or of the utility of the workshop. Craftsmanship means a fusion of both, so that the economic motive can never dominate its personal, qualitative and organic aspects.

Birch is an illiterate survivor from the old Bewdley; Parker, the modern business man, has become a resident in the old government building that once controlled it. Yet there is nothing incompatible between John Birch's unconscious pursuit of a way of life regarded as obsolete and John Parker's articulate ideas. On the contrary, the object of Parker is to restore the cultural setting of Birch's Bewdley, to enrich it and make it the bedrock of a new civilisation. The wheel has come full circle when the pioneer stretches out a hand to the living museum-piece. If the pioneer were but a crank, there would be nothing significant in this reunion between the representatives of the past and of the future. But industrial civilisation is breaking up because it has failed to satisfy human needs and has deserted the fundamental laws of human existence on earth. In periods of the breaking of nations such men as Parker appear to remind distracted man both of his own nature and that of reality. They look into the past not as antiquarians but in order to discover examples of that dual nature and of a stability that is the natural antidote of chaos. They are few but they are the voices of a new age.

CHAPTER XI

LITTLE MEN OF THE BORDER

"Earth's increase, foison plenty,
Barns and garners never empty;
Vines with clust'ring bunches gròwing;
Plants with goodly burden bowing:
Spring come to you at the farthest,
In the very end of harvest!
Scarcity and want shall shun you;
Ceres' blessing so is on you."

The Tempest.

I

THE COUNTY OF HEREFORDSHIRE, at any rate in the north, is full of contrasts and surprises. It remains much as it has always been, at any rate since the planting of hedgerows, and how many counties can claim that continuity to-day? Perhaps the most gratifying thing about it is the abundance of its hardwood timber. Most of it is still coppice (with a fourteen years' rotation) of ash and oak standards. The ash makes particularly sturdy and shapely growth along the seams and pockets of the limestone. I was astonished at the wealth of mixed woodlands, bitterly accustomed as the observer is to-day to the waste of this natural riches in a country better adapted in soils and climate for well-grown hardwoods than any other region in the temperate zone. I shall not easily forget what a royal range of timber captivated my sight in the neighbourhood of the Pyons in north-central Herefordshire. The long ridges swept across the large-hearted land in flowing curves and half-moons to the south, west and east. There Hampton Court, whose first stone was laid by Sir Roland Lenthal, a kinsman of Henry IV, lay snug on the banks of the Lugg at the north-eastern extremity of Dinmore Hill.

Dinmore itself, the Wellington and Pyon ridges and others

beyond them in a pattern of concentric and interlacing scroll-work, were cloaked with hardwoods from their crests far down their shoulders. They are a wonder to see in a modern England becoming naked or coniferous. The twin flattened cones of Robin Hood's Butts, so characteristic of this county of broken and tumultuous ridges, were themselves mantled in woodland, like a lavish sauce poured over a pudding. And this heartening density is repeated in many other areas, especially in the north-west. Nearly always it is upland, not valley, forest. But it is quite unlike the neat blocks of woodland conspicuous on the Chilterns. The Herefordshire woodlands make great sweeps and curves, though not over long distances. They look generous and free, especially in the Wormsley region south of Weobley, where the wooded steeps and brackened folds and hollows seem as wild as prehistory. The England of the Forestry Commission, commercial development and the factory farm seems very far away.

It is a county, too, of great views as well as of great woods, befitting its creased and crumpled surface. The yet greater ramp of the mountains from the Forest of Dean along the line of the Black Mountains to Radnor Forest and the Clun Heights make a kind of fretted Norman chancel arch for its more intimate beauties. I think of two of these views among so many in warmer retrospect. One is in the neighbourhood of the great houses of the Foleys and the Scudamores, Stoke Edith and Holme Lacey, more or less in the centre of the county. It is a region of the utmost confusion and diversity of contour. Its geology is disorderly, and abrupt outcrops of rock occur along the Wye where strawberries and gooseberries can be grown a month earlier than elsewhere. Hereabouts there is a queer sudden hill called the Cockshoot, where in Elizabethan times there was a landslide. From its summit the eye takes a buzzard flight from the Abberley Hills, along the Titterstone and Brown Clees and the Bromyard Downs to the Malverns. Beyond them follows the calm, clearly pencilled scarp-line of the Cotswolds as far as the multiform ridges of the Forest of Dean. That is the background, the curtain wall of the Midland shires. The foreground is filled with the oceanic Worcester plain between it and me. The spire of Ledbury under the Malverns and a cedar a hundred feet below are the only two

sharp points projecting from it. A few steps downhill and the
Border Marches burst into the scene from Radnor Forest to
Garway Hill and Craig, the gateposts of the Monnow Valley
beyond the Black Mountains. It is as though the heart of
England were beating within the ribs of Wales.

The second view is from the park of Croft Castle near the
Shropshire border and the Valley of the Teme. A little higher
up from Croft Ambrey (named from Ambrosius), the view is
over fourteen counties and from the Quantocks to Cader Idris.
In the Castle park I see only from the Brecon Beacon to the
Clees, and yet it is the grander spectacle. The reason is because
there is so much magnificence on the spot. The Castle is a
palimpsest of five centuries. Its fourteenth century flanking
towers match the vast spread of England and Wales below by
a pride that is not arrogance. The approach to the park is
unique, by a triple avenue, first of oak, then of beech and
lastly of seven hundred yards of Spanish chestnut, ending in a
grove of them. All are of an antiquity that can only be surmised
by their girth. One of the oaks measures thirty-five feet round
the bole and several of the chestnuts, which must be the oldest
in England, were over twenty feet, one of them reaching
twenty-six. No view, however spacious or varied, could dwarf
a mile of trees like these. The Castle among them is great
not by mere size but because it has been held by the same
family certainly from 1086 (and possibly earlier) to the present
day.

A family continuity that has impressed itself upon a
borderland tumultuous both in scene and in history for nine
centuries has its roots in the very bones of England. It is
impressive in its own right. Such a residence is organic, not
only because it has grown from Norman to eighteenth century
Gothic, but because, if the lands below once belonged to it,
now it belongs to them.

Nor is Croft the only such Castle. Further south on the
Radnorshire border near Presteigne, there are three minute
manors, Knill, Nash and Rodd, all Norman in origin and
within a couple of miles of one another. Many of the farmers
here are Welsh, but the labourers are pure Saxon. Rodd Court,
the home of the Rennell family, was built of wattle and daub
like the huts of the poorest villeins and "bordars," as Domesday

Book calls them. This is evidence of its attachment to the people, the land and the region. The population of this little valley near the source of the Lugg has not changed in numbers and hardly in occupation, since the eleventh century. The same is true of the Rodd demesne, which was and is a hide (120 acres). Even one of the water-mills is still running, though, of course, only to grind grist for cattle, not bread for men. The little valley has survived not only the raids and plunderings of Border warfare but almost the modern invasion of taking the bread out of the mouths of its inhabitants.

In my journeys over North Herefordshire, I observed the contrast between little and great running like a musical theme across the land. The huge fattening water-meadows along the banks of the Wye near Stoke Edith and of the Lugg at Lugwardine are still common lands. The authorities have made the usual mess of them, ploughing up some and preventing the flooding that once so enriched them. But the commoners, nearly all small men, still pay threepence a head grazing rights for sheep and fivepence for cows or horses.

But the contrast goes deeper and wider. Variety is the keynote of the Herefordshire scene. Its hop-yards make a mosaic of the valley floors, its orchards climb the multiform slopes, its lusty woodlands dip, float and rise with the hills that bear them. Its comely rivers, Wye, Lugg and Arrow, steal over the country like the great river of Eden in a mediæval woodcut. The stalwart, lazy Herefords, which Cobbett called "the finest and most beautiful of all horned cattle," decorate in small herds the soft permanent pastures. The brooks sidling out of the cross-valleys, the thick compact hedges, often of beech and embanked, the profusion of wild flowers, are all derived from the prodigal richness of the Old Red Sandstone. The whole land is like a banquet.

For that very reason it is pre-eminently and with the sole exception of the hop-yards a county for the modest yeoman and small-holder. This, of course, is heresy to the modern theoretic "agriculturalist," who claims the rich land for the big farmer and the poor land for the small. This view is inorganic, like most modern thought. The richer a county the more intensively it can be cultivated, and the big farmer is extensive only in his aims and methods. The friend with whom

I was staying, a farmer whose family has been planted in Herefordshire since the Conquest, said with truth that no farm in the county (leaving out of account the thin rye lands of the south) ought to be more than one hundred and fifty acres.

How right that considered opinion is can be seen almost anywhere in the northern part of the county. A good example is the course of the Lugg from Lugwardine close to Hereford up north to the pub of England's Gate, where the land opens out into the rolling hills and hanging woods of Dinmore. There is an endless string of tiny orchard closes, often with Welsh sheep in them (though the land is really too rich for sheep), flanked by coppices and pastures grazed by a few Herefords and hardly bigger than paddocks. Toy packhorse bridges cross the stream. Little farms and "magpie" cottages perched up on stone plinths are scattered over the expressive face of the land, so wealthy in grass, fruit and timber. The bower-like seclusion of these meadows and closes, posted with magnificent solitaries or small groves of hardwoods, gives a warm pastoral beauty to the series of miniature scenes. But this pastoral is embedded in the epic frame of the mountains and their foothills. Grandeur is the setting of littleness and the general effect is of a true prosperity. Prosperity must always be jerry-built and unreal unless it is founded upon the security and vocational skill of the small cultivator. North Herefordshire is an ideal home for him.

With the exception of Eardisley, whose street is like a winding river, where limestone slats, tiling, sandstone walls and magpie timbering accord as perfectly as alders with willows and reeds, I was a little disappointed with the villages. Barbarous modern intrusions are too common in them. But once they and the smaller market-towns fitted into the economy of the small farmstead, and indeed of the great house before it made war on the cottage. Leominster is very dilapidated. But the hood-moulds, the brackets, the decorative brick-work and other touches of homely elegance reveal what market-towns once were before they fell asleep or became ambitious to rise (like Tewkesbury with its Trading Estate) into a more pretentious sphere than is proper to the nature of a market-town. This craftsmanly ornamentation displays

the town. But its outskirts on the north side demonstrate its
affinity with the village. Here the Pinsley Brook, an affluent
of the Lugg and once celebrated for its eels and trout, flows
along the street with a riparian brick wall behind which are
cottages skirted with gardens and orchards and (in one) with
a dozen Large Black piglets.

It is one of the best sights in mutilated England to see this
unravished countryside still the bride of quietness. Royally
staged, it is set out by nature and was equipped by our forefathers to be the land of peasant and yeoman.

II

So in my mind's eye I people it with a new breed of farmers,
the breed that is yet to be. For the traditional small farmer's
hold on his native land is slipping. Though he has not
surrendered to factory farming like many a big farmer,
heedless of the *Mene Tekel* written over the dust-bowls of three
continents, he is rapidly becoming a depressed class. Bullied
by officials, plotted against by agricultural professors, compelled to upset his cropping economy by the agents of Whitehall, threatened by technicians, bewildered by all the ignorant
clamour against him, he feels that the very stars in their
courses contend against him. Many yield and become one-track
milk-exporters. The survivors cling valiantly to mixed
husbandry, but not in cheerful hope and freedom. Dogged
does it is their motto, anxiety their familiar. They resort to
expedients and take short cuts because no other way is open to
them. The genuine small farmer accepts overtime like every
craftsman. But the burden of excess overwork is like a millstone round his neck. The cultural graces are shed with his
autumn.

In Shakespeare's once yeoman county there is a parish
where ten small yeomen have been bought out by one farmer
who has turned the land into one vast cow-prairie, retailing
all the milk. The ten farmhouses are occupied by his foremen.
By the modern arithmetic, ten farms make one milk factory.
So the small mixed farmer is haunted by the voice which
threatens, "go modern or get out!" "A first bare notion

of technical progress," says a leading journal, "must be injected into primitive folk working a patch of land with a hand hoe." These are so ignorant that they are quite unaware of how profoundly the "new knowledge" will affect their "ways of life." Hence they "must" put heart and soul into applying the new techniques. They "must." But suppose that the rude clodhopper prefers to keep mixed stock, to use farmyard manure, to be a craftsman rather than a technician and to practise husbandry rather than factory farming? What then?

I happen to know a good many of these hand-hoeing primitives. One of them farms some of the most difficult land in the West of England and has had a tough year of it. Though his wife did what she could (namely, too much), he got badly behind with his cultivations from having poisoned his hand. When he recovered the use of both his hands, he had to plough when the earth was too hard and strained his horse which had to be destroyed. Then there was a flood which swept his lane into the road and blocked it. He worked so hard at getting the lane back again that he strained his heart. In the winter of 1944-45, with the snow three feet deep, he ran out of hay and could only get one cut. His in-calf cow died, and just at this time an unwanted baby was planted on the family. It was at once adopted, but it had dysentery which it imparted to the family. Recovering from that, this little farmer had bronchitis, followed by influenza. Weakened by this series of inflictions, he found it easier to cut his corn with a sickle than with a scythe. But, never having used one before, he nearly took his finger off. All through this period he could obtain no outside help; everybody was short-handed and no surplus labour was to be had. In the autumn of 1945, he was tackling an acre of potatoes, and trying to get an Italian to help him through the winter. But he feared that the W.A.E.C. would refuse him this boon owing to his small acreage. Not even a farmer's boy was available in his desperate need. All the same, he still found time to lend a helping hand to a neighbouring farmer.

I can well imagine what would be the orthodox view about this "case." But the two most important items of it have yet to be told. The first is that in actual yields per acre and in variety of produce this man, suffering under this load of misfortune, raises at least double the amount of food on his tiny farm in ratio to that produced on farms that follow big business methods. Secondly, he is a happy man. How many happy men has the age of technics and automatic progress produced? There never will be happy men in the world again until they can live by a way of life conforming to essential human nature and in an organic relation directly or indirectly with nature. Until they can " orgainise" their own lives instead of having them organised for them; until they can take pleasure in work worth doing instead of being bound to the conveyor-belt, turning out consumer goods in cut-price competition with those of other nations; until they can cultivate their own national heritages instead of exploiting them for export. There is no other way to live.

Here is an example of what is happening and has happened in the clash not between old and new but a time-honoured economy and its modern substitute. The site is some miles west of Croft Castle and in a region of traditional small farmers. Among them is an estate owned by the same family for generation after generation. The father of the present owner, who has lived more than seventy years on the property, managed the home-farm on self-supporting principles so radical that their application reads like a fairy tale. Up to 1914, the whole of the work of the farm, of the little industries allied to it and of the villages round was done by hand. Up to 1939, the home-farm and the small buildings both on the estate and in its neighbourhood were completely self-contained.

The family of the present owner baked its own bread from its own wheat-flour, churned its own butter from the Jersey cows and lived on its own beef and mutton from the cattle and the four-year old wethers of the mountain sheep. Only surplus butter was sold off the farm. The calves were reared by their dams and each child on the estate drank a pint of fresh milk every day. Abundant vegetables were grown and consumed by the residents. Turkeys, geese, ducks and fowls roamed over the fields and were fed on the grain and roots of the home-farm. None of the poultry were imprisoned for forced laying or fattening. Except for lime, locally burned, nothing was used on the fields but dung. Not only were tubercular diseases, abortion, swine-fever and other current maladies unknown but the soil and the plants were free from pest invasions and virus diseases.

The present owner still wears the suit spun by the village weaver and made up by the village tailor fifty years ago. This tailor, who always sat on a table with his legs crossed, is now over ninety and still hale. The suit itself has never lost a button in its half-century of life. The people made their own blankets and carpets and each village had its own cobbler. Among the small industries of the region the burning of lime in the local kiln had so great a reputation through the centuries that the Plantagenet kings used to send from overseas for it to build their great churches at Rouen, Fécamp and Caen.

Since 1939, how heavy a change! The War Agricultural Committee ordered so much of the land to be ploughed up that the present owner had to buy a tractor. His corn being compulsorily exported, he had to get rid of his horses. His livestock being further depleted by lack of pasture, he was forced to spend large sums on chemical fertilisers. He has seen his soil losing its crumb structure and his produce, especially the roots, deteriorating year by year. The County Council stopped the weaver's children from gathering seaweed for dyes and carding the wool. The lime-kiln was closed down. Owing to exorbitant taxation, the owner is now faced, as he told me, with having to abandon the home-farm and "dismiss the families who have been with us for four or five generations" and "had trusted in us" for their security.

It would be easy enough for the modern, educated in a certain way of thinking that admits no other, even if he is aware of it, to justify this strangulation of a whole small community. I know exactly what he would plead in extenuation of the deed. But the fact is that the deed is done or all but done. A wheel rides over a lapwing's nest and what was a happy family becomes a stain on the ground. Nobody is to blame; it just happened so. But that is what our modern civilisation is doing all the time—breaking the soil into dust, breaking families into nomadic gangs, breaking life itself to pieces.

Thus it is clear that the existing small farmer, suffering from external pressures, neglect and hostility that make misfortune desperate for him, needs the infusion of new blood. He is in the position of the Italian peasant that the Gracchi fought in vain to rehabilitate against the high tide of the *latifundia*. Still more urgently, our whole age needs the pioneer, the man of vision, who will bring to the cultivation of the earth that lost culture once inseparable from it. Horatius cannot hold the bridge much longer. The Border needs re-peopling with a new breed. It needs families who will embrace its ardours, its trials, its sterner virtues and its rewarding truth and beauty with a new spirit. They will take it to heart with a sacrificial conviction and a sense of vocation implicitly religious. One such family I know, though it is not of the Border. But it is of the happy breed the Border demands, and where two or three are gathered, others will follow.

The story is epic. A decade ago, a family of husband and wife, three small boys and a baby five weeks old returned from a disastrous enterprise in East Africa with coffee and maize. Accordingly, they had to look for the cheapest possible farm on the market. During the depression of the thirties, of course, farms were all but given away, and the family, through a friend, bought one of one hundred and eight acres. It had been derelict for seven years and empty for five. It had no water supply except for ponds, nothing but a green lane for the approach and nothing in the fields but ragwort, thistle, nettle and squitch. But the buildings were still good and, after the purchase of a mowing machine for a pound, two aged horses and a couple of cows, there were still fifteen pounds left. And the house welcomed the family, so that it minded less than it might have done bird's nests in the chimney, bindweed growing through the floors and the garden impassable for briars. As a member of it told me, "only a desperate soil-mad man could have taken it on." But after the first supper of cold boiled bacon and ginger cake, "such peace and certitude fell upon the house that made this the most vivid experience of my life." The farm seemed to know that the right kind of doctor had arrived.

For three years husband and wife fought grimly to bring the farm back to health. Not only were they unable to afford any hired labour on the farm but even their own. They had to take holiday-makers at very low rates. The husband made poultry houses and took on odd building jobs, the wife did a bit of journalism and broadcasting. In spite of such handicaps to a full-time job on the farm, they weeded a whole nine-acre field of ragwort by hand and carted it to a stack. All the ploughing, sowing and reaping were done by their two selves. In between-whiles they restored the homestead, exposing the old oak, making fireplaces out of old floor bricks and the like. After five years, the stock was increased by heifers and pigs and enough money was put by to spend on help at the peak periods. Several fields were sown down to first-class pasture. Then the war came and not only was the owner's economy of mixed farming disrupted but he very nearly lost his farm.

The best comment on this situation is to quote what his wife told me—"What would happen to a poor illiterate farmer terrified of authority? . . . To threaten to throw out a family with four sons, most of whom we hope will farm with and after us, four days before Christmas in a Christian country, and for no offence except having been forced to work beyond capacity and being late in consequence!" The records of other farmers (especially small ones) whose experience has been less fortunate would make interesting reading. But they will never be read.

By fortitude, courage and peasant virtues practised by a family that was not a peasant one, this story has a happier ending. In 1945 the farm had been completely reclaimed. A spring clover-lay, undersown to barley, plumps the cattle for the winter. The pedigree bull, Lord Bosmere of Wellesley, is the father of two calves, the bull-calf walking from the bottom meadows to the stable before he was dry. The overgrown hedges are pleached and the disciplined orchard bears in abundance. Seventeen acres of seed-clover, still fetching nine pounds a bushel, goes some way to filling that heart-aching financial void between June and September when the farmer who avoids cashing in on his fertility lives on a grudging overdraft. Straw-stacks stand by the corn-stacks while, the farms around are hidden under palls of smoke from the burning pea-haulm, barley and wheat-straw. But on this island of example, surrounded by a sea of factory farms, a pattern of orderly well-drained fields has been stamped upon

what they were when only a decade ago they were bought
for a song :

> " fallow leas
> The darnel, hemlock and rank fumitory
> Do root upon, while that the coulter rusts,
> That should deracinate such savagery;
> The even mead, that erst brought sweetly forth
> The freckled cowslip, burnet and sweet clover,
> Wanting the scythe, all uncorrected, rank,
> Conceives by idleness, and nothing teems
> But hateful docks, rough thistles, kecksies, burrs,
> Losing both beauty and utility."

The husband has now found his true place as the stockman
of a pedigree herd of Shorthorns. The sons, now ten, eleven,
thirteen and fifteen years old, with the help of one hired man,
cut, stooked and stacked the bumper harvest of that year.
Their health and energy are the admiration of the neighbours,
and with their help " we hope ultimately to ignore the fertiliser
makers . . . and to return all wastes to the land and garden."
This was the harvest supper on September 15th, 1945, par-
taken entirely out of the bounty of the farm: chicken, potatoes,
cabbage, onions in bread sauce, greengage and apple pies,
cream, farmhouse butter, cream cheese, wholemeal biscuits
and whole wheat bread (of course illegally ground!), toffee and
sweets made by the children. On the table was a miniature
wheatsheaf in a plinth of apples, tomatoes and pears wreathed
with bryony berries. There are still people left in England
who know how to live in the fullest sense of the term.

A family like this is a star in the spiritual darkness of our
age. But it is darkness which lights the stars, need which
brings forth response. No period in the world's history has
needed such an example as this one for ours. It closes the breech
between what is bread and more than bread. It restores culture
to husbandry. It reconciles the gentleman with the peasant,
the manual worker with the man of ideas. It raises from the
grave the principle of responsible property. It makes adventure
and exploration at one with tradition. This family is an
ambassador for England's future, an envoy of peace to heal

the division between the Englishman and his native land. It is a stimulant to the dormant rural instinct of the English people. But perhaps the greatest of its services lies in revealing the fusion by truth between beauty and utility. "Losing both beauty and utility"—Shakespeare understood that when he saw a derelict farm. We have an even richer experience than his. The dereliction of English land has been far greater in our time than his. But we view the same loss when that land is exploited by the methods of the factory.

When, therefore, I think of the great and generous land of Herefordshire and the Border, the paradox that it is essentially the home of the small farmer is resolved. For Blake infinity was held in the palm of the hand. For ourselves we see greatness and generosity in this experiment of one family on a small farm. They are by their nature infectious. Where one family leads others will follow. Not only on the Border, the stronghold of the small man, but in the heart of England.

CHAPTER XII

SAXONS OF SUSSEX

Tools with the comely names,
Mattock and scythe and spade,
Couth and bitter as flames,
Clean and bowed, in the blade,—
A man and his tools make a man and his trade.

Breadth of the English shires,
Hummock and kame and mead,
Tang of the reeking byres,
Land of the English breed,—
A man and his land make a man and his creed.

Leisurely flocks and herds,
Cool-eyed cattle that come
Mildly to wonted words,
Swine that in orchards roam,—
A man and his beasts make a man and his home.

Children sturdy and flaxen
Shouting in brotherly strife,
Like the land they are Saxon,
Sons of a man and his wife,—
For a man and his loves make a man and his life.

A Saxon Song by VITA SACKVILLE-WEST.

I

IN ARNOLD TOYNBEE'S *Study of History* there is a long section
devoted to examining the causes for the arrested development
of certain civilisations. The examples he takes are those of
the Esquimaux, the Nomads and the Spartans. The Esquimaux
have marvellously adapted themselves to the rigours of
northern latitudes largely by becoming mermen. They
invented the kayak, that frail canoe that can outride the
roughest seas. It can be righted in a moment after being
capsized and pursue the seal with an agility and a velocity

actually superior to those of the animal itself. The kayak is, in fact, the body of an artificial seal, its double-bladed paddle a pair of artificial flippers. For a man, that land-bound biped, to have invented a tool that can overcome a sea-mammal whose command of its own element is supreme is a miracle of human ingenuity. In fact, the humble Esquimau puts Watt with his steam-engine into the shade, for the kayak is one of the greatest achievements ever made by the dexterity of man. But, as the author remarks, a price has to be paid for the faculty of working miracles. This has been nothing less than "the determined and systematic repudiation of those very qualities of the human hand and the human eye and the human reason which are distinctive of human nature." The arrested development of the Esquimau civilisation is due to over-specialisation.

Now turn to the Nomad. If the northern hunter is a merman, the shepherd and herdsman of the Steppes is a centaur. His kayak is his horse or his camel and, in training his horse to herd his sheep, goats or kine, he has accomplished a feat as miraculous as that of the Esquimau. But he has paid the same penalty for this prodigy of skill as his northern brother. This can be most clearly seen in the consequences of his conquests. Our author takes as his example the subjugation of North Africa and Eastern and Central Europe by the Ottoman power. Instead of adapting itself to new surroundings and conditions, the Osmanli civilisation reproduced those of its ancestors on the Steppes. The shepherd of flocks became the shepherd of men; the place of the horse, the dog and the camel was taken by the corps of Janissaries. That rigidly trained and disciplined body of soldiers kept in subjection the conquered peoples, the human cattle who corresponded with the desert flocks and herds. The Ottomans had become so over-specialised that they were unable to adapt themselves to an entirely new environment. Their Empire became fossilised; in two centuries it disintegrated and has now disappeared.

The third example is the Spartans. Sparta never produced any art, culture or way of life. Its whole existence was centred upon military despotism, and its military despotism was conditioned by its conquest of the Messenians, free Greeks like the Spartans. In order to keep the Messenian helots down, *their* "human cattle," the whole education and organisation of the Spartan "peers" were concentrated on specialised and professionalised soldiering. As the Esquimau became a merman and the Nomad a centaur, the Spartan from the ages of seven to sixty was occupied in becoming and staying an animated spear-head. There is an entertaining story in Plutarch about the Spartans. Their military allies complained that, though their overlords were fewer in number than they, they were perpetually being dragged into one campaign after another by them. So King Agesilaus held a review of all the troops both of the allies and the Spartans, and ordered to drop out of the ranks all those who were builders or carpenters or potters or smiths. So many of the allies' soldiers dropped out that their numbers became fewer than those of the Spartans, whose ranks never lost a man.

The main interest of all this is, of course, the question whether modern civilisation is not also suffering from arrested development and is unable to find a way out of its blind alley. Like the Esquimau, it has "repudiated . . . the human hand and the human eye and the human reason" in its glorification of applied science and the machine. Its Janissaries are the corps of experts, technicians and bureaucrats who control, or want to control, human life from the cradle to the grave. The craftsman has become as much despised among us as he was among the Spartans. Among the totalitarian States at any rate, their populations are hardly one remove from "the human cattle" of the Ottomans. As the Esquimaux over-adapted themselves to the seal and the Nomads to the horse, so modern society has over-adapted itself to the social organisation of the ant. Aldous Huxley's *Brave New World* was a satire on that very theme. As the years go by since he wrote it, it looks less and less like an extravagance and more and more like an anticipation. Our confusion of growth with the technical advance we call progress is a further symptom of arrested development. Modern civilisation in the middle of our century is confronted with a set of entirely different challenges and conditions than those dominant in the nineteenth century. It responds to them only by desperate attempts to patch up, "modernise" and drive along the path of progress an era of industrial expansion that has become obsolete.

But adaptation means for human life the rediscovery of realities that have been lost, and reality only discloses itself through the medium of a way of life. Since the modern age lacks any way of life, one method of finding it must be looked for in times and places where it once existed. And architecture, from the pigsty to the palace always reveals a culture, a way of life by which permanent realities are perceived.

The infallible and unconscious art of adjusting buildings to the ground on which they stood has been utterly lost. To see a modern building in the country (unless it has been built by the squire) which so fits into the landscape as to be part of it as is rare as to see a bee-eater, waxwing or golden oriole. The reason goes deep; it is because we no longer live in organic relation with our native land. This contrast is best seen in the winter months when there is no leafage to veil the modern house in its crude heresy against the natural law of fitness to environment. The earth revenges itself for its urban conquest by an unsparing exposure of the gracelessness and irrelevance of houses built of imported materials and unsited. No satirist could reveal the sham and shame of these houses as does the nakedness of the earth on which they have been so blindly set. The conquest of the country by the town is achieved by them, but how barbarous a one the earth shows it to be! Contrast them with the traditional ones that do express an organic relation with their surroundings. The earth is in repose and all colouring is subdued, all tones are modulated to the moods of the wintry skies. The cottages, barns and farmsteads seem to sink into this patient relaxed earth, as though her cloak were thrown over them. They are subdued to earth as earth is to sky. Subdued too in the sense of accepting their limitations by the building of them in the local materials. But from this acceptance springs their variety and individuality.

To illustrate that variety, I will take a group of villages that lack the advantages of remoteness, of a spectacular countryside to show them off and of a guide-book notoriety that labels them as "picturesque." It consists of Bidford, Salford Priors, Harvington and Offenham along the Avon Valley and on or close to the main road between Stratford and

Evesham. Shakespeare must often have passed this way either for Dover's Hill to see the "Cotswold Games" and Justice Shallow's greyhound "outrun" or to visit his relations at Nibley. East and west are Cleeve Hill and the far more celebrated Lenches, villages which have the advantage over my group of not being on a main road. The geology of the region is the red marls of Worcestershire and the stubborn Lower Lias clay. What marvellous use of deposits by no means exceptional for building purposes were made by villages which, being strung along a highway, had no particular amenities of position!

The diversity of the largest of them, Bidford, almost goes to extremes. The most ambitious of the buildings on the main road is Church House. But, as decay reveals to the eye, it was originally built of lath and plaster. Later periods made it a stone and timber building with a stone plinth, a timber overhang, tiled end-gables, a modillioned cornice, a string-course, dripstones over the windows without the Cotswold technique of right-angled ends and chimney clusters of heavy stone stacks. But if Church House is the patrician of the street, it is not aloof from it, nor divided whether in idiom or site from its village neighbours. Its stone walls have a local mannerism peculiar to the region. They were built in alternate courses of thick and thin slabs, and this long-and-short phrasing is repeated over and over again in the village, including its street walls. Its houses vary in size from the cottage to the substantial dwelling of a prosperous middle-class, and have made use of the stone, brick, timber, tiling and reed-thatching in a series of variations. The stone plinth with timber upper storey is frequent, but with varying depths of the stone from the ground. One wall round a front garden is of upright monoliths.

Salford Priors, where the Nunnery has been converted into a Tudor mansion, is hardly more than a hamlet. But a like variety informs it, and here some gables are Dutch with finials on them. Harvington has a cruck-house and some highly distinctive timber houses on very lofty plinths of stone. The timber overhang occurs again here; gables are dormered; porches are thatched and the roofs are so steep and set at so many angles that they look like a Doré wood-engraving.

W.M.B.   Q

Offenham excels in weather-boarding. How could this variety have failed to impress itself upon Shakespeare's consciousness and so to foster his own?

Ruin is now devouring the smaller of these villages and sameness ousting their lively and individual characters. But not even dividends and interests, that modern building syndicate, have yet effaced the evidences of a dynamic tradition. Here as elsewhere, the vernacular cottages, however humble, are full of life and difference from their neighbours. The villas in the villages, with all the commercial resources of transport and alien materials at their disposal, look dead as mutton. Lacking biological and geological integrity, theirs is only a borrowed life.

Being now an urban civilisation, we regard ourselves as independent of nature. So we no longer build villages in the country but housing estates. Nature is regarded as just ground; water is pumped from a main; food is imported from a distance, usually as far as the Antipodes. Yet the means to live, water and food, are still the same for the housing estate as for the village. The difference between them is that the one makes its own living power, while the other passively receives it from elsewhere. The one is self-supporting, the other parasitic. And this difference is invariably followed by another: the one is beautiful and the other ugly.

In *Our Building Inheritance*, a professional architect, Mr. W. H. Godfrey, defends the beauty of our pre-industrial buildings, not on "sentimental" grounds, but in "the firm conviction that beauty is the only excuse for the existence of architecture." And why are our traditional English buildings almost invariably beautiful in any age except the Victorian and our own? They are beautiful because they express perfect fitness to their functions, their purpose and their surroundings. They obey certain general principles both of life and of architecture—a very different thing from planning and ideology. The materials were those provided by nature in a particular region, and the first consideration of all was not cost accountancy but good workmanship. Godfrey's object is twofold. It is the practical one of showing by example and precept how easily with a little care, taste and knowledge of the laws of structure we could recondition nearly all of our pre-industrial buildings, whether in town or country, devoting especial attention to the cottage.

A perfect example of where the healing hand of this wise architect might save a whole village from disfigurement and at the same time reconcile tradition with modernism is Castle Combe. It dips down in curves like lines of verse from the plateau of the southern Cotswolds near Bath, accompanied by its walled stream, to the Valley of the Bybrook. This is one of the most beautiful villages in the world, perfect both in form and environment, in the works of nature and of man. It belongs to a local small estate, and one of its trustees, a soldier back from the War, wrote to me and asked me how this village, devotedly fostered by successive owners of the estate, could be repaired from years of neglect during the War and its cottages reconditioned in the traditional materials. There were two formidable obstacles against this—the expense and the attitude of the Rural District Council. I instantly put him in touch with Godfrey's *Our Building Inheritance*. For, as that book demonstrates, the real obstacles to making our old cottages and other buildings commodious and agreeable to the moderns are not the cottages and not the materials of which they were built. They are our financial system, the pressure of vested interests and the ignorance and prejudice (words that continually occur in the book) of the local authorities. They prefer to demolish rather than to conserve.

Godfrey's more general argument is to give cogent reasons for the inevitable beauty of our old buildings, their organic structure, their obedience to certain principles and values, moral, architectural and æsthetic, their durability and the natural good taste and neighbourliness of the craftsmen who built them. In short, he reveals these buildings as an organic growth and so as the expression of a way of life, the door into reality.

II

The county of Sussex has remained truer to its Saxon foundations than any other in England. It has no Dutch nor Flemish nor Danish element as in Norfolk, its only rival as a

Saxon territory which retains its Saxon character. Though
Sussex was the centre of the flint industry in pre-Celtic times,
all traces of the Neolithic and Bronze Age colonists have
disappeared from the people, as they certainly have not in
Wessex. There is only one Celtic place-name in all Sussex—
Mount Caburn (Cær Bryn), east of Lewes. The Norman
castles on the rivers began and ended as fortresses in an alien
land and the knights of the Norman manors came and stayed
only as overlords. The vernacular buildings of Sussex are thus
stamped with the imprint of a single people with a specific
culture of its own. They are the manuscript of a way of life
written by a Sussex scribe on the parchment of Sussex earth.

Sussex and Wiltshire are the simplest of our southern
counties, and so perhaps the most satisfying. Not that they
lack variety. Sussex is full of it but not crowded with it, and
so the traveller never loses sight of the county's structural
design. In the west it is triune—wooded Weald (the Roman
Anderida Silva), the broad water-meads of Rother, Arun and
Adur and Downland scarp. The alluvial littoral between sea
and Downs was once a fourth character, but it is virtually
blotted out by resorts and ribbon development. The wooded
Weald, which is undulating and rarely a plain, has begun to
suffer the same process of levelling down into an equality of
ugliness. There is nothing simple about this: it is due to
the over-complexity of a decaying civilisation. Everywhere
the building estate and the poxing of villas and bungalows
are killing the diversity in simplicity of the Weald, while
the farmsteads are being separated from their farms by
speculative buying and selling.

The odd polarity of road, rail and river between north and
south stresses this simplicity. It is a perplexing job to work
your way between east and west. The Iron Age Underhill Lane
under the feet of the Downs and corresponding with the
Icknield Way of Berkshire, Oxon and Bucks, is almost the
only road that so runs. The rivers cleave the Downs and in
surpassing beauty confer upon them the resemblance to a
school of porpoises, rising and falling in a multiplicity of
line in headland, col, hollow way, dry vale and bottom, valley
and flying buttress. The large areas of parkland—Parham,
Arundel, Cowdray and their brothers, also make for simplicity.

But the extensive blocks of woodland are by no means mono-cultural. The woods round Greatham, for instance, are of as mixed a timber as sound principles of husbandry could desire —fine stands of Scots pine, oak, spruce, Spanish chestnut, poplar, beech and ash. I know no more lovely experience than to burst out of these woodlands and confront the calm, pure, linear masses of the Downs, say, from Amberley Mount along the crests of Rackham and Kithurst. One moves at a step from the pent to the free, from multitude to amplitude, from mystery to candour, from luxury to austerity, from the romantic to the classic, from profusion to the bare archaic grandeur of what Gilbert White called this "majestical chain of mountains." The intense white of the chalk-pits above Amberley Bridge contrasts with the green domes, the silver oats and amber wheat mounting into the blue sky. But the colours are all primary, as the county itself looks joyously, innocently primitive. It is right that Sussex should be *the* home in our island of the simple, tenacious Saxon. The Celts were a subtle people.

If the great houses be excepted, the vernacular building is also simple because it is domestic. This domesticity covers the churches of flint or local stone, graciously dollish with their shingled spirelets or squat triangular belfries. They are nearly always smaller than the black weather-boarded and tiled barns on plinths of clunch or flint. Domesticity even covers castles like those of Bramber and Amberley, which look like folio editions of the churches. The modesty and minuteness of these Norman and Early English churches, many or most of them risen from Saxon foundations, have communicated their spirit to the buildings of market-town and village, with their quietude, reticence and even diffidence. Yet how rich and various they are in their economical usage of the materials available at their doors! They are so ingeniously assembled that one thinks of the flint, stone, Horsham slats, tiling and brick as regional crops grown by a natural husbandry like the straw and timber by a human. The patterns of external timbering are never florid, like the magpie style of the West Country, and the infillings are sometimes flint, stone and brick in the same house. Occasionally I saw the ponderous Horsham slats, tiles and thatch on the same roof. A cottage at Bignor has one wall of timbering, flint, brick and ironstone under a thatched hat and as inconsequently fitted together as a patchwork quilt.

Individual mannerisms abound. At North Chapel (where that great Hambledon cricketer, Noah Mann, was born), in the northern Weald, for instance, the local tile-hanging proliferates into ornamental designs surpassing the norm of square, round and fish-tail. It is noticeable that most of the modern houses that attempt tile-hanging are ugly: the sense of structure, seemliness and natural taste has gone. The weight of the Horsham slat-roofs at Bramber does not prevent timber over-hangs. At Burpham, half clustered, half strung out on a slope looking across the Arun meads to Arundel Castle, poised on its wooded ridge, the style is penny plain thatch and stone or flint, and of a sedate country comeliness. At Amberley, now an artist colony and with the immemorial right of way to the Castle arbitrarily closed and the view of the primeval Wild Brooks shut out, roughcast, tile-hang, weather-boarding, flint, stone walls with brick quoins, brick walls with stone quoins, make a discreet festival. And the walls of stone or flint or both with flat or arched copings, they are everywhere; nowhere but in West Sussex have I seen flint field-walls. A notable thing about these villages and little towns is that the barns and farmsteads more often than not congregate in them, bringing in the fields on which village and market-town once depended.

In the same sense of neighbourly communication, founded upon the essential unity between husbandry and community, the market-towns are but expanded villages. Few enough of them are not all but submerged by a mob of unsightly and flimsy intruders. But Petworth, Midhurst and Lindfield remain largely unviolated. They look like and doubtless were enlargements of a village like, say, Chiddingfold, once home of the Sussex glass-makers. The little squares of Midhurst are the urban idiom of the greens of Chiddingfold, and the local and native architectural style prints itself upon both village and town. The most remarkable of the towns, I think, is Lindfield, punctiliously end-stopped by the pond at the bottom of the slope and the broach spire at the top. The houses are generously spaced and constructed; bow windows, overhangs, porches, cornices, grey and rosy brick, green shutters, tiled and Horsham stone roofs, fish-tail tile-hanging, rich but restrained timbering, white weather-boarding and even thatch, localised Tudor, Jacobean, Georgian and the purely and almost changeless local styles, make this little town as diverse in appearance as was Cleopatra in moods.

A house steeped in character is East Mascalls, with a roof of Horsham slats, carved barge boards and iridescent diamond-paned windows. The church, like Gulliver among the men of Lilliput, overlooks a cluster of diminutive Tudor houses. One, the Bouveries, retains the old Saxon hall-place as it was without the customary second floor added to it. Another has in its attics the encrusted soot of the Tudor central fires, gone hard as bog oak and with a surface like black satin. The very names of the older Lindfield houses, the Bouveries, East Mascalls, Pax Hill, Buxshalls, Old Place and others, are windows into their characters. This village-town is as faithful to the domestic vernacular as the tiniest hamlet sequestered in the Downland folds. Yet it is in perilous proximity to spurious, suburban Hayward's Heath. It seems that the identity of Lindfield was saved by one person who exercised the proper and noble use of wealth by keeping it true to itself and Sussex. She followed the tradition of the Quaker, William Allen, a resident of Lindfield who taught its children handicrafts, built good cottages for small rents, encouraged allotments and so kept the land-workers on the land.

To crown the whole, the white weather-boarded Dean's Water Mill on the Ouse still grinds humus-grown local corn between millstones powered by a water-wheel.[1] The whole grain is milled and baked by Mr. and Mrs. Horsfield, not as traditional survivors but pioneers with a public conscience. The integrity of the town is not a mere outward semblance when the fields, the mill and the bread it makes still interact in an honest wholeness.

Not even the age of destruction has yet knocked the South Downs out of shape. What it has done by military exercises and the removal of the "uneconomic" sheep is radically to change their surface. Now the lower slopes are grazed by cattle, and the plateau, seamed by shells and tanks, is either

[1] See Page 209.

abandoned or in corn. As this corn has been successively grown almost entirely on artificials, the upland soil, thin at the best of times, is poverty-stricken and rapidly becoming worthless. One field on Bury Hill is a kind of cemetery of flints. The departure of the sheep has made these Downs ragged and beggarly with bents and the weedier grasses, and gone are the "fairy flora" that W. H. Hudson once trod. Over miles of once good pasture the ragwort now flaunts its barbarian banners, and is by no means confined to the steeper slopes, where it is more difficult to control by good pasture management. The cattle-grazing make a patchy surface that is nothing like the former turf when it was properly sheeped into a resilient pile.

I went to see Mitchell of Pyecombe, the last of the Sussex crook-makers, in his sixteenth century barn-smithy. His father had been a blacksmith—he died at ninety-eight—and his grandfather a wheelwright, so that his craftsmanship was bred in the bone. He told me that there were now only forty-five apprentices for the smiths of the whole United Kingdom. "You don't mean to tell me you still make crooks?" "A few." "But the sheep have left the Downs." "Oh, I don't make 'em for shepherds, only for bishops." With a resigned irony he quoted me what he had read in Gilbert White, that "no self-respecting Sussex shepherd should be without a Pyecombe crook." He had had one order from the Bishop of Tristan da Cunha, but, since these crooks have become an ecclesiastical monopoly, he could not make one for the great sheepless shoulder of down opposite his smithy. He remembered a thousand Southdowns grazing on it. He remembered the days when farmers farmed, not just pulled teats and emptied the chemical bag. A man, he said, could in the old days walk for nine miles on the Downs from Pyecombe to Lewes on a sward "like a billiard table." Now the grass is up to the knees.

By chance I found a corner of old Sussex which seemed to give me the essence of its Saxon history and character, as one grain is the history of a cornfield. This place was the hamlet of Sullington, lying between Chantry Hill and sombre Chanctonbury, in whose grove, the full stop of West Sussex, no birds sing. Like all of these Downland parishes, Sullington is a strip between north and south, the higher chalk slopes in

the south for sheep-grazing, the lower slopes and fields below
the springs for cattle and corn and the northern heath and
woodland for timber, as a swine-run and a warren, and, before
the Enclosures, for the common or waste. How deep are the
agricultural associations of Sullington when its southern
boundary is scored with "shepherd's stairs"—namely, the
irrigation terraces of prehistory! They are the ancient
representatives of the most modern methods of soil-conserva-
tion—contour ploughing.

The hamlet consists of a church, a manor farm with bartons
and a sprinkle of cottages. It must always have been so, for
the entry in Domesday Book values the manor of Sillinstone,
belonging to the Norman Aquillons, at two shillings, a revenue
derived from one villein and half a plough. In Henry III's
time it belonged to Sir William de Covert, whose effigy in
chain armour reposes in the church. No matter how tiny
might be a settlement in the Middle Ages, it was usually
dignified by a proud name. But the pride of Sullington in later
days was the farm. The farm buildings, placed by the springs
where the down becomes steep, certainly cover an area at least
four times that of the combined two-gabled farmstead of
ironstone and tiles on a knoll above the farm and the little
flint church beside it, mainly Norman but with Saxon long
and short work at the coigns of the tower. The bartons consist
of a great rectangular courtyard, once no doubt the midden.
One of the greatest barns in Sussex occupies one whole side,
of black weather-boarding on a flint and stone plinth and
roofed with russet and lichened tiling, sweeping like a downland slope within a few feet of the ground. The rest of the
rectangle and a smaller one adjoining it is enclosed by the
byres and cow-houses, the granary, a dovecot, cartsheds and
the like. A lofty grove of beech, elm and sycamore screens the
steading from the winds. And the builders of this noble
group? They were the Saxon Standens and ten of their tombstones take up a corner of the churchyard, dated from 1730 to
1942. But the last of the Standens was no longer the owner of
the farm whose midden to-day is dungless. One of the tombstones reads—"In Memory of Joseph Standen, Yeoman, who
departed this life the 16th day of August, 1780." No more,
but all the eighteenth century tombstones are richly orna-

mented with coronets, cherubs like angels or angels like cherubs, urns and (in one) a wheat-sheaf. The shapes and carvings and style of these tombstones are some of the handsomest I have ever seen. It was to be noted how they became uglier and uglier as they advanced into the nineteenth century.

I tarried long at Sullington. A speck of a place, but how spacious and large-minded its conception! An insignificant hamlet lost among the Downs, but how masterful its continuity through the ages! A mere cluster of buildings but housing a complete community, polarised, as man was meant to be, between "the kindred points" of heaven and earth. A lonely and a homely working farm, but so rich in natural and human beauty interfused. A "picturesque" groping, but organically productive for a thousand years. Here was the very core of human life on earth, the pillar of human stability, the nurse of human culture; here were home and peace and reality in a world of nightmares.

CHAPTER XIII

WHERE MAN BELONGS

"Do not despise matter, for it is not despicable. Nothing is that which God has made. This is the Manichæan heresy. That alone is despicable which does not come from God, but is our own invention, the spontaneous choice of will to disregard the Natural Law."

St. John Damascene.

WHERE DOES man belong? The modern answer is that he belongs to the State, to Cosmopolis, to the money-market, to material and technical progress. Only as conditioned to the pace of the industrial machine, whose vortex now revolves quicker than thought, can he hope to attain the millennium promised by these huge impersonal forces. At long last, a highly specialised technical research has led to the invention of the atomic bomb. The news of this victory over the inorganic forces of nature was received in a duality of mood, each the opposite extreme of the other. The one mood climbed to the apex of the Utopian dream which has always accompanied the theory of automatic progress. It was the mood of Dr. Faustus. "Unimaginable vistas" of the earthly paradise and its "undreamt-of riches" were evoked by the opiate of material power to be released to infinity by disintegrating the structural fabric of the cosmic frame. The immeasurable powers of destruction already conferred were translated into an immeasurable prosperity to come. The builders of the Tower of Babel had laid the first stone.

The other mood was the mood of Hamlet when the full revelation of the horror at the court of Denmark corroded his will and unnerved his arm. His nature turned in upon itself and in an introverted brooding saw what all but turned his reason—the vision of chaos. The Greeks recorded the same frustration of despair in their legend of Medusa, who turned men to stone. The one mood saw the Tower of Babel being rebuilt, the other saw it consumed. And with it the whole earth according to the words of Prospero in *The Tempest*:—

> "The cloud-capped towers, the gorgeous palaces,
> The solemn temples, the great globe itself,
> Yea, all which it inherit, shall dissolve
> And like this unsubstantial pageant faded,
> Leave not a rack behind."

It may well be that Shakespeare's prophecy will be fulfilled in our time. But it certainly will not be if the middle way be chosen between the vulgar vainglory of man in his possession of inorganic powers and its contrary, the fatalistic disruption of his will to overcome the forces of death. For it used to be said of him that, being man, he possessed another power, not subject to change. By this power the life of nature means more to him than the senseless atom and the life of the spirit more than the fear and the arrogance of material power. By this power he perceives that the modern answer is not an answer to the real needs of man nor can satisfy his real nature. If man belongs neither to heaven nor to earth nor to himself, he belongs nowhere and to nothing. He is dooming himself to exist in a vacuum. Once the sources of life that poised him between heaven, earth and himself fail to reach him, the life has gone out of him. Only by renewing himself at the sources of life can he recover himself, the earth his heritage and heaven his star. Otherwise, as Shakespeare foretold of man at division with himself and the cosmic order, chaos is come again.

Where does man belong? He belongs to his own place which he has almost lost. In his own place he is able to be himself; in his own place he is in touch with what is beyond space and time. The simple Christmas story affirms this to be so. Its tale of the infinite lodged in a village is absolute truth in a nutshell. Otherwise, it is no more than a fable.

In this book I have given examples of how Englishmen worked or work each in his own place. The very great are in company with the very small, and yet all react according to their different functions and capacities in the same way. This is a creative way of life transcending the economics of self-interest, and so each one who lives or has lived it is himself.

Whether professing to do so or not, all express in their works a wholeness between the organic and the spiritual, or, in older phrase, a commerce between heaven and earth. The proof of this triple relationship is not in argument but in the lives and works of the individuals described. It is true of them all from Shakespeare himself who dramatised part of the Christian philosophy in his plays to the unregarded company whose works would not have been despised by a Master who was exalted from their ranks. At the same time, these least among men in an age which drives its machines over them are also one with Shakespeare in living and working from a creative harmony with nature. The craftsman in his generations is, like Shakespeare, not of an age but for all time.

Thus, these three things in one, the person, the place and their sanction in ultimate truth, are the foundations of man's life on earth. When he tries another way, the present way, which is not a way of life at all, a shadow falls upon uprooted man which frustrates his enterprises and darkens our age.

THE END

INDEX